Camper's Guide to
DELAWARE, MARYLAND, VIRGINIA, AND WEST VIRGINIA

Parks, Lakes, and Forests

Where to Go and How to Get There

Mickey Little

Gulf Publishing Company

Gulf Publishing Company
Book Division
P.O. Box 2608 □ Houston, Texas 77252-2608

10   9   8   7   6   5   4   3   2   1

This title and graphic design are a trademark of
Gulf Publishing Company.

Library of Congress Cataloging-in-Publication Data
Little, Mildred J.
    Camper's guide to Delaware, Maryland, Virginia & West Virginia parks, lakes, and forests : where to go and how to get there / Mickey Little.
        p.   cm.
    Includes index.
    ISBN 0-88415-028-3
    1. Camping—Delaware—Guidebooks.   2. Camping—Maryland—Guidebooks.   3. Camping—Virginia—Guidebooks.   4. Camping—West Virginia—Guidebooks.
5. Delaware—Guidebooks.   6. Maryland—Guidebooks.
7. Virginia—Guidebooks.   8. West Virginia—Guidebooks.
I. Title.
GV191.42.D32L48   1996
796.54′0974—dc20   95-47509
                                                    CIP

Photo Credits

All photos are by the author unless otherwise credited:
Marsha Elmore, 110, 141
Florida Division of Tourism, 45
Judy Hallmark, 81
Rena Koesler, 112
Lillian Morava, 129
National Park Service, 41, 66, 83, 140
U.S. Forest Service, 117, 176

Contents

Introduction — 1

How to Use This Camper's Guide, 2
Delaware, 3
Maryland, 5
Virginia, 7
West Virginia, 9
Federal Recreation Passport Program, 12
Reservation System, 13
Appalachian National Scenic Trail, 14
New River Gorge, 16
Backcountry Country Ethics, 19
Camping/Backpacking Supplies Checklist, 20
Map Symbols, 23

Delaware — 24

Blackbird State Forest, 25
Brandywine Creek State Park, 26
Cape Henlopen State Park, 27
Carpenter State Park, 28
Delaware Seashore State Park, 29
Killens Pond State Park, 30
Lums Pond State Park, 31
Trap Pond State Park, 32

Maryland — 34

Assateague Island National Seashore, 36
Assateague State Park, 38
Big Run State Park, 39
Catoctin Mountain Park, 40
Chesapeake and Ohio Canal National
   Historical Park, 42
Cosca Regional Park, 45
Cunningham Falls State Park, 46
Deep Creek Lake State Park, 47
Elk Neck State Park, 48
Fort Frederick State Park, 49
Gambrill State Park, 50
Garrett State Forest, 65
Greenbelt Park, 51
Green Ridge State Forest, 65
Greenbrier State Park, 52
Hart-Miller Island State Park, 53
Janes Island State Park, 54
Little Bennett Regional Park, 55
Martinak State Park, 56
New Germany State Park, 57
Patapsco Valley State Park, 58
Pocomoke River State Park, 59
Point Lookout State Park, 60
Potomac State Forest, 65
Rocky Gap State Park, 61
Savage River State Forest, 65
Smallwood State Park, 62
South Mountain State Park, 63
State Forests, 65
Susquehanna State Park, 67
Swallow Falls State Park, 68
Watkins Regional Park, 69
Youghiogheny River Lake, 71

Virginia — 72

Bear Creek Lake State Park, 73
Blue Ridge Parkway, 74
Breaks Interstate Park, 77
Bull Run Regional Park, 79
Claytor Lake State Park, 80
Clinch Mountain Wildlife Management
   Area, 81
Cumberland Gap National Historical Park, 82
Douthat State Park, 84
Fairy Stone State Park, 85
False Cape State Park, 86
Flannagan (John W.) Dam & Reservoir, 87
Gathright Dam & Lake Moomaw, 88
George Washington National Forest, 90
Grayson Highlands State Park, 105
Holliday Lake State Park, 106
Hungry Mother State Park, 107
Jefferson National Forest, 108
Kerr (John H.) Dam & Reservoir, 114
Kiptopeke State Park, 115
Mount Rogers National Recreation Area, 116
Natural Chimneys Regional Park, 119
Natural Tunnel State Park, 120
North Fork of Pound Lake, 121
Occoneechee State Park, 122
Philpott Lake, 123
Pocahontas State Park, 124
Pohick Bay Regional Park, 125
Prince William Forest Park, 126
Seashore State Park and Natural Area, 129

Shenandoah National Park, 130
Sky Meadows State Park, 133
Smith Mountain Lake State Park, 134
Staunton River State Park, 135
Twin Lakes State Park, 136
Westmoreland State Park, 137

West Virginia ——— 138

Audra State Park, 139
Babcock State Park, 140
Beech Fork State Park, 142
Blackwater Falls State Park, 143
Bluestone State Park, 144
Bluestone Lake Wildlife Management Area, 145
Burnsville Lake, 146
Cabwaylingo State Forest, 147
Camp Creek State Park, 148
Canaan Valley Resort State Park, 149
Cedar Creek State Park, 150
Chief Logan State Park, 151
Coopers Rock State Forest, 152
East Lynn Lake, 153
Greenbrier State Forest, 154
Holly River State Park, 155
Jennings Randolph Lake, 156
Kanawha State Forest, 157
Kumbrabow State Forest, 158
Laurel Lake Wildlife Management Area, 159

Moncove Lake State Park, 160
Monongahela National Forest, 161
North Bend State Park, 167
Panther State Forest, 168
Pipestem Resort State Park, 169
Pleasant Creek Wildlife Management Area, 170
Plum Orchard Lake Wildlife Management Area, 171
R. D. Bailey Lake, 172
Seneca State Forest, 173
Spruce Knob-Seneca Rocks National Recreation Area, 174
Stonewall Jackson Lake State Park, 177
Summersville Lake, 178
Sutton Lake, 179
Teter Creek Lake Wildlife Managment Area, 180
Tomlinson Run State Park, 181
Twin Falls Resort State Park, 182
Tygart Lake State Park, 183
Watoga State Park, 184

Resources for Further Information, 185

Index, 186

Acknowledgments ———————

I am grateful to the following for their cooperation in providing information through maps, photographs, brochures, telephone conversations, and personal interviews. Thank you for helping make the guide possible for others to enjoy.

Appalachian Trail Conference
Delaware Department of Agriculture, Forestry Section
Delaware Division of Parks & Recreation
Delaware Tourism Office
George Washington National Forest & all ranger districts
Hammond Almanac
Jefferson National Forest & all ranger districts
Maryland Department of Natural Resources, State Forest & Park Service
Maryland-National Capital Park and Planning Commission
Maryland Office of Tourism Development
MISTIX Reservation System
Monongahela National Forest & all ranger districts

National Park Service, U.S. Department of the Interior
National Recreation Reservation System
Northern Virginia Regional Park Authority
U.S. Army Corps of Engineers: Baltimore, Norfolk, & Huntington Districts
Virginia Department of Conservation and Recreation, Division of State Parks
Virginia Division of Tourism
Virginia State Forest Superintendent
West Virginia Division of Natural Resources, Wildlife Resources Section
West Virginia Division of Tourism and Parks, Parks and Recreation

While every effort has been made to ensure accuracy of the information in this guide, neither I nor the publisher assume liability arising from the use of this material. Because park facilities and policies are subject to change, campers may want to verify the accuracy of important details before beginning a trip. Happy Camping!

Mickey Little

Introduction

The proximity of Delaware, Maryland, Virginia, and West Virginia and their many similarities make it quite appropriate for this *Camper's Guide* to include these four states. Three of the states share the Delmarva Peninsula, and all four are mid-Atlantic states within a short drive of the District of Columbia. Several share various geographical features with one another, such as the Appalachian Plateau, Piedmont Plateau, Great Appalachian Valley, Shenandoah Valley, Allegheny Mountains, Blue Ridge Mountains, and the Atlantic Coastal Plain, also called the Tidewater Region. There is no doubt about it—the diversity of this area along with its four-season climate definitely provide the local folks, as well as out-of-state visitors, countless opportunities for outdoor recreation.

Consider these facts: the state and federal agencies in these four states combined provide camping facilities at 64 state parks, 8 national parks, 2 national recreation areas, 3 national forests, 12 lakes, and 6 regional parks, as well as 12 state forests and 6 wildlife management areas that offer primitive or rustic camping. These 113 recreation sites are the focus of this guide. Yes, opportunities for experiencing the outdoors abound in this area—not only in parks that provide camping facilities, but in day-use-only parks, as well. But, what better way is there to really see and enjoy the great outdoors in this four-state area than by camping?

Visitors from other states who drive to this area should be aware that there are numerous information centers, often called Welcome Centers, located, most often, at the state line on interstate highways or other major highways entering the state. These centers provide official state maps, details on state attractions, accommodations, historic sites, parks, and events. They are usually open from 8 or 9 a.m. to 4 or 5 p.m. year-round, but are closed on major holidays; some have extended hours during the summer. The locations are too numerous to list here, but at last count, Delaware had 2, Maryland had 9, Virginia had 11 and West Virginia had 7. Welcome Centers are often marked on the official state map. Out-of-state visitors should plan ahead and order the state map from the appropriate Office of Tourism prior to traveling; these maps often contain a wealth of "extra" information. Please notice that the addresses and telephone numbers of more than 20 agencies are included in the Appendix to aid you in your quest for related information.

This *Camper's Guide* shows you where to go and how to get to the popular, well-known campgrounds, as well as the lesser-used camping areas. The public campgrounds presented in this guide are provided and operated by state and federal agencies, and afford varied options for outdoor recreation: fishing, boating, canoeing, backpacking, swimming, sailing, picnicking, bicycling, horseback riding, water skiing, or walking along a nature trail. In season, you can also alpine ski, cross-country ski, snow shoe, or snowmobile. You can pursue your favorite hobby as a bird watcher, photographer, botanist, geologist, or naturalist. You may choose to rough it along a backpacking trail or enjoy all the comforts of home in a recreational vehicle. You can spend a day, a weekend, or an entire vacation doing what you like best, no matter how active, or inactive.

There are rules and regulations encountered at all public campgrounds, whether administered by a national, state, or county agency. Please keep in mind that policies, fees, regulations, and available facilities change from time to time. Campers must stay informed by requesting updated information from the parks they visit, by reading the material posted or distributed at the parks, and by reading newspaper articles reporting policy changes. And while we are on the subject of staying informed— take time to get acquainted with the rest of the information in this introduction. You'll find a variety of related topics. In other words—keep reading, don't stop now!

Surely the adage "Train up a child in the way he should go . . ." is applicable to youngsters whose parents are camping enthusiasts.

How to Use This Camper's Guide

Information in this guide is arranged by states: Delaware, Maryland, Virginia, and West Virginia. The parks, lakes, and forests within each state are arranged alphabetically and are cross-listed by name and city in the index. The first page for each state locates the park, lake, or forest on the map and gives the page number where you can find more detailed information and maps of that specific area.

All the information in this *Camper's Guide* has been supplied by the respective operating agency, either through literature distributed by them, through verbal communication, or through secondary sources deemed reliable. The information presented is basic—it tells you how to get there, cites outstanding features of the area, and lists the facilities and the recreational activities available. Mailing addresses and telephone numbers are given in case you want additional information prior to your trip. For some parks, it may be a good idea to confirm weather and road conditions before heading out. Although many campgrounds are open year-round, keep in mind that during the off-season, some camping areas may be closed or some facilities may be discontinued. Also keep in mind that reservation systems are in effect at some parks.

The maps showing the location of facilities within a park or campground should be of considerable help. These maps are often available to you at the park headquarters, but they can also aid you in planning a trip to an unfamiliar park. Arriving at a park after dark can be exasperating if you don't know the layout of the campground. And, those of you who have attempted to meet up with friends at a predetermined spot at a large campground can readily appreciate the value of having such a map prior to your arrival. Most parks are easily found with the help of a good road map, but vicinity maps have been included in some instances. Signs along the way can also be relied upon after you reach the general vicinity of a park.

Because each ranger district within a national forest operates somewhat independently of the national forest as a whole, distributes its own materials, and in many ways has its own "personality" because of terrain, recreational opportunities, etc., information on each national forest is arranged by ranger districts. Most national forest lands are available for primitive camping; those wishing to travel off-the-beaten path should consider purchasing the official national forest map, because even the best road map often does not show the many back roads of the forest.

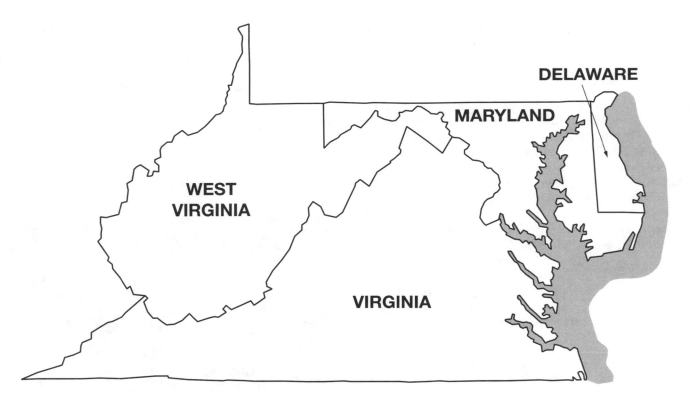

The facilities at a campground are always changing, but a change in status usually means the addition of a service rather than a discontinuation. In other words, a camper often finds better and more facilities than those listed in the latest brochure.

The average camper usually doesn't need help deciding what activities to engage in. Obviously, water-related sports are the most popular activities at a lake, river, or beach setting. Other possible activities have been listed to indicate the availability of nature trails, hiking trails, horseback trails, boat ramps, etc. During the summer camping season, many parks offer interpretive programs, including nature walks, guided tours, and campfire talks, conducted by park personnel.

Whether you camp for a day, a weekend, or longer, whether you are a beginner or a seasoned camper, may this *Camper's Guide* serve you well in the years ahead. Take time to camp, to fish, and to hike the trails, to become truly acquainted with nature, and with yourself, your family, and your friends! Don't put off until tomorrow what can be enjoyed today!

Delaware

The state of Delaware is part of the Delmarva Peninsula separating Delaware Bay and Chesapeake Bay; the peninsula is shared with Maryland and Virginia. Delaware has the nation's lowest mean elevation; almost all of the state consists of a part of the Atlantic Coastal Plain, other than a 10-mile wide part of the Piedmont Plateau that crosses the northern tip. It is hilly and wooded in the north, but becomes nearly level in the south where the coastal plain is smooth. Aided by fertile soil and an abundant water supply, agriculture has long been an important part of Delaware's economy. There is a 30,000-acre cypress swamp along the southern border that is thought to be the northernmost swamp in the country. The most distinctive topographic feature of Delaware is the 18-mile long beach that separates Rehoboth Bay, Indian River Bay, and Assawoman Bay, from the Atlantic Ocean.

Miles of beaches have made Delaware's eastern shore a major resort center. Surfing enthusiasts generally find the best waves on the ocean beaches of Indian River Inlet. Sailing has become a primary recreational activity on the inland bays—Rehoboth, Indian River, and Little Assawoman—and is catching on in the Delaware Bay. Numerous tranquil creeks and rivers in Kent and Sussex counties offer settings for leisurely inland canoeing. One of Delaware's unique boating attractions is the wilderness canoe trail at Trap Pond State Park. A portion of the Great Cypress Swamp lies within the park's 966 acres; the canoe trail is on the 90-acre pond. Hiking is also popular in Delaware; the Division of Parks and Recreation awards the "Golden Boot" award to those hiking 15 nature walks in the state's parks and nature preserves.

Lums Pond is one of Delaware's 3 inland state parks that offer camping facilities; it's open April 1 through October 31.

Boating enthusiasts can challenge the Atlantic Ocean and Delaware Bay or explore the numerous coves of the more protected southern bays. Excellent saltwater fishing begins as early as April and continues through November. Little Creek, Bowers, Mispillion Light, Lewes, and Indian River Inlet are surf fishing centers. Freshwater fishing opportunities are also abundant because lakes and streams are stocked. Several designated trout streams are located in northern Delaware.

Delaware has 12 state parks and 3 state forests. Five of the state parks offer public camping facilities: Cape Henlopen and Delaware Seashore are near the ocean, and Lums Pond, Killens Pond, and Trap Pond are inland. Two other state parks have been included in this guide because they offer youth camping—Brandywine Creek and Carpenter.

Camping Season: Killens Pond State Park is open year-round, while Lums Pond and Cape Henlopen are open from April 1 through October 31. Trap Pond is open from April 1 through November 27. Delaware Seashore State Park is open from March 11 through November 12 for "regular" camping, but the campground is available for fully self-contained units year-round. However, only electric hook-ups are available on-site. A dumping station is open and water is available in a special area.

Delaware State parks do not accept **reservations** for most family campsites. Most campsites are registered on a first-come, first-served basis. The Killens Pond cabins and Trap Pond rent-a-camp sites may be reserved. Between Memorial Day weekend and Labor Day, camping is permitted for a maximum of 14 days within a 21-day period.

Pets are permitted in state park campgrounds but must be on a leash not to exceed 6 feet; they must be attended and under control at all times. Pets are not allowed at the Killens Pond cabins.

Entrance fees for state parks are collected daily from Memorial Day weekend through Labor Day, and on weekends in May, September, and October.

Annual permits allow your vehicle and its occupants unlimited entrance into 10 state parks during the fee season; annual permits are not valid at Fox Point State Park and Fort Delaware State Park. The annual permit fee differs for Delaware citizens, out-of-state visitors, senior citizens, and military personnel.

The three state forests are Blackbird, Ellendale, and Redden. According to one forest manager, the Tybout Tract on the Blackbird State Forest is the only area that has designated family campsites and group campsites. Camping is free of charge, year-round; campsites are primitive and available on a first-come, first-served basis. However, some printed materials from the Forestry Section of the Delaware Department of Agriculture indicate that overnight camping is allowed on any of the state forest lands, but that a written permit for camping in excess of one day is required. Contact the Forestry Section for current policies.

STATE FACTS

	Delaware	Maryland
Capital:	Dover	Annapolis
Inhabitant:	Delawarean	Marylander
Nickname:	The First State	Old Line State
	The Diamond State	Free State
Entered Union:	1787 (1st)	1788 (7th)
Total Area:	2,057 square miles; ranks 49th	10,577 square miles; ranks 42nd
Population:	666,200; ranks 47th	4,781,500; ranks 19th
Extreme Length:	96 miles	198.6 miles
Extreme Breadth:	35 miles	125.5 miles
Highest Point:	448 feet; Ebright Road, Brandywine	3,360 feet; Backbone Mountain
State Motto:	Liberty and Independence	Manly deeds, womanly words
State Flower:	Peach blossom	Black-eyed susan
State Bird:	Blue hen chicken	Baltimore oriole
State Tree:	American holly	White Oak

Maryland

Maryland ranges from above 3,300 feet in the western reaches of the state to sea level in the coastal and Chesapeake Bay regions. The state's coastline along the Atlantic Ocean is short, but Chesapeake Bay, which divides the state into an Eastern and Western Shore, provides many fine harbors, and several important islands dot the bay. The width of the bay varies from 3 to 30 miles and is a primary channel of commerce. The Eastern Shore is predominantly low, rolling farmland, and pine forests interspersed with marshy bottomlands; this section of the Atlantic Coastal Plain is sometimes called "Tidewater Maryland." Southern and central Maryland rise gradually in the rich agricultural belt of the Piedmont Plateau, broken by the ridges of the Catoctins. The Eastern Continental Divide passes through Western Maryland, and the Youghiogheny River water drains north to the Ohio River System.

Recreational areas in Maryland are scattered from the Atlantic shore to the Allegheny Mountains in the western part of the state. Seaside pastimes can be pursued at Assateague Island on the Atlantic shore, while alpine skiing is available in the winter in the mountains of the west. Wisp Mountain, located near McHenry in Garrett County, rises over 3,080 feet above sea level and overlooks Deep Creek Lake. With 23 slopes and 14 miles of trails from novice to expert, the Wisp ski area offers great Eastern skiing. Snowmakers can cover 90% of the trails on the mountain with deep, light snow every winter so skiers don't have to depend on Mother Nature. Cross-country skiing is popular throughout Northern and Western Maryland after snowfalls. Popular trails are located in state parks such as Herrington Manor and New Germany. Snowmobile trails are located at the 4 state forests; facilities for sledding, ice skating and ice fishing are available at many state parks.

Boating ranges from shooting the upper Potomac rapids in a kayak to yachting along the bay, the lower Potomac and Patuxent rivers. More than 20 state parks have lakes/streams suitable for canoeing; many offer canoe rentals. Canoe trails are located at Assateague Island, Patuxent River State Park, and the C & O Canal National Historic Park. Whitewater rafting on the Potomac and Youghiogheny rivers is an exciting and challenging activity; the inexperienced should raft with a professional outfitter. Gunpowder Falls State Park, Patapsco State Park, and Savage River State Forest list whitewater canoeing as available activities.

Anglers can choose from swift mountain streams, well-stocked lakes and reservoirs, the Chesapeake Bay, the Atlantic Ocean, and such large rivers as the Patuxent and Potomac. Surf fishing is popular at Assateague Island. Ocean fishing is best from mid April until late October. Ocean City is known as the "White Marlin Capital of the World."

Maryland's unique geography provides scuba divers with a wide variety of underwater activities in different aquatic environments year-round. The ocean off the coast of Maryland is the most popular diving spot because of the number and variety of shipwrecks found there. The Chesapeake Bay is another popular diving area; wreck diving is enjoyed there as well as harvesting oysters in the fall and winter months. Surfers enjoy riding the waves at Ocean City and Assateague Island.

Hundreds of miles of maintained trails are located in Maryland—self-guided nature trails, hiking trails, bicycle trails, and horseback trails. Two of the longest continuous hiking trails are the 40-mile section of the Appalachian Trail along the ridge of South Mountain, and the 184.5-mile towpath trail of the C & O Canal National Historical Park from Georgetown in Washington, DC, to Cumberland on the Allegheny Plateau. This trail is also used for cycling and horseback riding. Two other cycling trails are the 13.3 miles of paved trails of the Baltimore and Annapolis Trail Park from Dorsey Road to Route 50 in Arnold, and the 21-mile Northern Central Railroad Hike and Bike Trail from Cockeysville to the MD/PA state line. The Maryland Department of Transportation publishes a map called *The Bicycle Touring Map;* it is free from the Maryland Office of Tourism, or from any of the 10 Visitor Information Centers.

Horseback trails exist at the 4 state forests, 10 of the state parks, and 3 of the national parks in Maryland. Maryland has a singular official state sport: jousting. In the modern version of this medieval pursuit, competitors on horseback charge down an arena, catching rings of decreasing size on a lance.

Maryland has 20 state parks, 4 state forests, 4 national parks, 1 lake, and 3 regional parks that offer public camping facilities. The 4 parks operated by the National Park Service are Assateague Island National Seashore, Catoctin Mountain Park, Chesapeake and Ohio Canal National Historical Park, and Greenbelt Park. Youghiogheny River Lake is operated by the US Army Corps of Engineers. The 3 regional parks are located in Montgomery and Prince George's counties in the proximity of Washington, DC; they are included in this guide because they have camping facilities and also offer a wide variety of recreational activities. Because the rules and regulations pertaining to camping at these 8 assorted agency-operated recreation areas differ in many ways from the rules and regulations for state-operated parks, information on them is provided in the Maryland section of this guide.

The State Forest and Park Service of the Maryland Department of Natural Resources operates 55 parks, forests, natural environment areas, national resource management areas, demonstration forests, and wildlife sanctuaries. Camping facilities are provided at 20 of the state parks and 4 of the state forests. The following information pertains specifically to these recreational sites.

The main **camping season** in state parks appears to be mid-April through October. However, it varies according to weather conditions. Some camping areas are open all year with limited facilities; several parks keep only one loop open for self-contained units. Garrett, Green Ridge, Potomac, and Savage River state forests remain open for camping all year. Call (410) 461-0052 for campground opening and closing dates and for the day-use operating schedule. Many parks are open year-round but may have limited facilities part of the time.

About three-fourths of the state parks take telephone **reservations** at the park office Monday through Friday during office hours; a $5 fee is charged. Because the camping reservation list may change from time to time, campers should obtain an updated copy of the current reservation list each year. **Camping fees** are charged; discounts are given when camping before Memorial Day and after Labor Day, and during the week (Sunday through Thursday) Memorial Day through Labor Day, excluding holidays.

Day use fees are charged at many state parks—generally, March through October. However, some parks charge a day use fee only on weekends.

Cabins may be rented at 6 state parks: Cunningham Falls, Elk Neck, Herrington Manor, New Germany, Janes Island, and Martinak. Reservations can be made one calendar year in advance, with a $5 reservation fee, by calling the park office directly. They must be made for one week intervals from Memorial Day through Labor Day, and 2 nights minimum stay for the remainder of the operating season. For detailed information about cabin rental, phone headquarters (410) 974-3771 and request the brochure on cabin rentals.

Generally, **pets,** under the control of their owners, are permitted in state forests and some undeveloped areas of state parks, such as roadways, and trails. Pets are not allowed at any bathing beaches, picnic areas, cabin areas, or other developed day use areas. Presently, the 4 state forests and 9 other camping parks allow pets; some restrictions apply. Obtain the list of parks that allow pets from the State Forest and Park Service, or phone the park directly for their policy.

Maryland's forests and parks are "trash-free." All trash barrels, receptacles, and dumpsters have been removed from picnic and beach areas. Visitors to day-use areas are provided with bags when they enter parks and are asked to take home their own refuse and to recycle. When you visit a state park, remember to pack your picnic in reusable containers and to carry out what you carry in. Those persons renting shelters or having large groups should bring their own large trash bags with their other picnic or camping supplies.

Swallow Falls State Park is located in the western part of Maryland in the Allegheny Mountains along the Youghiogheny River. The park is a mountain paradise of scenic beauty—a place of rushing water and towering trees, of cliffs and rocks and wildflowers.

Virginia

Virginia, somewhat triangular in shape, has 4 principal land regions (west to east): the Appalachian Plateau, the Great Appalachian Valley, the Piedmont Plateau, and the Atlantic Coastal Plain. The Appalachian range includes the Allegheny Mountains along the western border and the Blue Ridge range, which rises between the Valley and Piedmont sections. The rolling Piedmont Plateau, which extends from the fall line that runs from Washington, D.C. through Richmond, covers nearly half the state. The eastern fourth of the state is the Coastal Plain, also called by its historic name, the "Tidewater Region." This region includes the 750-square-mile Dismal Swamp on the North Carolina border. The Eastern Shore, east of Chesapeake Bay and separated from the rest of the state, is on the southern tip of the Delmarva Peninsula.

Some of the finest scenery in the east is found in the George Washington and Jefferson national forests, which include much of the state's western mountains and plateaus. Mount Rogers National Recreation Area in the Jefferson National Forest boasts the state's highest peak—Mt. Rogers, at 5,729 feet. On the northern end of the Blue Ridge Mountains is Shenandoah National Park. Spectacular in every season, its 105-mile Skyline Drive winds along the crest from Front Royal south to Afton, where it connects with the Blue Ridge Parkway. The Blue Ridge Parkway crosses the Virginia/North Carolina state line at Mile 216.9.

Recreational opportunities are numerous in Virginia. The center for beach activities is the ocean resort of Virginia Beach and the more primitive Assateague Island National Seashore. Assateague is an undeveloped barrier island that offers swimming, surfing, and surf fishing along its 37 miles of land that parallels the shores of Virginia and Maryland. The saltwater fishing spots are in 2 distinct areas: The Chesapeake Bay (bayside) and the Atlantic Ocean (offshore and coastal). Both bay and ocean produce a large variety of fish. The 17.6-mile Chesapeake Bay Bridge-Tunnel connecting the Eastern Shore to the Virginia mainland is often referred to as the world's largest and most productive man-made reef.

Whitewater canoeing is popular on the Shenandoah, Maury, and James rivers. Rapids as high as Class 4 are along urban Richmond's stretch of the James River. Boating and fishing are popular on Virginia's 15 major lakes. The largest boating lakes are the 50,000-acre Kerr Reservoir, also called Buggs Island Lake, and the 22,000-acre Smith Mountain Lake. The state boasts 185 trout streams covering 2,100 miles with more than 850,000 trout released annually into streams and lakes.

Some of the best skiing in the southeast can be found in Virginia. Five ski areas in the state offer downhill skiing: Bryce in Basye, Cascade Mountain near Galax, the Homestead in Hot Springs, Wintergreen near Waynesboro, and Massanutten near Harrisonburg. Accommodations range from rustic

Reconstructed cabins, at Virginia's Grayson Highlands State Park, recapture the lives of the hardy pioneers who settled this rugged land.

to luxurious. All ski areas are equipped with 100% snowmaking ability and offer night skiing. Cross-country skiing is offered at one of the ski resorts, and several state and national parks.

Virginia has 9 rails-to-trails statewide, with one of the longest US rails-to-trails bikeways (45 miles) located in Northern Virginia. Two of the country's major interstate bicycle routes bisect Virginia. The 600-mile Virginia Loop Trail takes cyclists through some of Virginia's most scenic areas. For Information on bicycle trails, contact the State Bicycle Coordinator at the Virginia Department of Transportation.

Hiking opportunities in Virginia are abundant—in the state and national parks as well as in the 2 national forests. One-fourth of the Appalachian Trail (AT) lies in Virginia. Shenandoah National Park has 100 miles of the AT; it crosses the Skyline Drive 32 times. A very beautiful section of the AT passes through the Jefferson National Forest. The 57-mile New River Trail State Park stretches through 4 counties in the Southwest Blue Ridge Highlands as it follows the scenic and historic New River.

Virginia has 19 state parks, 4 national parks, 1 national recreation area, 2 national forests, 5 lakes, 1 wildlife management area, and 3 regional parks that offer public camping facilities. The 4 parks operated by the National Park Service are Blue Ridge National Park, Cumberland Gap National Historical Park, Prince William Forest Park, and Shenandoah National Park. The Mount Rogers National Recreation Area is administered by the US Forest Service, as are the 2 national forests, Jefferson and George Washington. Gathright Dam and Lake Moomaw is a US Army Corps of Engineers lake but the management of the 2 recreational areas is shared by 2 ranger districts of the George Washington National Forest. The other 4 lakes, namely, Flannagan, Kerr, North Fork of Pound, and Philpott, are operated by the US Army Corps of Engineers. The 3 regional parks are included in this guide because they have camping facilities and also offer a wide variety of recreational activities. Because the rules and regulations pertaining to camping at these 15 assorted agency-operated recreation areas differ in many ways from the rules and regulations for state-operated parks; information on them is provided in the Virginia section of this guide.

The Piedmont State Forests of Virginia total about 50,000 acres. The Cumberland, Appomattox-Buckingham, Prince Edward-Gallion, and Pocahontas are administered by the Virginia Division of Forestry. A state park that offers camping facilities and a variety of recreational activities is located in each of these state forests. Therefore, information about the 4 forests, other than the state parks located there, is not included in this guide. Anyone desiring maps, or information on these forests, should contact the Division of Forestry (see Appendix for address.)

According to a Virginia Department of Conservation and Recreation brochure, the names of the areas managed by them include the following: park, historic park, wildlife management area, natural area, and natural area preserve. There are 40 such areas listed; camping facilities are provided at 19 of them. The following information pertains specifically to these 19 recreation sites.

STATE FACTS

	Virginia	West Virginia
Capital:	Richmond	Charleston
Inhabitant:	Virginian	West Virginian
Nickname:	Old Dominion State	Mountain State
Entered Union:	1788 (10th)	1863 (35th)
Total Area:	40,817 square miles	24,232 square miles
	ranks 36th	ranks 41st
Population:	6,187,400; ranks 12th	1,793,500; ranks 34th
Extreme Length:	440 miles	265 miles
Extreme Breadth:	200 miles	237 miles
Highest Point:	5,729 feet, Mount Rogers	4,861 feet, Spruce Knob
State Motto:	Thus ever to tyrants	Mountaineers are always free
State Flower:	Dogwood	Big rhododendron
State Bird:	Cardinal	Cardinal
State Tree:	Dogwood	Sugar maple

State parks are open year-round but the **camping season** usually runs from March through November. Parking fees are collected daily year-round; the fee differs on the park and day of the week. An annual parking pass is available for $20. The maximum camping period is 14 days in any 30-day period.

All campsite **reservations** are made by calling the Virginia State Parks Reservation Center weekdays from 9 a.m. to 4 p.m. at 1-800-933-PARK (7275) or in the Richmond calling area (804) 225-3867. A $6 fee is charged for each reservation. Reservations are not accepted by individual state parks. Any campsites not reserved are available on a first-come, first-served basis.

Boat rentals, including rowboats, paddleboats, and canoes, are available at many state parks; they are generally available daily from Memorial Day weekend through Labor Day weekend. Swimming areas generally operate daily from Memorial Day weekend through Labor Day weekend, as do horse rentals at Hungry Mother State Park.

Climate-controlled housekeeping **cabins** are located at 7 state parks: Claytor Lake, Douthat, Fairy Stone, Hungry Mother, Seashore, Staunton River, and Westmoreland. They are available in different sizes. Douthat State Park has a lodge with 6 bedrooms that will accommodate a maximum of 15 persons. In the past, cabins had to be rented by the week between Memorial Day and Labor Day

weekend, and could be rented with a two-night minimum in the "off-season" between Labor Day weekend and Memorial Day weekend. A new policy allows two-night minimum stay reservations throughout the season on a limited basis. These reservations may be made no earlier than one month in advance of your intended stay. Any cabins not reserved will become available on a first-come, first-served basis for a minimum of two nights. To learn of cabin availability, phone the park directly no sooner than the Friday before you would like the cabin. Cabin reservations for 6 of the parks are made by calling the Virginia State Parks Reservation Center at the phone number listed in this section. However, reservations for the rustic overnight cabins at Westmoreland State Park must be made through the park directly; call (804) 493-8821. These 6 cabins can be rented for a minimum of 2 nights and a maximum of 2 consecutive weeks; they are available Memorial Day weekend through Labor Day weekend.

Pets are allowed in cabins and campgrounds; they are not allowed on swimming beaches. Rabies shots are a must for dogs brought into state parks. Your dog must wear a tag certifying that it has been innoculated. Pets must be kept in cabins, tents, or vehicles at night or on a leash no longer than 6 feet at all times. Cabin and campsite guests will be charged $3.00 per pet per night, paid upon arrival at the park.

West Virginia

West Virginia has rugged, ravine-slashed terrain and highly irregular boundaries. There are 2 main land regions: the Appalachian Plateau constitutes more than 80% of its area, and the Great Appalachian Valley consists of a wide strip along the eastern border that includes a small section of the Blue Ridge. The Allegheny Plateau slopes toward the northwest, sending the Monongahela, Little Kanawha, and Big Sandy rivers into the Ohio River; the Big Sandy serves as part of the boundary with Kentucky. West Virginia is bounded on the northwest by the Ohio River, and on the northeast by the Potomac River. The highest section of the state is the Allegheny Front, just inside the Virginia/West Virginia border, where elevations range from 3,500 to more than 4,000 feet. Between its ridges lie valleys that are deep and fertile but often difficult to reach. The Spruce Knob Unit of the Spruce Knob-Seneca Rocks National Recreation Area in the Monongahela National Forest boasts the state's highest point—Spruce Knob, at 4,861 feet.

West Virginia's parks, forests, wildlife management areas, rivers, and lakes, offer a wide array of **recreational facilities** in a wide range of scenic settings. Boating can be enjoyed at Sutton Lake, Summerville Lake, Bluestone Lake, Tygart Lake, and several smaller reservoirs, as well as the Ohio and Kanawha rivers. Lakes are suitable for row, paddle, motor, and sailboats. Boating equipment may be rented at several parks that have access to lakes and rivers. Anglers may choose from numerous lake, rivers, and streams. Mountain streams, which flow through many parks and forests, provide the habitat for many native and specially stocked fish. Nearly all state parks have swimming pools, while some offer river and lake swimming on supervised beaches.

The whitewater rafting industry is thriving in West Virginia; the state claims to be the whitewater capital of the East. Seven of the 22 major rivers in the East suitable for rafting are in West Virginia—the Gauley, New, Cheat, Tygart, Potomac, Bluestone, and Shenandoah. A 15-mile section of the New River Gorge from

Thurmond to Fayette Station provides the most challenging rapids in the East. This section is named "The Grand Canyon of the East." A detailed whitewater rafting brochure listing various outfitters is available by calling 1-800-CALL WVA.

Virtually every state park in West Virginia has hiking trails. In fact, the state has a program called "Hiking West Virginia" whereby a one-time registration fee of $10 is paid, and mileage is accumulated on a hiking trail located in a state park, forest, or wildlife management area. Various hiking plateaus have been set, whereby hikers reaching these plateaus from 25 to 1,000 miles are recognized. Winding from Caldwell to Cass, the 76-mile Greenbrier River Trail is popular for hiking, mountain biking, and cross-country skiing; contact Watoga State Park for information. The North Bend Rail-Trail is a 61-mile trail from Wolf Summit to Walker for hiking, biking, and horseback riding; contact North Bend State Park for information. Equestrian trails and riding stables are at several state parks and state forests. There are several extensive hiking trail systems in the state suitable for backpacking. Call the West Virginia Scenic Trails Association (304) 744-5157, for information.

The best alpine and nordic skiing in the mid-Atlantic states can be found at Snowshoe, Canaan Valley, Silver Creek, and Winter Place resorts and neighboring cross-country ski centers. A 7.9-mile portion of the long-distance Allegheny Trail makes an inn-to-inn connection through the national forest from Canaan Valley Resort State Park to Blackwater Falls State Park, where the Nordic Ski Center opens miles of backcountry ski touring. Many other state parks and state forests, too numerous to mention here, offer cross-country ski trails. Blackwater Falls and

Pipestem Resort feature sled runs with rope tows, rental sleds, and toboggans. Canaan Valley operates an ice skating rink and rental skates are available. A complete guide to alpine and nordic skiing in West Virginia is available by calling 1-800-CALL WVA.

West Virginia has 18 state parks, 1 national recreation area, 6 lakes, 7 state forests, 5 wildlife management areas, 1 national forest in its entirety and several segments of another national forest, that offer public camping facilities. The Spruce Knob-Seneca Rocks National Recreation Area is administered by the US Forest Service. Monongahela National Forest lies entirely within West Virginia; 3 relatively small sections of the Jefferson National Forest lie along the WV/VA state line. All 6 of the lakes are operated by the US Army Corps of Engineers. Because the rules and regulations pertaining to camping at these 9 assorted agency-operated recreation areas differ in many ways from the rules and regulations for state-operated parks, information on them is provided in the West Virginia section of this guide.

In addition to the thousands of acres of land already managed, protected, and developed for recreational use within the jurisdiction of the state park system, the recreational facilities on seven of the state's wildlife management areas have been placed under the supervision of the Department of Natural Resources. Five of these 7 wildlife management areas provide camping facilities: Laurel Lake offers standard campsites; Pleasant Creek, Plum Orchard, and Teter Creek offer rustic campsites; and Bluestone offers primitive campsites. There are other wildlife management areas that offer rustic or primitive camping, but information about them is not included in this guide. For information on them, contact the Wildlife Resources Section of the West Virginia Division of Natural Resources.

The following information pertains specifically to the 30 recreation sites that are operated by the state: namely, the 18 state parks, 7 state forests, and the 5 wildlife management areas that offer camping. The state operates many other historical parks, day-use parks, forests, and wildlife management areas. For information on all of these areas, as well as up-to-date detailed information on camping regulations, phone or write to the West Virginia Division of Tourism and Parks. The information given here should be considered as an overview, and, of course, is subject to change.

Operation of state-owned campgrounds is variable and dependent upon the weather. It is advisable to

Twin Falls Resort State Park offers 5 rent-a-camp sites. Designed for the novice or sometime camper, they are completely equipped.

check with the individual facility in advance of stated opening and closing dates for confirmation. In most cases, recreational facilities operate only from Memorial Day weekend to Labor Day. The **camping season** for state parks usually runs from mid-April to October with a few exceptions (Watoga, Moncove Lake, and Holly River are open through deer rifle season.) Cannan Valley, Beech Fork, and Pipestem, are open-year round but have few or no water hookups in the winter. Due to the primitive to rustic classifications, the wildlife management areas are open nearly year-round to accommodate the hunting season.

Twin Falls Resort and Tomlinson Run offer **rent-a-camps.** Designed for the novice or sometime camper, a completely equipped site can be rented. Reservations are accepted for the period from Memorial Day weekend through Labor Day and are handled in the same manner as renting a regular campsite.

While most state parks and forest campsites are rented on a first-come, first-served basis, up to 50% of the sites can be reserved at 15 of the 18 state parks. **Reservations** are not accepted at Audra, Moncove Lake, and Tygart Lake. Sites can be also be reserved at Greenbrier and Kanawha state forests. With the exception of Canaan Valley Resort, where the season extends through October, the camping reservation season generally begins the Friday before Memorial Day and ends Labor Day. A minimum stay of 2 nights, up to a maximum of 14, is required when making a reservation. Reservations must be made at least 7 days in advance; a $5 fee is charged. Reservations may be obtained by writing or calling the park directly or by calling 1-800-CALL WVA.

All state park and forest **cottages/cabins** are completely furnished and equipped for housekeeping. Cabins are classified as modern, standard, economy, and rustic. Facilities are thoroughly modern throughout with the exception of rustic cabins. There are 4 parks that offer cabins or lodge rooms but not camping facilities, so are not included in this guide. They are Cacapon Resort, Cass Scenic Railroad, Hawks Nest, and Lost River. At certain state parks, cottages and modern cabins are open year-round while standard cabins open April 15 and close October 31. Only weekly reservations are taken from the second Monday in June to Labor Day; the cottage/cabin week is Monday to Monday. However, they may be rented by the day or longer from Labor Day to the second Monday in June, with the exception of Canaan Valley during ski season. Some lodges may require more than one night as a minimum stay on holiday and

Photographers are always in abundance at this park in West Virginia, named for the falls of the Blackwater River. Its waters plunge 5 stories, then tumble through an 8-mile-long gorge.

prime weekends. Reservations may be made up to one year in advance from the first day of the month. Lodge, cottage, or cabin reservations may be made by calling or writing a park or forest directly, or by calling 1-800-CALL WVA. A $15 handling fee is is charged for cottage/cabin reservations. A detailed brochure is available on rates and reservation procedure for cabins, cottages, and lodges.

The state's 8 lodge and **resort parks** are known throughout the region for their outstanding accommodations and recreational activities. Each of them has a restaurant, and rooms are available to accommodate everything from intimate gatherings of 20 to groups of 300. Six of the resort parks have campgrounds and are included in this guide. The 2 that do not offer camping facilities are Cacapon Resort, and Hawks Nest. The state park lodges are open year-round with the exception of the lodge at Tygart Lake; it is closed November 1 to March 31, or Easter weekend, whichever comes first. At both Pipestem and Cacapon resorts, one of their two lodges closes and one remains open during the winter. Restaurants at the resort parks are open all year, other than Tygart Lake. In other parks, restaurants or snack bars generally observe operating seasons from Memorial Day weekend through Labor Day, and some remain open on weekends only through the fall color season. Check in advance for exact dates and operating hours.

With regard to **pets,** only dogs and cats are permitted in camping areas, but must be restrained on a leash not more than 10 feet in length. Pets are not allowed in the lodges, cottages, or cabins. Campers must pay a small fee for the use of swimming and game court facilities.

Federal Recreation Passport Program

Some federal parks and facilities can be entered and used free of charge. Other areas and facilities require payment of entrance fees, user fees, special recreation permit fees, or some combination. A brochure by the U.S. Department of the Interior entitled *Federal Recreation Passport Program* explains the five entrance pass programs, Briefly stated below, these beneficial programs can provide a savings to park visitors.

Passports are obtainable at all National Park System areas where entrance fees are charged, all National Forest Service supervisor's offices, and most Forest Service ranger station offices.

Golden Eagle Passport—an annual entrance pass to all federally-operated parks, such as national parks, monuments, historic sites, recreation areas and national wildlife refuges. It admits free of charge the permit holder and acccompanying persons in a private, noncommercial vehicle. For those not traveling by private car, it admits the permit holder and family group. The pass costs $25, is good for one calendar year (January 1 through December 31), and permits unlimited entries to all federal entrance fee areas.

Golden Age Passport—for a one-time fee of $10, a lifetime entrance pass for citizens or permanent residents of the United States who are 62 years or older. It admits the permit holder and any accompanying passengers in a single, private, noncommercial vehicle. Where entry is not by private car, the passport admits the permit holder, spouse, and children. It provides a 50% discount on federal use fees charged for facilities and services except those provided by private concessioners. It must be obtained in person, with proof of age.

Golden Access Passport—a free lifetime entrance pass for citizens or permanent residents of the U.S. who have been medically determined to be blind or permanently disabled and, as a result, are eligible to receive benefits under federal law. It offers the same benefits as the Golden Age Passport, and must be obtained in person with proof of eligibility.

Park Pass—an annual entrance permit to a specific park, monument, historic site or recreation area in the National Park System that charges entrance fees. The Park Pass is valid for entrance fees only and does not cover user fees. The cost varies between $10 and $15 depending upon the area; is good for one calendar year (January 1 through December 31); and permits unlimited entries to the park unit where it is purchased.

Federal Duck Stamp—officially known as the Migratory Bird Hunting and Conservation Stamp and still required of waterfowl hunters, the Federal Duck Stamp now also serves as an annual entrance fee permit to national wildlife refuges that charge entrance fees. The Duck Stamp is valid for entrance fees only and does not cover user fees. The stamp costs $15, is good from July 1 through June 30 of the following year, and permits unlimited entries to all national wildlife refuges that charge an entrance fee. It can be purchased at most post offices.

Rocky Knob Campground is located at mile 170 on the Blue Ridge Parkway; it has 109 campsites for RVs and tents. Other campgrounds along the parkway in Virginia are at Otter Creek (mile 60.9), Peaks of Otter (mile 86.0), and Roanoke Mountain (mile 120.4).

Reservation System

Although many campgrounds operate on a first-come, first-served basis, it is best to check with the operating agency of a campground to assure campsites are available. The list of campgrounds requiring reservations and their reservation season may change from year to year; even the agency handling the reservations may change. Perhaps the best procedure for a camper, each year, is to obtain an up-to-date brochure describing the reservation procedure with the reservation application. The brochure also serves as a valuable source of information on current fees and facilities available. Be reminded that the reservation systems differ for state parks, national parks, and national forests.

State Parks

Delaware

Delaware state parks do not accept reservations for family campsites other than the rent-a-camp sites at Trap Pond; campsites are available on a first-come, first-served basis. The Killens Pond cabins at Killens Pond and the rent-a-camp sites may be reserved by phoning the park.

Maryland

About three-fourths of the state parks take telephone reservations at the park office Monday through Friday during office hours; a $5 fee is charged. Campground users should obtain an updated copy of the current reservation list each year. Reservations for cabins can be made one calendar year in advance, with a $5 reservation fee, by calling the park office directly. They must be made for one week intervals from Memorial Day through Labor Day, and 2 nights minimum stay for the remainder of the operating season.

Virginia

All campsite reservations are made by calling the Virginia State Parks Reservation Center weekdays from 9 a.m. to 4 p.m. at 1-800-933-PARK (7275) or in the Richmond calling area (804) 225-3867. A $6 fee is charged for each reservation. Reservations are not accepted by individual state parks. Any campsites not reserved are available on a first-come, first-served basis. In the past, cabins had to be rented by the week between Memorial Day and Labor Day weekend. A new policy allows two-night minimum stay reservations throughout the season on a limited basis. These reservations may be made no earlier than one month in advance of your intended stay. Any cabins not reserved will become available on a first-come, first-served basis for a minimum of two nights. To learn of cabin availability, phone the park directly. Reservations for the rustic overnight cabins at Westmoreland State Park must be made through the park directly; call (804) 493-8821. Cabin reservations in the other parks are made through the Reservation Center.

West Virginia

Up to 50% of the state park campsites can be reserved except those at Audra, Moncove Lake, and Tygart Lake; the other sites are rented on a first-come, first-served basis. Sites can also be reserved at Greenbrier and Kanawha state forests. The camping reservation season generally begins the Friday before Memorial Day and ends Labor Day. A minimum stay of 2 nights is required. Reservations must be made at least 7 days in advance; a $5 fee is charged. Reservations may be obtained by writing or calling the park directly or by calling 1-800-CALL WVA.

Reservations for the rent-a-camps are handled in the same manner as renting a regular campsite. From the second Monday in June to Labor Day, cottages and cabins must be rented for a week that runs from Monday to Monday. However, they may be rented by the day or longer from Labor Day to the second Monday in June, with the exception of Canaan Valley during ski season. A $15 handling fee is charged for cottage/cabin reservations. Some lodges may require more than one night as a minimum stay on holiday and prime weekends. Lodge, cottage, or cabin reservations may be made by calling or writing the park or forest directly, or by calling 1-800-CALL WVA.

National Parks

Assateague Island National Seashore in Maryland, and Shenandoah National Park in Virginia have campsites on the MISTIX reservation system. Reservations are available through MISTIX by telephone from 7 a.m. to 6 p.m., Pacific Time, 7 days a week. Visa, Mastercard, Discover and personal checks are accepted. Reservations may be made no sooner than 8 weeks in advance, and up to the day before your planned arrival. Phone reservations made within 10 days of arrival will be held at the campground; all others will be mailed. For reservations, procedures, restrictions and cancellation charges, write or call:

MISTIX
P.O. Box 85705
San Diego, CA 92138-5704
1-800-365-CAMP (2267)

National Forests

The US Forest Service provides a nationwide reservation system for selected campgrounds throughout the United States. Jefferson National Forest and George Washington National Forest are located in Virginia; Monongahela National Forest and 3 relatively small areas of George Washington National Forest are in West Virginia. Most national forest campgrounds still operate entirely on a first-come, first-served basis. However, because the campgrounds on the reservation system may change periodically, it is recommended that you contact the respective forest supervisor or district ranger for a current list. Campgrounds that are on the system usually have about 50% of the campsites available for reservations, while other sites are first-come, first-served. Reservations for some group campsites may be handled directly through the ranger district, or, for family sites, through a concessionaire.

The National Recreation Reservation System offers customer payment through Visa, Discover, MasterCard, and personal checks/money orders. The center operates during the following hours:

January–September:
Monday–Friday, 9 a.m.–9 p.m., E.S.T.
Saturday–Sunday,   11 a.m.–7 p.m. E.S.T.
October–December:
Monday–Friday, 11 a.m.–7 p.m., E.S.T.

Reservations can be made up to 360 days (for group sites) and up to 180 days for family sites) in advance of your first night of arrival. For details, reservations, procedures, restrictions and cancellation charges, write or call:

National Recreation Reservation System
P.O. Box 900
Cumberland, MD 21501-0900
1-800-280-CAMP (2267)
TDD number for hearing impaired:
1-800-879-4496   FAX: (301) 722-9802

Appalachian National Scenic Trail

For Information

Appalachian Trail Conference
P.O. Box 807
Harpers Ferry, WV 25425-0807
(304) 535-6331

The Appalachian National Scenic Trail is a public footpath across 2,144 miles of Appalachian Mountain ridgelines from Maine to Georgia. It was designed, constructed, and marked in the 1920s and 1930s by volunteer hiking clubs joined together by the Appalachian Trail Conference. The Appalachian Trail (AT) was one of the first two national scenic trails named after the National Trails System Act was passed in 1968.

From Maine's Mount Katahdin to Georgia's Springer Mountain, this footpath winds through the scenic, wooded, pastoral, and wild lands of the Appalachian Mountains. Motor vehicles are illegal on all sections of the AT. Horses are prohibited except where expressly permitted. Dogs are prohibited in Great Smoky Mountains National Park and must be leashed in Shenandoah National Park.

Appalachian Trail Conference (ATC) headquarters is located in Harpers Ferry, WV near the Trail's halfway point. From here, the ATC coordinates maintenance of the AT through 31 affiliated clubs and 4 ATC field offices.

The ATC is the central clearinghouse for guidebooks and maps covering every section of the AT, and educational brochures for trail users. ATC also sells nearly 60 other publications on related subjects, including backpacking techniques and equipment, first aid, and trail food. Thru-hikers stop at ATC headquarters in Harpers Ferry, WV to write in the AT log book and to have their picture taken. When they complete the entire trail, they contact the ATC and they then qualify as 2,000-milers.

The Appalachian Trail Project Office (ATPO) of the National Park Service is also located in Harpers Ferry. ATPO is responsible for the trail's overall administration. The National Park Service has overall responsibility for the AT through its Project Office. Actual operations affecting use of the Trail are shared responsibilities of the National Park Service, the US Forest Service, various agencies in the 14 states through which it passes, the ATC, and dozens of hiking conferences and clubs. The forest service administers 850 miles of trail and states administer 420 miles. In 1984, the National Park Service delegated the day-to-day responsibility for managing the lands through which the AT is routed, to the Appalachian Trail Conference.

You do not need a permit to walk the AT. However, overnight camping permits are necessary in Shenandoah and Great Smoky Mountains national parks and parts of the White Mountain National Forest. The trail is marked with 2-inch by 6-inch vertical white paint blazes. A double blaze—one above the other—is placed before turns, junctions, or other areas that require that hikers be alert. Blue blazes mark AT side trails. Usually these lead to shelters, water supplies, or special vistas.

Maryland Section—The 40 miles of the AT in Maryland are characterized by a 38-mile walk along the ridge crest of South Mountain. This offers a good choice for a 3- or 4-day trip with good views and is never too far from towns and highways. The trail joins the Chesapeake and Ohio Canal towpath at the Potomac River.

West Virginia Section—The AT crosses the Potomac River into West Virginia at Harpers Ferry on a new footbridge built onto a railroad bridge. The ATC headquarters is at the corner of Washington and Jackson Streets, uphill from Harpers Ferry National Historical Park. The trail soon leaves West Virginia across the Shenandoah River opposite Harpers Ferry; it briefly touches WV again near Pearisburg, VA.

Virginia Section—One-fourth of the AT lies in Virginia. Shenandoah National Park has 100 miles of the trail—it crosses Skyline Drive 32 times—and many side trails. Views here are extraordinary. The AT crosses the Blue Ridge Parkway twice in one 70-mile stretch, and it crosses several sections of the Jefferson National Forest for short distances. From here the AT crosses west of the Shenandoah Valley. The portion in southwest Virginia affords a splendid wilderness trip. In both Jefferson and George Washington national forests, the floral displays in June and July of rhododendron and azalea are outstanding.

The Appalachian National Scenic Trail is a public footpath across the Appalachian Mountain ridgelines from Maine to Georgia; portions of the trail lie in Maryland, West Virginia, and Virginia.

New River Gorge

For Information

New River Gorge National River
P.O. Box 246
104 Main Street
Glen Jean, WV 25846
(304) 465-0508

The New River and its gorge and 40 miles of its tributaries are preserved as New River Gorge National River, Gauley River National Recreation Area, and Bluestone National Scenic River, all units of the National Park System. The New River is one of the most renowned fishing streams in the state, and nowhere else in the US can one find such a concentration of premiere whitewater.

The **New River Gorge National River** was established in 1978 to preserve and protect 53 miles of the New River as a free-flowing waterway. This unit of the National Park System lies along the New River between the towns of Hinton and Fayetteville in southern West Virginia. Here the free-flowing New River falls 750 feet in 50 miles from Bluestone Dam to Gauley Bridge creating one of the

Map #1—North Half

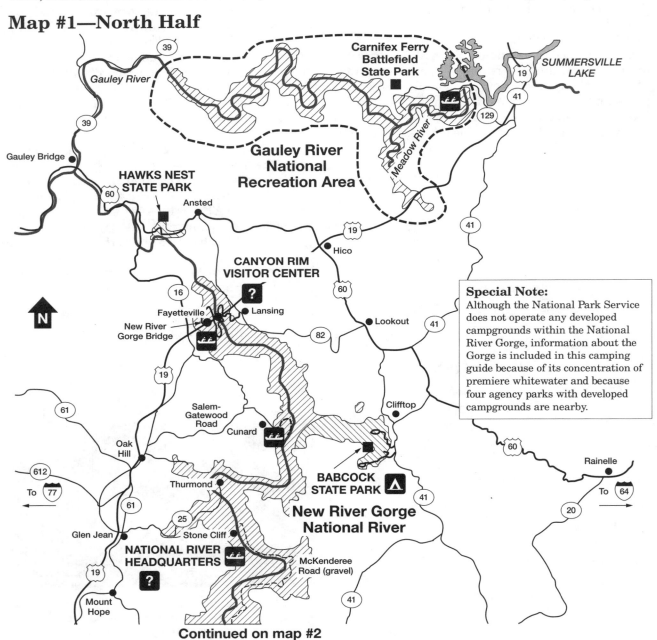

Special Note:
Although the National Park Service does not operate any developed campgrounds within the National River Gorge, information about the Gorge is included in this camping guide because of its concentration of premiere whitewater and because four agency parks with developed campgrounds are nearby.

Continued on map #2

finest whitewater rivers in the eastern United States. In the southern end of the park, the river is more placid. Except for a few Class III rapids that challenge the intermediate canoeist, this section is ideal for beginning boaters who look for a leisurely float with occasional smaller rapids and excellent fishing from the banks or shallows. North of Thurmond, the whitewater begins in earnest with rapids in varying heights and combinations ranging from Class I to V. This last 13-mile section is named "the Grand Canyon of the East" and hosts the famous "Big Water Canyon," renowned for its roller coaster ride. Only experienced and properly equipped boaters should attempt to navigate these waters; it is advisable to go with an outfitter. The New River is a large volume river with reliable flows year round. The high water season peaks in the spring but rises quickly with local rainfall throughout the summer.

The park maintains a list of all active commercial whitewater outfitters who run trips down the New River from early April to late October. Ask at one of the visitor centers or at park headquarters in Glen Jean for the listing. Within or near the boundaries of the park are 5 West Virginia state parks. Babcock and Grandview are within the park, and Hawks

Map #2—South Half

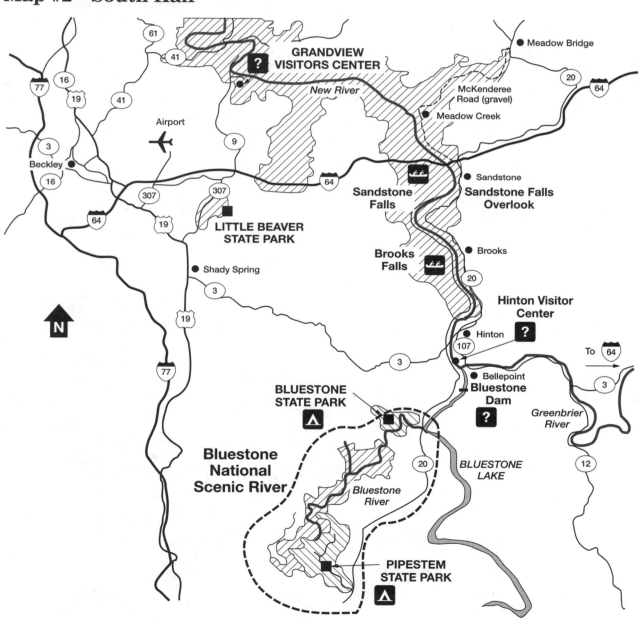

Nest, Pipestem, and Bluestone are nearby. All but Grandview, a day-use park, have accommodations.

The best place to begin your visit to the park is at one of the 3 visitor centers; they provide information services, exhibits, and interpretive activities. Books, slides, postcards, posters, maps, and other materials are sold at all centers. **Canyon Rim Visitor Center** is on US 19, just north of Fayetteville and the New River Gorge Bridge. This facility is open year-round and features museum exhibits, an illustrated program, and bus tours throughout the summer season. The overlooks provide spectacular views into the gorge and of the US 19 bridge. This is the world's longest single steel arch bridge with a central span of 1,700 feet and a total length of 3,030 feet. It rises 876 feet above the riverbed. Phone: (304) 574-211.

Grandview Visitor Center is northeast of Beckley; travel east from Beckley on I-64, take the Grandview exit (#129) and travel north on WV9. This center is open seasonally; it offers overlooks, hiking trails, picnic facilities (reservations required), and outdoor drama presentations during the summer. Phone: (304) 763-3715.

Hinton Visitor Center is located on the Route 3 bypass in Hinton on the banks of the New River, and is open seasonally; it features an illustrated program and summer canoe programs. Phone: (304) 466-0417.

Gauley National Recreation Area: The 25 miles of free-flowing Gauley River and the 6 miles of the Meadow River pass through scenic gorges and valleys. Both rivers provide excellent fishing and hiking opportunities. From April through August the Gauley reacts and fluctuates like a free-flowing river, running anywhere from 500 to 5,000 cubic feet per second. In the fall, the Corps of Engineers pulls the plug on the dam and releases high flows for a period of 22 days. People come from around the world to challenge the Gauley during the fall drawdown. There are two sections, the "Upper Gauley" named Lost Paddle Canyon and the "Lower Gauley" named Cliffside Canyon. Together they host over 100 major rapids. To navigate both canyons is to drop more than 670 feet through 26 miles of rugged terrain. The Upper Gauley is the most powerful and relentless stretch of the river with torrents of water, steep slopes, and a rugged river bed. The Lower Gauley, though not as formidable as the Upper Gauley, hosts roller coaster waves and hard-hitting holes.

Bluestone National Scenic River: This river preserves relatively unspoiled land and contains natural and historic features of the Appalachian plateau. In its 11 miles the lower Bluestone River offers excellent warm water fishing, hiking, boating, and scenery. Pipestone and Bluestone state parks and Bluestone Lake Wildlife Management Area are located along this segment of the river.

The New River Gorge National River, a unit of the National Park System, protects 53 miles of the New River as a free-flowing waterway; it is one of the finest whitewater rivers in the eastern United States.

Backcountry Ethics

Rules for backcountry camping are common-sense rules meant to control actions that may damage natural resources or take away from the enjoyment of an outdoor experience. In recent years, the term "going light" has taken on new meaning. To a backpacker, "going light" is the skill of paring down the load and leaving at home every ounce that can be spared. Today, "going light" also means to spare the land and travel and camp by the rules of "low impact." The US Forest Service suggests the following "low impact" rules. Although these suggestions were written for the hiker and backpacker, they are quite appropriate for anyone camping in the backcountry, whether traveling by foot, canoe, bicycle, or horse.

General Information

▲ Keep noise to a minimum; exceptions may exist for areas inhabited by bears.
▲ Respect the privacy of other campers.
▲ Do not short-cut trails or cut across switchbacks. Trails are designed and maintained to prevent erosion.
▲ Trampling meadows can create confusion and damage vegetation.
▲ Do not pick flowers, dig up plants, or cut branches from live trees. Leave them for others to enjoy.
▲ Remember, it is unlawful to take, damage or deface any park objects, such as rocks, plants, and artifacts.
▲ It is unlawful and dangerous to feed animals, large or small.

Planning a Trip

▲ Keep camping groups small.
▲ Take a gas stove to help conserve firewood.
▲ Bring sacks to carry out trash.
▲ Take a light shovel or trowel to help with personal sanitation.
▲ Carry a light basin or collapsible bucket for washing.
▲ Before traveling, study maps of the area, get permits if necessary and learn the terrain.
▲ Check on weather conditions and water availability.

Setting Up Camp

▲ Pick a campsite that does not require clearing away vegetation or leveling a tent site.
▲ Use an existing campsite, if available.

▲ Camp 300 feet from streams or springs. Law prohibits camping within ¼ mile of an only-available water source (for wildlife or livestock).
▲ Do not cut trees, limbs, or brush to make camp improvements. Carry tent poles.

Breaking Camp

▲ Before leaving camp, naturalize the area. Replace rocks and scatter needles, leaves, and twigs around the campsite.
▲ Scout the area to be sure nothing is left behind. Everything packed into camp should be packed out. Try to make it appear as if no one has been there.

Campfires

▲ Even when campfires are permitted, use gas stoves when possible to conserve dwindling supplies of firewood.
▲ If a campfire is needed and allowed, use an existing campfire site. Keep it small.
▲ If clearing a new fire site is needed, select a safe spot away from rock ledges that would be blackened by smoke; away from meadows where it would destroy grass and leave a scar; away from dense brush, trees and duff, where it would be a fire hazard.
▲ Clear a circle of all burnable materials. Dig a shallow pit for the fire. Keep the sod intact.
▲ Use only fallen timber for firewood. Even standing dead trees are part of the beauty of wilderness, and are important to wildlife. Put fires cold out before leaving. Let the fire burn down to ashes, mix the ashes with dirt and water. Feel it with your hand. If it is cold out, cover the ashes in the pit with dirt, replace the sod, and naturalize the disturbed area.

Pack It In—Pack It Out

▲ Bring trash bags to carry out all trash that cannot be completely burned.
▲ Aluminum foil and aluminum-lined packages will not burn completely in a fire. Compact it and pack it out in trash bags.
▲ Cigarette butts, pull-tabs, and gum wrappers are litter, too. They can spoil a campsite and trail.
▲ Do not bury trash! Animals dig it up.
▲ Try to pack out trash left by others. A good example may catch on!

Keep The Water Supply Clean

▲ Wash yourself, dishes, and clothes away from any source of water.
▲ Pour wash water on the ground away from streams and springs.
▲ Food scraps, toothpaste, even biodegradable soap will pollute streams and springs. Remember, it is your drinking water, too!
▲ Boil water or treat water before drinking it.

Disposing of Human Waste

▲ When nature calls, select a suitable spot at least 100 feet from open water, campsites, and trails. Dig a hole 4 to 6 inches deep. Try to keep the sod intact. After use, fill in the hole, completely burying waste. Then tramp in the sod.

Emergency Items

▲ According to conditions, carry rain gear, extra warm clothing such as a windbreaker, wool jacket, hat and gloves. Sunscreen lotion is important to use in warm and cold conditions.
▲ Keep extra high-energy foods like hard candies, chocolate, dried fruits, or liquids accessible. Do not overload yourself, but be prepared.
▲ Travel with a first-aid kit, map, compass, and whistle. Know how to use them.
▲ Always leave a trip plan with a family member or a friend. File a trip plan with park rangers.
▲ Mishaps are rare, but they do happen. Should one occur, remain calm. In case of an accident, someone should stay with the injured person. Notify appropriate officials.

Camping/Backpacking Supplies Checklists

Camping Equipment Checklist

The following checklists are designed to guide you in planning your next camping trip. Your needs will vary according to the type, length, and destination of your trip, as well as personal preferences, number of persons included, season of the year, and budget limitations.

Obviously, all items on the checklists aren't needed on any one trip. Since using checklists helps you think more methodically in planning, these extensive lists should serve merely as a reminder of items you may need.

When using these checklists to plan a trip, the item may be checked (√) if it needs to be taken. Upon returning, if the item was considered unnecessary, a slash could be used: ✕. If a needed item was forgotten, a zero could be used (0); if the item has been depleted and needs to be replenished, an encircling of the check could be used; ✓. This is of particular importance if you camp regularly and keep a camping box packed with staples that can be ready to go on a moment's notice.

Cooking equipment needs are quite dependent on the menu—whether you plan to cook and eat three balanced meals a day or whether you plan to eat non-cooked meals or snacks the entire trip. Many campers find it helpful to jot down the proposed menu for each meal on a 4″ × 6″ index card to help determine the grocery list as well as the equipment needed to prepare the meal. By planning this way, you'll avoid taking equipment you'll never use and you won't forget important items.

It's important for backpackers to use checklists; their goal is to carry everthing essential, but no more than they need.

Typical Menu with Grocery and Equipment Needs

MEAL: Saturday breakfast		Number of Persons: 5
MENU	GROCERY LIST	EQUIPMENT
orange juice	Tang	camp stove
bacon	10 slices bacon	gasoline, funnel
eggs	8 eggs	folding oven
(scrambled)	1 can biscuits	frying pan
biscuits	peach jelly	baking pan
	honey	pitcher
	margarine	mixing bowl
	salt	cooking fork, spoon
	pepper	

Shelter/Sleeping:

_____ Air mattresses
_____ Air mattress pump
_____ Cots, folding
_____ Cot pads
_____ Ground cloth
_____ Hammock
_____ Mosquito netting
_____ Sleeping bag or bed roll
_____ Tarps (plastic & canvas)
_____ Tent
_____ Tent stakes, poles, guy ropes
_____ Tent repair kit
_____ Whisk broom

Extra Comfort:

_____ Camp stool
_____ Catalytic heater
_____ Folding chairs
_____ Folding table
_____ Fuel for lantern & heater
_____ Funnel
_____ Lantern
_____ Mantels for lantern
_____ Toilet, portable
_____ Toilet chemicals
_____ Toilet bags
_____ Wash basin

Clothing/Personal Gear:

_____ Bathing suit
_____ Boots, hiking & rain
_____ Cap/hat
_____ Facial tissues
_____ Flashlight (small), batteries
_____ Jacket/windbreaker
_____ Jeans/trousers

_____ Pajamas
_____ Pocket knife
_____ Poncho
_____ Prescription drugs
_____ Rain suit
_____ Sheath knife
_____ Shirts
_____ Shoes
_____ Shorts
_____ Socks
_____ Sweat shirt/sweater
_____ Thongs (for showering)
_____ Toilet articles (comb, soap, shaving equipment, tooth brush, toothpaste, mirror, etc.)
_____ Toilet paper
_____ Towels
_____ Underwear
_____ Washcloth

Safety/Health:

_____ First-aid kit
_____ First-aid manual
_____ Fire extinguisher
_____ Insect bite remedy
_____ Insect repellant
_____ Insect spray/bomb
_____ Poison ivy lotion
_____ Safety pins
_____ Sewing repair kit
_____ Scissors
_____ Snake bite kit
_____ Sunburn lotion
_____ Suntan cream
_____ Water purifier

Optional:

_____ Binoculars
_____ Camera, film, tripod, light meter

_____ Canteen
_____ Compass
_____ Fishing tackle
_____ Frisbee, horseshoes, washers, etc.
_____ Games for car travel & rainy day
_____ Hobby equipment
_____ Identification books: birds, flowers, rocks, stars, trees, etc.
_____ Knapsack/day pack for hikes
_____ Magnifying glass
_____ Map of area
_____ Notebook & pencil
_____ Sunglasses

Miscellaneous:

_____ Bucket/pail
_____ Candles
_____ Clothesline
_____ Clothespins
_____ Electrical extension cord
_____ Flashlight (large), batteries
_____ Hammer
_____ Hand axe/hatchet
_____ Nails
_____ Newspapers
_____ Pliers
_____ Rope
_____ Saw, bow or folding
_____ Sharpening stone/file
_____ Shovel
_____ Tape, masking or plastic
_____ Twine/cord
_____ Wire
_____ Work gloves

An unexpected snow during the night can test the backpacker's preparedness for possible changes in weather conditions.

Cooking Equipment Checklist

**Food Preparation/
Serving/Storing:**

____ Aluminum foil
____ Bags (large & small,
     plastic & paper)
____ Bottle/juice can opener
____ Bowls, nested with lids
     for mixing, serving &
     storing
____ Can opener
____ Colander
____ Fork, long-handled
____ Ice chest
____ Ice pick
____ Knife, large
____ Knife, paring
____ Ladle for soups & stews
____ Measuring cup
____ Measuring spoon
____ Pancake turner
____ Potato & carrot peeler
____ Recipes
____ Rotary beater
____ Spatula
____ Spoon, large
____ Tongs
____ Towels, paper

____ Water jug
____ Wax paper/plastic wrap

Cooking:

____ Baking pans
____ Charcoal
____ Charcoal grill (hibachi or
     small collapsible type)
____ Charcoal lighter
____ Coffee pot
____ Cook kit, nested/pots &
     pans with lids
____ Fuel for stove
     (gasoline/kerosene/liquid
     propane)
____ Griddle
____ Hot pads/asbestos gloves
____ Matches
     Ovens for baking:
____ Cast iron dutch oven
____ Folding oven for fuel
     stoves
____ Reflector oven
____ Tote oven
____ Skewers
____ Skillet with cover
____ Stove, portable

____ Toaster (folding camp
     type)
____ Wire grill for open fire

Eating:

____ Bowls for cereal, salad,
     soup
____ Cups, paper
____ Forks
____ Glasses, plastic
____ Knives
____ Napkins, paper
____ Pitcher, plastic
____ Plates (plastic,
     aluminum, paper)
____ Spoons
____ Table cloth, plastic

Clean-Up:

____ Detergent (Bio-
     degradable soap)
____ Dish pan
____ Dish rag
____ Dish towels
____ Scouring pad
____ Scouring powder
____ Sponge

Hiking/Backpacking Checklist

This list is not meant to be all inclusive or necessary for each trip. It is a guide in choosing the proper gear. Although this list was prepared for the hiker/backpacker, it is quite appropriate for anyone using the backcountry, whether they are traveling by foot, canoe, bicycle, or horse. Parentheses indicate those optional items that you may not want to carry depending upon the length of the trip, weather conditions, personal preferences, or necessity.

Checklists should be used by day-hikers to assure that essential items are carried that will make the trip safe and enjoyable.

Ten Essentials for Any Trip:

— Map
— Compass
— First-aid kit
— Pocket knife
— Signaling device
— Extra clothing
— Extra food
— Small flashlight/extra bulb & batteries
— Fire starter/candle/waterproof matches
— Sunglasses

Day Trip (add to the above):

— Comfortable boots or walking shoes
— Rain parka or 60/40 parka

— Day Pack
— Water bottle/canteen
— Cup
— Water purification tablets
— Insect repellant
— Sun lotion
— Chapstick
— Food
— Brimmed hat
— (Guide book)
— Toilet paper & trowel
— (Camera & film)
— (Binoculars)
— (Book)
— Wallet & I.D.
— Car key & coins for phone
— Moleskin for blisters
— Whistle

Overnight or Longer Trips (add the following):

— Backpack
— Sleeping bag
— Foam pad
— (Tent)
— (Bivouac cover)
— (Ground cloth/poncho)
— Stove
— Extra fuel
— Cooking pot(s)
— Pot scrubber
— Spoon (knife & fork)
— (Extra cup/bowl)
— Extra socks
— Extra shirt(s)
— Extra pants/shorts
— Extra underwear
— Wool shirt/sweater
— (Camp shoes)
— Bandana

— (Gloves)
— (Extra water container)
— Nylon cord
— Extra matches
— Soap
— Toothbrush/powder/floss
— Mirror
— Medicines
— (Snake bite kit)
— (Notebook & pencil)
— Licenses & permits
— (Playing cards)
— (Zip-lock bags)
— (Rip stop repair tape)
— Repair kit—wire, rivets, pins, buttons, thread, needle, boot strings

Map Symbols

 AMPHITHEATER

 BACKCOUNTRY CAMPSITE

 BOAT LAUNCH

 CABINS

 CAMPGROUND

 FISHING

 FITNESS TRAIL

 FOOD

 GENERAL STORE

 GROUP CAMPING

 HIKING TRAIL

 HORSEBACK TRAIL

 INFORMATION

 LODGING

 MARINA

 NATURE TRAIL

 PARKING

 PICNIC AREA

 PICNIC SHELTER

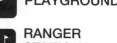 PLAYGROUND

RANGER STATION/PARK OFFICE

 RESTROOMS

 PUBLIC RIVER ACCESS

 SHOWERS

 SKI TRAIL

 SWIMMING

TRAILER SANITATION STATION

VC VISITOR CENTER

Delaware

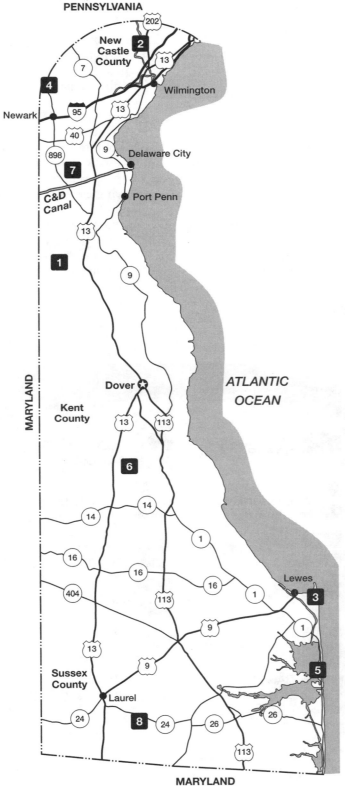

PENNSYLVANIA

202

2 New Castle County

13

7

Wilmington

4

95

13

Newark

40

898

9 Delaware City

7

C&D Canal

Port Penn

13

1

9

MARYLAND

Dover ✮

Kent County

13

113

6

14

14

14

16

1

16

16

16

113

404

16

1

Lewes

9

1

3

13

9

1

5

Sussex County

Laurel

24

8

24

26

26

113

MARYLAND

ATLANTIC OCEAN

1—Blackbird State Forest, page 25
2—Brandywine Creek State Park, page 26
3—Cape Henlopen State Park, page 27
4—Carpenter State Park, page 28
5—Delaware Seashore State Park, page 29
6—Killens Pond State Park, page 30
7—Lums Pond State Park, page 31
8—Trap Pond State Park, page 32

The 66-acre picturesque mill pond is the main attraction at Killens Pond State Park, offering fishing and boating opportunities.

Blackbird State Forest

For Information

Blackbird State Forest
RD 2, Box 2186
Smyrna, DE 19977
(302) 653-6505

Map Legend:
— Roads
▬ Boundary Lines
--- Trails
= Streams
+++ Railroad Tracks
●● Ponds

To 13

OLIVER GUESSFORD ROAD

CR 472

CR 36

CR 471

BLACKBIRD FOREST ROAD

N

FOREST BOUNDARY

DEXTER'S CORNER ROAD

To 15

Location

Blackbird State Forest, located northwest of Smyrna, consists of 5 separate tracts. These tracts are north of DE 6 and west of US 13/DE 1. Camping is permitted on the Tybout Tract only. County Road 471 traverses this 676.5-acre tract; travel southwest on CR 471 from US 13 at Blackbird, or travel north on CR 471 from DE 15 at Prices Corners. Camping is free of charge, year-round, and is restricted to the map-designated campsites. However, a permit, available at the office during office hours, is required. Campsites are on a first-come, first-served basis. Limit of stay is 3 nights per month. Pets are permitted, but should be leashed. Camping is not recommended during hunting seasons.

Camping is restricted to the 4 designated primitive campsites at Blackbird State Forest, and is limited to tent, van, or pickup.

Facilities & Activities

4 primitive campsites
  tent, van or pickup only
  NO travel trailers or motor homes
group camping (limit: 25/campsite)
tables, trash barrel
fire pits, charcoal grills
drinking water available at picnic pavilion

portable toilets in summer
3 picnic areas
picnic pavilion
horseback riding
hiking trails
nature study

Brandywine Creek State Park

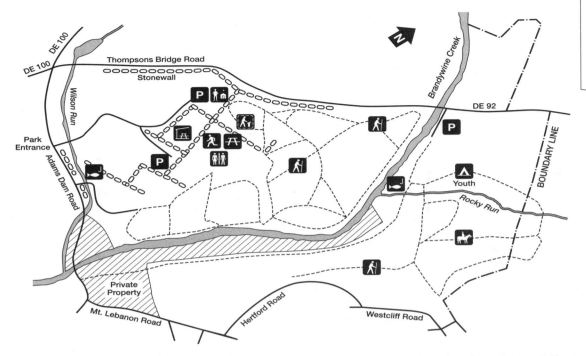

For Information

Brandywine Creek State Park
P.O. Box 3782
Wilmington, DE 19807
(302) 577-3534
(302) 655-5740 (nature center)

Location

This park is 3 miles north of Wilmington at the intersection of DE 100 and DE 92. The entrance is on Adams Dam Road. Delaware's first 2 nature preserves are located within this 795-acre park: Tulip Tree Woods, a majestic stand of 190-year-old tulip poplar, and Freshwater Marsh, home to the elusive Muhlenberg Bog Turtle. Canoeing and tubing on the Brandywine River is a popular activity during the hot summer months.

Facilities & Activities

Primitive youth camping ONLY

picnicking/pavilion
fishing
canoeing/tubing
18-hole disc golf course
equestrian center/stables

Although Brandywine Creek State Park is limited to primitive youth camping only, anyone may enjoy using the trails and other facilities during the day.

equestrian/bicycle trails
nature/hiking trails
fitness trail
X-country skiing/sledding
nature center

Cape Henlopen State Park

For Information

Cape Henlopen State Park
42 Cape Henlopen Drive
Lewes, DE 19958
(302) 645-8983
(302) 645-2103 (campground)
(302) 645-6852 (nature center)

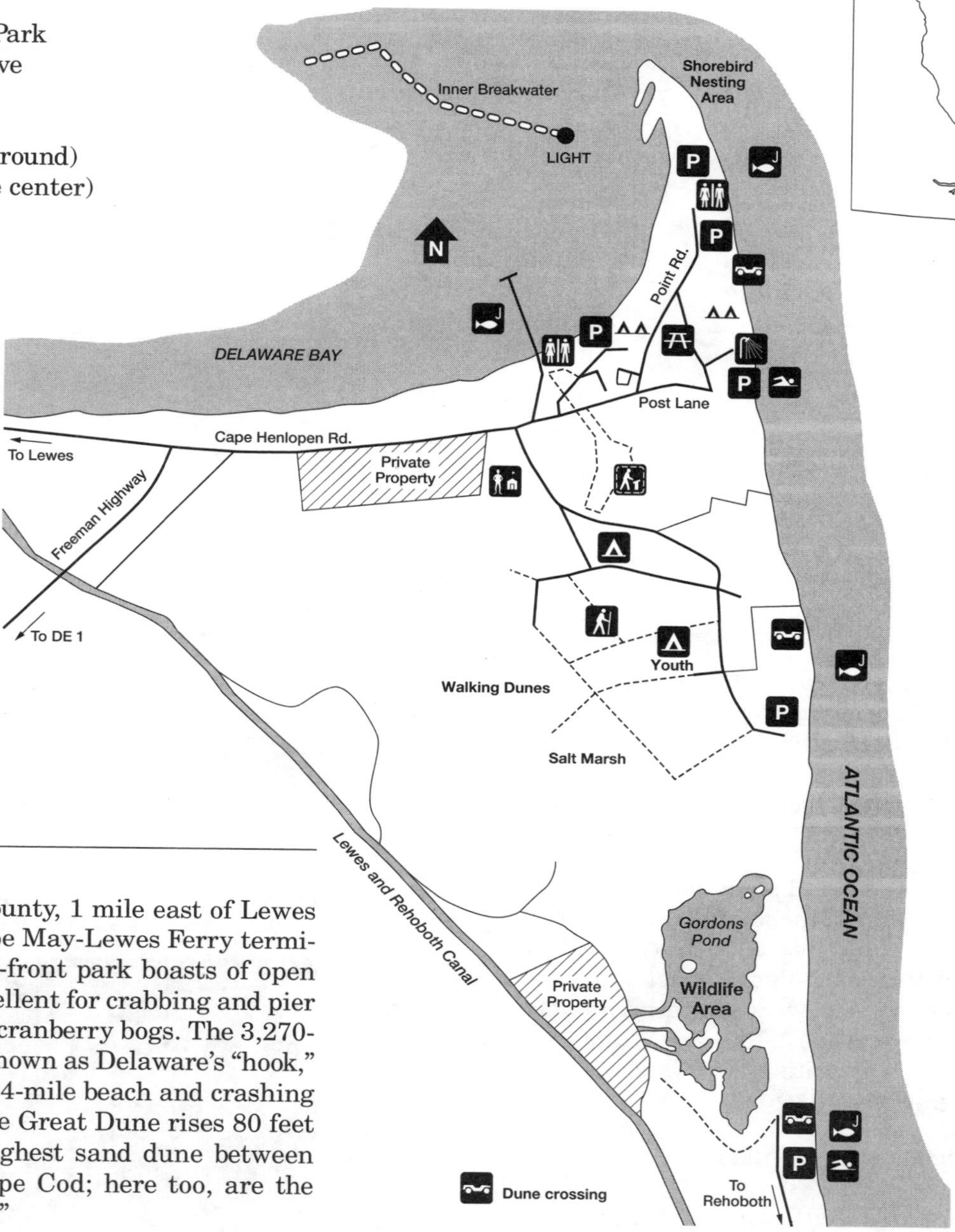

N

Inner Breakwater

LIGHT

Shorebird Nesting Area

DELAWARE BAY

Point Rd.

Post Lane

Cape Henlopen Rd.

To Lewes

To DE 1

Freeman Highway

Private Property

Private Property

Walking Dunes

Youth

Salt Marsh

Lewes and Rehoboth Canal

Gordons Pond

Wildlife Area

ATLANTIC OCEAN

To Rehoboth

Dune crossing

Location

Located in Sussex County, 1 mile east of Lewes and ½-mile past the Cape May-Lewes Ferry terminal, this popular ocean-front park boasts of open shoreline, bayshore excellent for crabbing and pier fishing, pinelands, and cranberry bogs. The 3,270-acre sandy peninsula, known as Delaware's "hook," lures its visitors with a 4-mile beach and crashing Atlantic waves. Here the Great Dune rises 80 feet above the shore, the highest sand dune between Cape Hatteras and Cape Cod; here too, are the famous "walking dunes."

Facilities & Activities

159 campsites
   water hookups
   showers
dump station
primitive youth camping
dormitory for youth groups
picnicking/pavilion
food/beach equipment concession
2 swimming beaches/bathhouse

fishing/surf fishing
¼-mile fishing pier
bait & tackle concession
game courts/ball fields
9-hole disc golf course
nature/hiking trails
observation tower/overlooks
nature/visitor center

Carpenter State Park

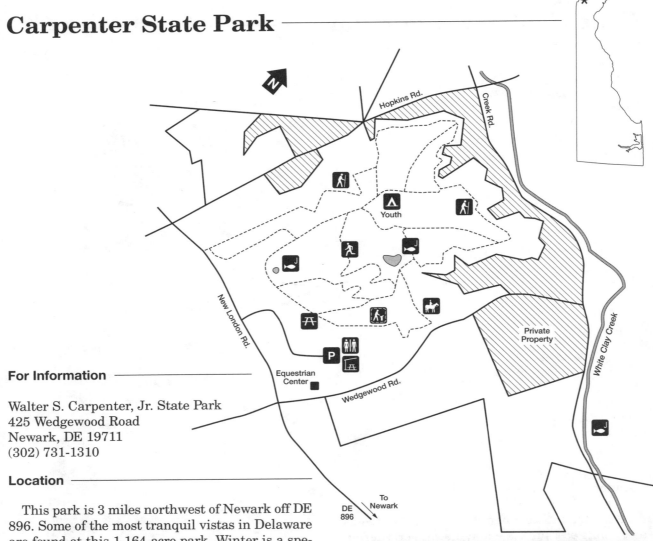

Youth

For Information

Walter S. Carpenter, Jr. State Park
425 Wedgewood Road
Newark, DE 19711
(302) 731-1310

Location

This park is 3 miles northwest of Newark off DE 896. Some of the most tranquil vistas in Delaware are found at this 1,164-acre park. Winter is a special time at the park, when cross-country skiing, sledding, and ice skating are available. Adjacent to the park is the 1,700-acre White Clay Creek Preserve, a favorite of birdwatchers and nature photographers alike.

Facilities & Activities

Primitive youth camping ONLY

picnicking/pavilion
fishing
9-hole disc golf course
equestrian center/riding ring
2 miles of equestrian trails
nature/hiking trails
fitness trail
3.1-mile cross country trail
X-country ski/snowmobile trail
sledding/ice skating
visitor center

Carpenter State Park has 2 miles of equestrian trails. Like Brandywine Creek State Park, it is limited to primitive youth camping only.

Delaware Seashore State Park

For Information

Delaware Seashore State Park
Inlet 850
Rehoboth Beach, DE 19971
(302) 227-2800
(302) 539-7202 (campground)
(302) 277-3071 (marina)

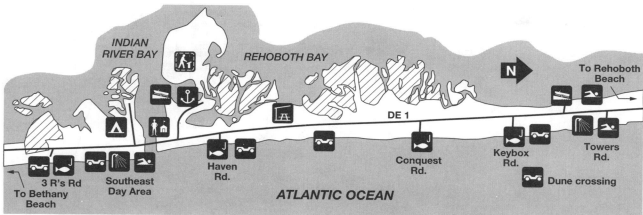

INDIAN RIVER BAY

REHOBOTH BAY

N

To Rehoboth Beach

DE 1

Conquest Rd.

Keybox Rd.

Towers Rd.

Dune crossing

3 R's Rd
To Bethany Beach

Southeast Day Area

Haven Rd.

ATLANTIC OCEAN

Location

The park, located in Sussex County, begins 1 mile south of Rehoboth Beach on DE 1. The park office and campground are 5 miles south at the Indian River Inlet. This 2,018-acre beachland paradise features availability to both the crashing surf of the Atlantic Ocean and the cool, still waters of Rehoboth Bay. Along the Atlantic Ocean, beachgoers have more than 6 miles of glistening sand and sparkling water to enjoy. A full-service marina is located at the Indian River Inlet. Ospreys, terns, and gulls use the bayside marsh islands for nesting; the inlet is an active winter birding spot. Fully self-contained units may camp year-round. However, only electric hook-ups are available onsite. A dumping station and water are available in a special area. Contact the park office during the off-season for information.

This park has more than 6 miles of beach along the Atlantic Ocean; surf fishing is popular.

Facilities & Activities

145 campsites with full hookups
133 campsites with no hookups
156 overflow campsites (self-contained units only; summer, Thurs.-Sun.)
showers
dump station
picnicking/pavilion

food/beach equipment concession
swimming beaches/bathhouses
surfing/windsurfing/sailing
non-motorized boat launch
fishing/surf fishing
handicapped fishing pier
boating
marina/snack bar/launching ramp (fee)
295-boat rental slips/charter fishing boats
nature trail

Killens Pond State Park

For Information

Killens Pond State Park
RD 1, Box 858
Felton, DE 10043
(302) 284-4526
(302) 284-3412 (campground)

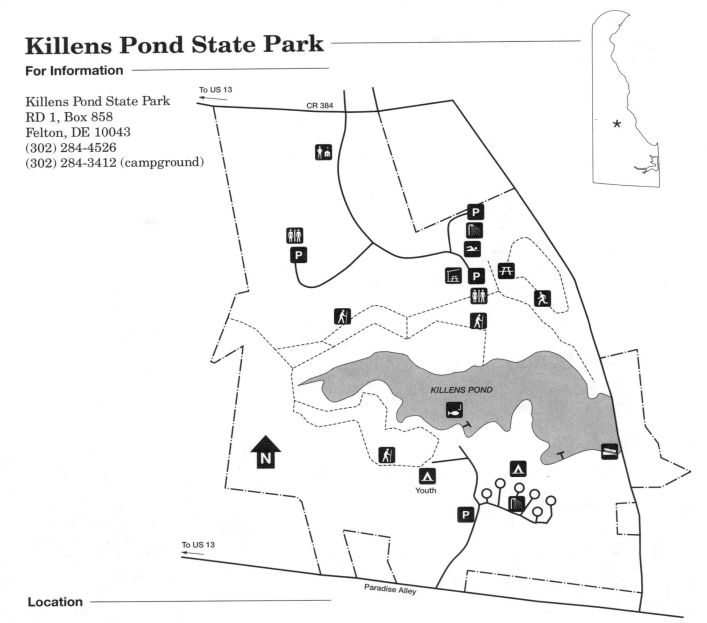

Location

Killens Pond State Park is located 1 mile southeast of Felton, about ½ mile off of US 13 in Kent County. The park's main entrance is on County Road 384; the campground entrance is on County Road 426. The 66-acre picturesque mill pond is the main attraction at this 878-acre park, offering fishing and boating opportunities. The Lakeside Nature Trail winds along the pine-wooded slopes of the pond to its source, the Murderkill River.

Facilities & Activities

59 campsites with electric/water hookups
showers
dump station
6 cabins (kitchenette, bath, 4 single beds)
primitive youth camping

picnicking/pavilion
snack bar
25-meter swimming pool/wading pool
bathhouse
fishing/fishing piers
boating/boat ramp
rowboat/canoe/paddle boat rentals
pontoon boat rides on weekends
game courts/ball fields
18-hole disc golf course
canoe trail
nature/hiking trails
fitness trail/cross country course
bike path

Lums Pond State Park

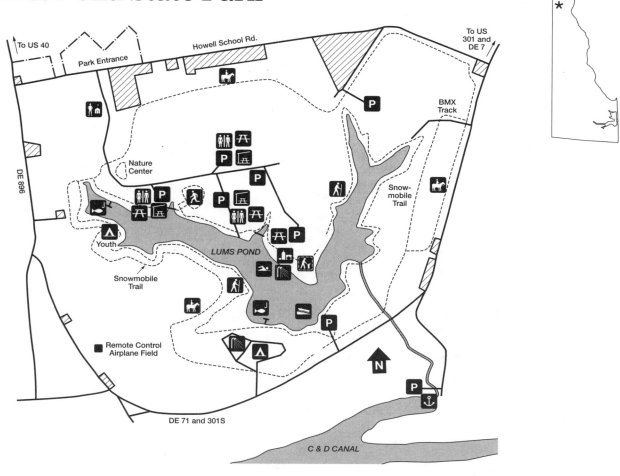

For Information

Lums Pond State Park
1068 Howell School Road
Bear, DE 19701
(302) 368-6989
(302) 836-1800 (marina)

Location

This park is located 2 miles south of Glasgow on DE 896 in the woodlands of New Castle County. The main entrance is on Howell School Road; the campground entrance is on DE 71. A 200-acre pond is the centerpiece of this diverse 1,757-acre park. A full-service marina is located along the Chesapeake and Delaware Canal.

Facilities & Activities

68 campsites with no hookups
showers
dump station
primitive youth camping
picnicking/pavilion
snack bar
swimming beach/bathhouse
fishing/piers
boating/boat ramp
canoeing/sailing
marina/250-boat rental slips
rowboat/canoe/paddleboat/sailboat rentals
game courts/ball fields
18-hole disc golf course
BMX bike track
equestrian trails
nature/hiking/fitness trails
X-country ski/snowmobile trail
remote control airplane field
nature/visitor center

Trap Pond State Park

For Information

Trap Pond State Park
RD 2, Box 331
Laurel, DE 19956
(302) 875-5153
(302) 875-2392 (campground)

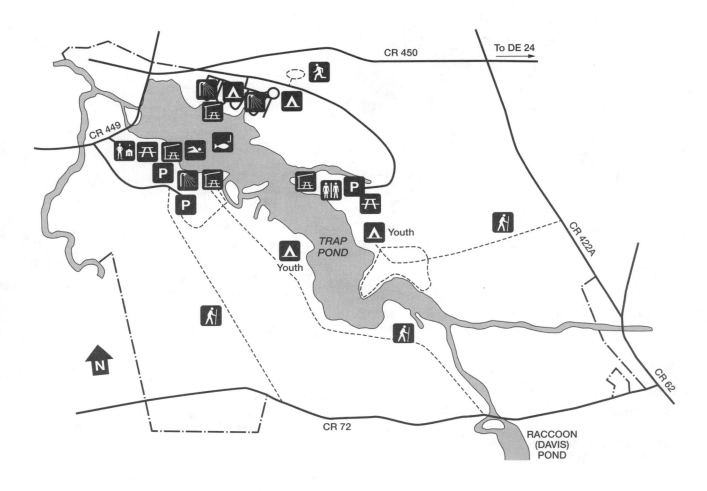

Location

Delaware's first state park, Trap Pond, is located 4 miles east of Laurel in Sussex County. The main entrance to the park is 1 mile down County Road 449 from DE 24; the campground entrance is on County Road 450. A portion of the Great Cypress Swamp lies within the park's 966 acres and holds the northernmost stand of bald cypress trees in the US. The park has a wilderness canoe trail on the 90-acre pond and both self-guided and unmarked hiking trails wind along the pond's banks and through the adjacent woods. A section of the Cypress Point Trail is adapted for wheelchair use.

Facilities & Activities

62 campsites with electric/water hookups
70 campsites with no hookups
8 secluded primitive campsites
2 rent-a-camp sites
showers
dump station
primitive youth camping
picnicking/pavilion

snack bar
swimming beach/bathhouse
fishing
boating/boat ramp
rowboat/canoe/paddleboat/sailboat rentals
pontoon boat rides on weekend
canoe trail
nature/hiking trails
equestrian/bicycle trails

A portion of the Great Cypress Swamp lies within Trap Pond State Park's 966 acres; a wilderness canoe trail is located on its 90-acre pond.

Maryland

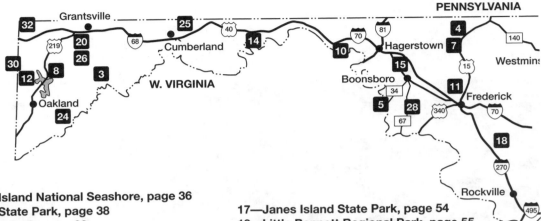

PENNSYLVANIA

Grantsville

32

20

26

219

30

12

8

3

Oakland

24

W. VIRGINIA

25

40

68

Cumberland

14

10

70

81

4

Hagerstown

7

140

15

15

Westmins

15

Boonsboro

34

11

Frederick

5

28

340

70

67

18

270

Rockville

495

1—Assateague Island National Seashore, page 36
2—Assateague State Park, page 38
3—Big Run State Park, page 39
4—Catoctin Mountain Park, page 40
5—Chesapeake and Ohio Canal National Historical Park, page 42
6—Cosca Regional Park, page 45
7—Cunningham Falls State Park, page 46
8—Deep Creek Lake State Park, page 47
9—Elk Neck State Park, page 48
10—Fort Frederick State Park, page 49
11—Gambrill State Park, page 50
12—Garrett State Forest, page 65
13—Greenbelt Park, page 51
14—Green Ridge State Forest, page 65
15—Greenbrier State Park, page 52
16—Hart-Miller Island State Park, page 53
17—Janes Island State Park, page 54
18—Little Bennett Regional Park, page 55
19—Martinak State Park, page 56
20—New Germany State Park, page 57
21—Patapsco Valley State Park, page 58
22—Pocomoke River State Park, page 59
23—Point Lookout State Park, page 60
24—Potomac State Forest, page 65
25—Rocky Gap State Park, page 61
26—Savage River State Forest, page 66
27—Smallwood State Park, page 62
28—South Mountain State Park, page 64
29—Susquehanna State Park, page 67
30—Swallow Falls State Park, page 68
31—Watkins Regional Park, page 69
32—Youghiogheny River Lake, page 71

Martinak State Park is located at the confluence of the Choptank River and Watts Creek, both tidal waters; a boat launch makes boating and fishing easily accessible after a short run up Watts Creek.

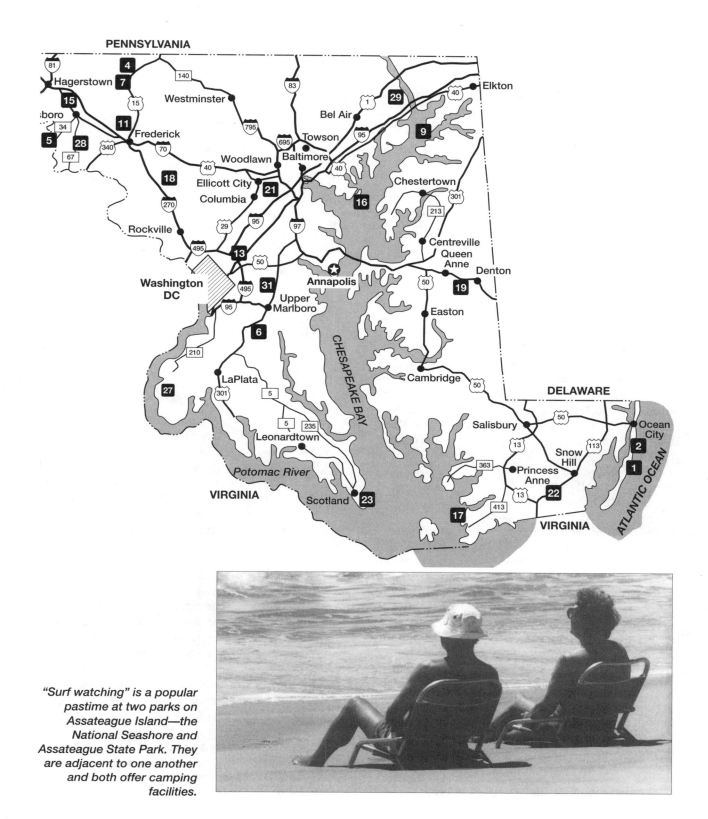

PENNSYLVANIA

81
Hagerstown
4
7
15
15
boro
34
11
5
28
67
340
270
Rockville
Westminster 140
83
Frederick
70
40
Woodlawn
18
Ellicott City
Columbia
29
95
495
13
50
Washington DC
495
31
95
Upper Marlboro
6
210
LaPlata
27
301
5
5 235
Leonardtown
Potomac River
VIRGINIA
Scotland **23**

Bel Air
1
29
95
Towson
Baltimore
695
795
40
9
40
Elkton
40

CHESAPEAKE BAY

Chestertown
301
213
Centreville
Queen Anne
50
Denton
19
Easton
Cambridge
50
DELAWARE

Annapolis ★

Salisbury
50
13
Snow Hill
113
Ocean City
2
1
ATLANTIC OCEAN
363
Princess Anne
13
22
17
413
VIRGINIA

"Surf watching" is a popular pastime at two parks on Assateague Island—the National Seashore and Assateague State Park. They are adjacent to one another and both offer camping facilities.

Assateague Island National Seashore

For Information

Assateague Island National Seashore
7206 National Seashore Lane
Berlin, MD 21811
(410) 641-1441

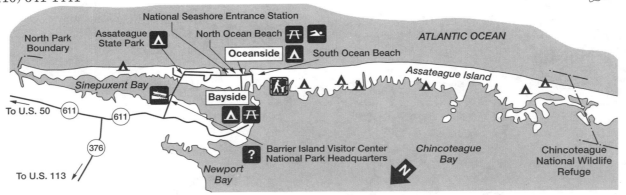

Location

Assateague Island is a 37-mile barrier island located off Maryland and Virginia's mainland, with sandy beach, pine forest, salt marsh, migratory waterfowl, wild ponies, and sheltered coves on Chincoteague Bay. The island consists of 3 major public areas: Assateague Island National Seashore, managed by the National Park Service; Chincoteague National Wildlife Refuge, managed by the US Fish and Wildlife Service; and Assateague State Park, managed by Maryland's Department of Natural Resources. The National Seashore, located on the north end of Assateague Island near Ocean City, is accessible via MD 611 off US 50 or via MD 376 & 611 from US 113 at Berlin.

Points of Interest

▲ Wild ponies make their home at the park; they are free to roam and may be anywhere. They are descendants of domestic animals that have reverted to a wild state. Feeding the ponies is strictly prohibited.

▲ Three self-guiding nature trails are available: Life of the Marsh, Life of the Forest, and Life of the Dunes. Longer hikes can be made north to Ocean City inlet or south on the ORV inner-dune road.

▲ Park rangers offers guided walks, talks, canoe trips, children's programs, and seashore recreation demonstrations daily in summer and on weekends in the fall and spring.

▲ Shell collecting is one of the many activities enjoyed. Although shells can be found along the entire beach, the extreme north or south tips of Assateague Island are best due to tidal action associated with the inlets.

▲ A driving tape tour that begins in the parking lot of the Barrier Island Visitor Center and continues for about an hour before concluding at the beach provides a colorful description of many wildlife-enriched Assateague environments.

General Information

▲ An entrance fee is charged and is valid for 7 days. Camping fees are charged for the 2 campgrounds. There is no fee for backcountry camping.

▲ The Barrier Island Visitor Center features exhibits, an aquarium, and maps. Numerous informative brochures are available on topics such as: surf fishing, shellfishing, seashells, mammals, wild horses, and off-road vehicles. Also featured and shown regularly is the Assateague nature film, *A Very Special Place*. A naturalist is available to answer questions.

▲ The park has 2 campgrounds: Oceanside and Bayside. Primitive outdoor facilities include chemical toilets, central location of drinking water, and cold, rinse-off showers. Any size camping unit can be accommodated. Oceanside also has walk-in, tent-only sites, located 100–200 feet from centralized parking areas. Upright grills are provided in Oceanside; at Bayside, ground fires may only be built in fire ring grills.

▲ Oceanside is open year-round while Bayside operates late spring to early fall. The limit of stay is 7 days from Memorial Day to Labor Day, with a limit of 30 days for the calendar year. A campsite reservation system is available through MISTIX from May 15 to October 31; sites are first-come, first-served the rest of the year.

▲ Five tent-only group campsites are open year-round for organized groups. Facilities include the same as in the family campground section. A group size of 12–25 can be accommodated at each site. An advance reservation with deposit is required. Contact the park for details.

▲ Each of the 6 backpack and canoe-access campsites in the backcountry has a chemical toilet and picnic table but no drinking water. The 2 oceanside sites are open year-round and are available to hikers. The 4 bayside camps are also available year round and may be used by hikers or canoeists. Biting insects can be fierce from May 20 to the first killing frost.

▲ Reservations for backcountry campsites are not necessary but parking and backcountry use permit are required. Obtain the permits at the campground registration office. Ocean sites are in open inner-dunes; bay sites sit among pine trees. The nearest site from the overnight parking area is 2½ miles by canoe or 4½ miles by backpack.

▲ North Ocean Beach is lifeguarded in the summer. A bathhouse with rinse-off showers, changing stalls, toilet facilities, and drinking water is located next to the day-use parking lot at this beach.

▲ No saltwater license is required for surf fishing along this coast. Surf fishing is best in late spring and fall. Naturalists present demonstrations in summer for anglers new to ocean fishing.

▲ In Maryland, certain waterfowl and game species may be taken under state and federal regulations. Contact the park for details.

▲ Clamming is better at the Maryland end of the park than at the Virginia end. The favored method is raking while wading in the generally shallow bay. The limit is one bushel a day year-round.

▲ Limits are placed on the number of off-road vehicles (ORV) allowed on the beach at any one time. The park area zoned for ORV use is from South Ocean Beach south to the state line. Permits are required and a fee is charged; they are issued at the ranger station/campground office or may be obtained by mail. Phone: (410) 641-3030.

▲ Chincoteague Bay waters are ideal for canoeing; use the canoe launch at Old Ferry Landing. Large boats should use one of the three launch facilities available on the mainland at the Maryland end. One is near the visitor center at the MD 611 bridge.

The nearest backcountry campsite from the overnight parking area is 4½ miles by backpack or 2½ miles by canoe.

▲ Bicyclists can use 3 miles of bike path along Bayberry Drive and Oceanside Campground.

▲ Guard against poison ivy, mosquitos, and ticks; all are abundant on Assateague from spring through autumn. Bring plenty of repellent.

▲ It is recommended that pets be left at home. They are permitted in the park's campground and the beach area south of South Ocean Beach if they are on a leash, but they are not permitted in other areas.

▲ The 2 herds of wild ponies on Assateague Island are separated by a fence at the Maryland/Virginia state line and the population size of each herd is kept below 150 animals to lessen their impact on island ecology. These herds have divided themselves into bands of two to ten animals and each band occupies a home range.

Facilities & Activities

2 RV & tent campgrounds
    104 sites at Oceanside Campground
    48 sites at Bayside Campground
chemical toilets/water/rinse-off showers
sanitary dump
5 tent group campgrounds
2 oceanside backcountry campsites (hike-in)
4 bayside backcountry campsites (canoe-in/hike in)
2 picnic areas
swimming/lifeguarded beach
bathhouse/rinse-off showers
boating/canoeing/launches
fishing/hunting
surf fishing/crabbing/clamming
hiking/backpacking
3 self-guided nature trails
bicycle trail
off-road vehicle use
self-guided auto tour route
ranger-led talks/walks/demonstrations
museum/exhibits
visitor center

Assateague State Park

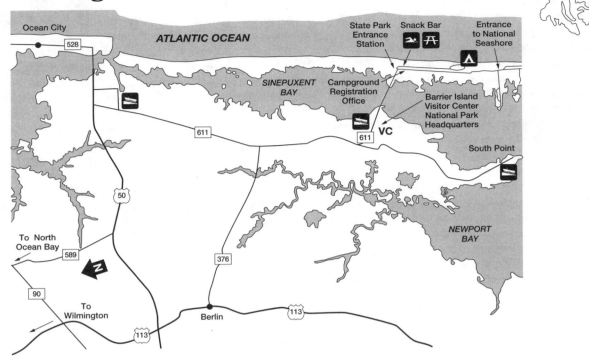

For Information

Assateague State Park
7307 Stephen Decatur Highway
Berlin, MD 21811
(410) 641-2120

Location

Covering 756 acres in Worcester County, Assateague State Park is located on Assateague Island on the Atlantic Coast, adjacent to Assateague Island National Seashore. The park is 8 miles south of Ocean City, accessible from US 50 via Maryland Route 611. Maryland's only ocean park has 2 miles of Atlantic Ocean frontage plus marshes and forests on Sinepuxent Bay. Campsites among the dunes are available for camping units. The 8 loops comprising the camping area have blacktop access roads and individual camping pads. A fire ring and picnic table are provided at each of the campsites.

Facilities & Activities

311 improved campsites*
dump station
picnicking/picnic shelters
food/drinks/camp store
swimming
fishing

Boardwalks through the sand dunes on Assateague Island provide access to the beach; the state park has 2 miles of Atlantic Ocean frontage.

boat launch/rental
bicycle trail
campfire program
visitor center

*Reservations: one week only (Sat. through Sat.) from 3rd Sat. in June through 1st Sat. in Sept. Contact park office.

Big Run State Park

For Information

Big Run State Park
c/o New Germany State Park
Route 2, Box 63-A
Grantsville, MD 21536
(301) 895-5453

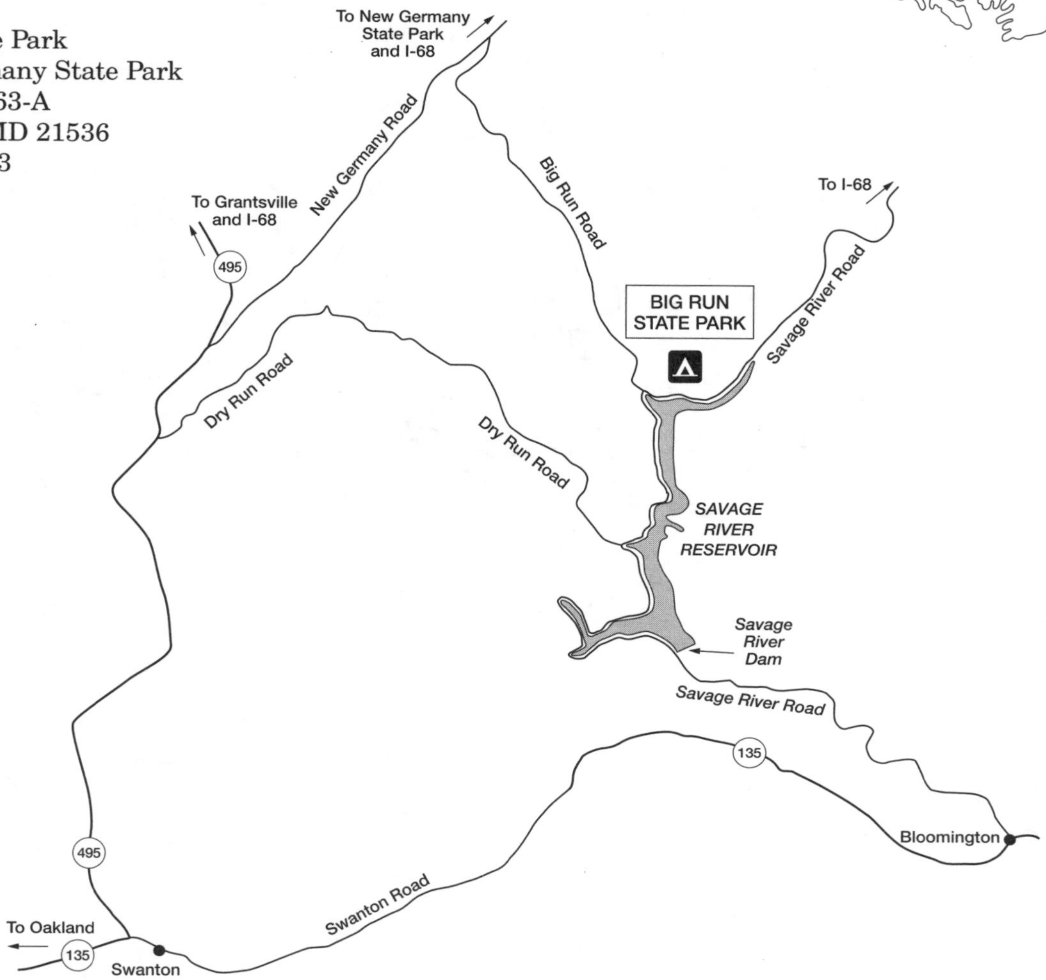

Location

This park covers 300 acres in Garrett County, on the northern tip of the Savage River Reservoir within the Savage River State Forest. Rustic camping is offered in this wilderness park where many forms of wilderness, water and forest activities are enjoyed. The park is accessible from several directions. From WV 135 at Bloomington, travel Savage River Road to the Savage River Dam. Continue along this road as it goes along the north end of the lake, and then along the west side of the lake. The park is at the extreme north end of the lake on Savage River Road.

Another approach from the south is to take WV 495 north from WV 125 at Swanton. From WV 495, take the right fork to New Germany Road. Big Run Road intersects this road; turn right and continue to the park. One approach from the north is to take New Germany Road from US 40A or exit 22 from I-68 just east of Grantsville and travel south to Big Run Road.

Facilities & Activities

30 unimproved campsites
picnicking/picnic shelters
fishing
boat launch
flatwater canoeing
hiking trail
historic interest

Catoctin Mountain Park

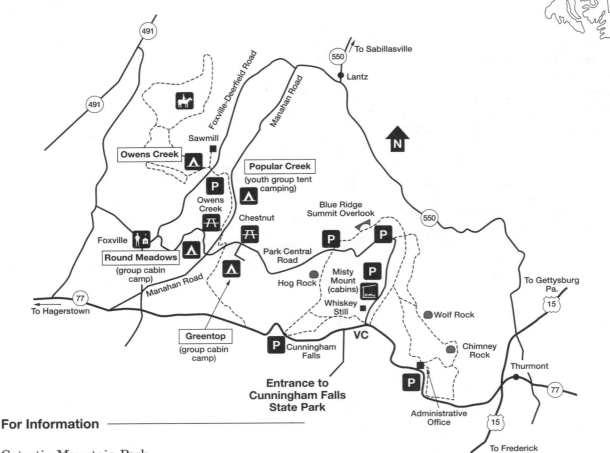

For Information

Catoctin Mountain Park
6602 Foxville Road
Thurmont, MD 21788-1598
(301) 663-9388

Location

Catoctin Mountain Park is part of the forested ridge that forms the eastern rampart of the Appalachian Mountains in Maryland. In 1935, more than 10,000 acres were designated as the Catoctin Recreational Demonstration Area to demonstrate the possibilities of creating parks from wornout land. In 1954, the area was divided into 2 parts, separated by MD 77. The federal government retained the area to the north (Catoctin Mountain Park) and the remaining acreage was deeded to the state of Maryland to be managed for recreational use (Cunningham Falls State Park). Tradition says that the name "Catoctin" came from a tribe of Indians, the Kittoctons, who lived at the foot of the mountains near the Potomac. To reach the 5,770-acre park from the east, travel north from Frederick on US 15, then west on MD 77 for approximately 3 miles; the visitor center is on the right. From Hagerstown, travel east on MD 77.

Points of Interest

▲ The roads of Catoctin Mountain Park offer scenic driving at all seasons of the year. The park staff at the visitor center can offer suggestions on routes and times as some roads are unpaved.

▲ Cunningham Falls, located in the state park, has trail access from Catoctin via 3 different trails. However, the shortest access to the falls is from the parking lot on MD 77.

▲ Hikers in Catoctin Mountain Park can enjoy seven different self-guiding trails; the trailhead to each is near a parking area. The nature-oriented trails are classified as "easy to moderate" and most take from ½ to 1 hour.

▲ About 25 miles of trails are available for hiking, cross-country skiing, and snowshoeing; many lead to outstanding vistas. The trail is steep leading to Chimney Rock, but the panoramic view is worth the effort.

▲ Rangers present a variety of seasonal activities including cross-country ski seminars, orienteering, wildflower walks, and campfire programs.

Activities are scheduled for the entire year; registration is required for some of the activities.

General Information

▲ A park entry fee is not charged; fees are charged for RV and tent camping, and for cabin camping.

▲ The visitor center is open year round. During the winter period there may be additional weekday closings. The center contains a small museum. Park literature is available.

▲ Owens Creek Campground is located on Foxville-Deerfield Road and is open from April 15 through the third Sunday in November. Maximum trailer length is 22 feet; there is no length restriction on motor homes. No hook-ups are provided; no dump station is available. Tents, no larger than 9′ x 12′ must be completely on the tent pads, when available.

▲ All sites at Owens Creek are first-come, first-served, on a self-registration system. Camping is limited to 7 consecutive days and a total of 14 days per season. Each site has a picnic table and grill. The comfort stations have flush toilets and cold water. Ground fires are not allowed; fireplaces are provided.

▲ Poplar Grove is a group tent camping area for youth not exceeding high school age. It is open year-round except March 1 through April 15. There are 3 sites with a limit of 25 persons per site. Reservations are required.

▲ Rustic cabins at Camp Misty Mount are available to families from mid-April until the end of October. Modern restroom and shower facilities are centrally located. Each cabin is equipped with single beds, a fire circle, grill, and picnic table. Cooking is not allowed in the cabins.

▲ Camp Misty Mount has 18 four-bed cabins, 6 three-bed cabins, 1 six-bed cabin, and 3 eight-bed lodges. A dining hall and kitchen may be rented separately. The pool is open during the summer; hours will be posted.

▲ For information and reservations on the cabin area at Camp Misty Mount, call (301) 271-3140. Walk-ins will be accepted based on cabin availability.

▲ Greentop and Round Meadow are both for organized groups only. Both are Environmental Education Cabin Camps and are available in the spring and fall. Groups must include at least 60 persons. Reservations are required; contact the park for information.

▲ Permits are required for the use of the 2 Adirondack shelters (hike-in) and for rockclimbing; helmets are required for rockclimbing. Both permits are available free of charge at the visitor center.

▲ The 2 picnic areas have restrooms, tables, and grills. Isolated picnic tables are scattered throughout the park, but fires are permitted only at the developed areas.

▲ A horse trail is open in the Owens Creek area from April 1 to December 1; horses are not allowed on any other trails. Riders must supply the horses; there are no rentals in the area.

▲ Pets are permitted to stay overnight at Owens Creek but must be on a leash. They are not allowed in buildings or in group camps.

Facilities & Activities

51 RV & tent campsites at Owens Creek
youth group tent camping at Poplar Grove
group cabin camping at Greentop and Round Meadow
25 cabins & 3 lodges at Misty Mount
2 Adirondack shelters in backcountry
2 developed picnic areas
swimming pool at Misty Mount
fishing
25 miles of hiking trails
7 self-guided nature trails
rock climbing
horseback riding (no rentals)
cross-country skiing/snowshoeing
ranger-led talks/walks
visitor center/museum/exhibits

The trail is steep leading to Chimney Rock, but the panoramic view is worth the effort.

Chesapeake and Ohio Canal National Historical Park

For Information

C & O Canal National Historical Park
P.O. Box 4
Sharpsburg, MD 21782
(301) 739-4200 (Headquarters)

Map #1

(continued on map 2)

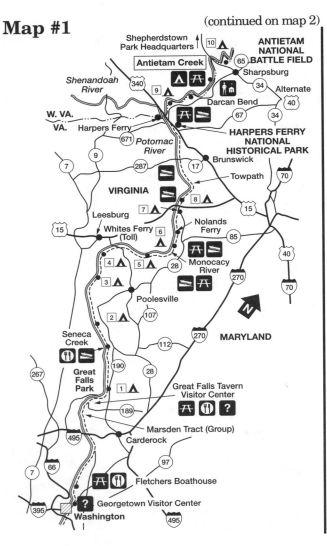

Map #2

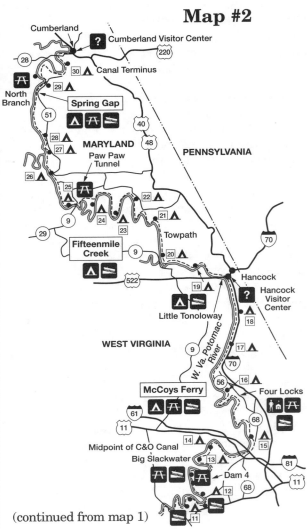

(continued from map 1)

Location

Beside the Potomac River, the C&O Canal stretches from the mouth of Rock Creek in Georgetown to Cumberland, MD. The canal, built between 1828 and 1850, ceased operation in 1924; its 74 lift locks raise it from near sea level to an elevation of 605 feet at Cumberland. Its towpath today provides a nearly level byway for hikers and bicyclists. Its watered sections provide quiet waters for canoeists, boaters, and anglers. The canal was proclaimed a national monument in 1961 and named a national historical park in 1971. Its 184.5-mile length preserves both history and nature. From tidewater at Georgetown in Washington, D.C., to Cumberland on the Allegheny Plateau, the canal winds through the Piedmont, past the dramatic Great Falls of the Potomac, and then through the ridge and valley section of the Appalachian Mountains.

Points of Interest

▲ The canal's towpath is an elevated trail 184.5 miles long. It was originally built 12 feet wide as a path for mules that pulled canal boats. Today it provides through-travel opportunities for hikers and bicyclists.

▲ Visitors can relive the canal's heyday afloat under mulepower and lock-through with a crew of costumed interpreters. Boats run at Georgetown and Great Falls from mid-April to mid-October.

▲ A museum in the historic Great Falls Tavern includes a lock model and canal era artifacts.

▲ A trail system that runs south from Great Falls Tavern provides scenic but rugged hiking opportunities to Mather Gorge and the site of the Maryland Gold Mine.

▲ Canal canoeing and boating are popular in sections between Georgetown and Violettes (Lock #23). Above Violetees Lock only short, isolated stretches can be canoed. Only experienced canoeists should attempt to canoe on the Potomac River. Obtain information at Great Falls Tavern.

General Information

▲ There is no entrance fee or camping fee.

▲ The National Park Service operates information centers at Georgetown, Great Falls Tavern, Hancock, and Cumberland. Maps and books about the canal are sold at some information centers. Walks and evening programs are conducted year-round; ask for a schedule.

—The Georgetown Information Center is in the Foundry Mall between 30th and Thomas Jefferson Streets; phone: (202) 653-5844.

—The Great Falls Information Center is in the Great Falls Tavern, 11710 MacArthur Blvd., Potomac; phone: (301) 299-3613.

—The Hancock Visitor Center is at 180 W. Main Street, Hancock; phone: (301) 678-5463.

—The Cumberland Visitor Center is at the Western Maryland Station Center on Canal Street in Cumberland; phone: (301) 722-8226.

▲ The center at Great Falls can provide information specific to Mile 0-31 and the centers at Hancock and Cumberland can provide information specific to Mile 106-184.5. For information on Mile 31-106, contact the Antietam Creek Ranger Station on Canal Road in Sharpsburg; phone: (301) 739-6179.

▲ There are 3 RV and tent campgrounds and 1 walk-in campground with primitive facilities that operate on a first-come, first-served basis. They are open May 1-October 15; limit of stay is 14 days per season, whether cumulative or consecutive. Maximum trailer length is 20 feet.

▲ Each of the 30 hiker-biker campsites has a grill, trash can, portable toilet, picnic table, and a hand water pump. Water is available from mid-April until mid-November with one exception. At any time the water quality is below acceptable standards, pump handles are removed. Camping is allowed all year on a first-come, first-served basis. Limit of stay is 1 night.

▲ Group campgrounds are found at Marsden Tract, Antietam Creek, and adjacent to Fifteen Mile Creek. Four sites are available at the Marsden Tract; maximum group size is 35; a free permit is required from the park ranger at Great Falls Tavern.

▲ For the boat trips, tickets go on sale 2 hours before each trip. Reservations are taken for organized groups only. For Georgetown tickets, go to the canal information center or phone (202) 472-4376. For Great Falls, go to the tavern visitor center, or phone (301) 299-2026.

▲ All boating on the Potomac is subject to Maryland regulations because the river is not within the park. However, 15 public access boat ramps are provided by the park. Only experienced canoeists should attempt to canoe on the Potomac River as some sections are extremely hazardous. Obtain canoeing information at Great Falls Tavern.

▲ There are at least 10 recreational equipment places that rent canoes, boats, and bicycles for use along the towpath, including 4 in the Georgetown/Great Falls area. Ask for the list at a visitor center.

▲ Bicycles should have wide mountain-bike type tires as opposed to narrow racing tires. They should be walked across aqueducts and foot bridges and walked through the Paw Paw Tunnel.

▲ Horseback riding is permitted from Swains Lock to Cumberland. Horse parties are limited to 5 riders. Horses are not permitted in picnic areas, campgrounds, or the hiker-biker campsites. For overnight camping, horse riders should contact park headquarters for regulations.

▲ There are 14 designated picnic areas. Although you may picnic anywhere along the canal, fires are permitted only where fireplaces are provided.

▲ All motor vehicles, including mopeds, motocycles, snowmobiles, and horse-drawn vehicles, are prohibited on the towpath.

▲ Swimming and wading are prohibited in the canal. Fishing is subject to Maryland or Washington, D.C. regulations.

Chesapeake and Ohio Canal National Historical Park *(continued)*

Facilities & Activities

3 drive-in campgrounds
1 walk-in campground
30 hiker-biker campsites
3 group campgrounds
14 picnic areas
canoeing/boating
15 boat ramps
canoe/boat/bicycle rental
fishing
hiking/backpacking
self-guided nature trails
bicycling
horseback riding
mule-powered boat trip
ranger-led walks/evening programs
historic buildings/museum/exhibits
4 visitor centers

Originally built as a path for mules that pulled canal boats, today it provides through-travel opportunities for hikers and bicyclists.

Campgrounds	Total Sites	RVs	Tents	Drinking Water
Antietam Creek (walk-in) (69.3)	20		•	•
McCoys Ferry (110.4)	14	•	•	
15-Mile Creek (140.9)	10	•	•	•
Spring Gap (173.3)	19	•	•	

All campgrounds have pit toilets

Hiker-Biker Campsites*

1—Swains Lock (16.6)
2—Horsepen Branch (26.1)
3—Chisel Branch (30.5)
4—Turtle Run (34.4)
5—Marble Quarry (38.2)
6—Indian Flats (42.5)
7—Calico Rocks (47.6)
8—Bald Eagle Island (49.9)
9—Huckleberry Hill (62.9)
10—Killiansburg Cave (75.2)
11—Horseshoe Bend (79.7)
12—Big Woods (82.7)
13—Opequon Junction (90.9)
14—Cumberland Valley (95.2)
15—Jordan Junction (101.2)

16—North Mountain (110.0)
17—Licking Creek (116.0)
18—Little Pool (120.6)
19—Leopards Mill (129.9)
20—Capapon Junction (133.6)
21—Indigo Neck (139.2)
22—Devils Alley (144.5)
23—Stickpile Hill (149.4)
24—Sorrel Ridge (154.1)
25—Purslane Run (157.4)
26—Town Creek (162.1)
27—Potomac Forks (164.8)
28—Pigmans Ferry (169.1)
29—Iron Mountain (175.3)
30—Evitts Creek (180.1)

* Access only by towpath; campsite numbers/names correspond to numbers on map; numbers in ( ) are locations according to canal milepost numbers.

Cosca Regional Park

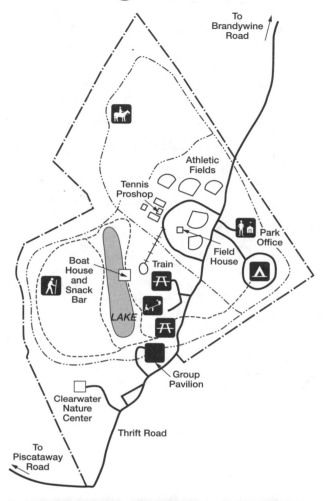

Athletic
Fields

Tennis
Proshop

Park
Office

Field
House

Boat
House
and
Snack
Bar

Train

LAKE

Group
Pavilion

Clearwater
Nature
Center

Thrift Road

To
Piscataway
Road

For Information

Louise F. Cosca Regional Park
11000 Thrift Road
Clinton, MD 20735
(410) 868-1397

Location

Louise F. Cosca Regional park is located 2 miles south of Clinton. At the intersection of MD 5 with MD 223 (Piscataway Road), turn west and go about 1 mile to Clinton; turn left on Brandywine Road and go to Thrift Road; turn right on Thrift Road to the park. This regional park is situated on 500 acres of rolling, wooded terrain. The Clearwater Nature Center (297-4575), located at the southern end of the park, provides a nature program to suit the needs of all ages. For year-round fishing and seasonal boating there is a 15-acre lake in the park. The year-round campground has family sites and 2 group sites. The group sites are designated for scout, church, etc. groups. There are over 5 miles of hiking and horse trails in the park.

Facilities & Activities

23 campsites with electrical/water hookups
flush toilets/hot showers
dump station
2 youth group camping areas (max. 30 each)*
picnicking/picnic shelters
group pavilion
snack bar
playground
fishing
paddleboat/flatboat rental in summer
hiker/equestrian trails
hiker/biker trails
10 tennis courts
   4 are lighted
   4 are enclosed for winter
tennis pro shop
3 softball/2 baseball fields
miniature train
interpretive activities
Clearwater Nature Center

*Reservations required: phone park office

A nature program that suits the needs of all ages is provided through the Clearwater Nature Center. The center is located at the southern end of the park.

Cunningham Falls State Park

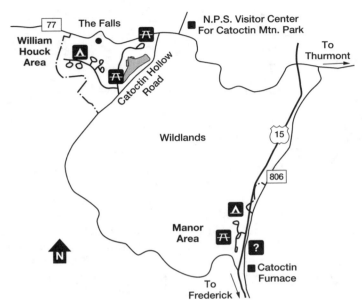

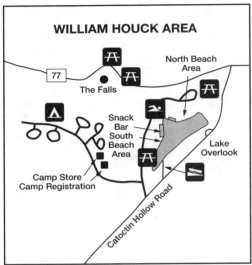

For Information

Cunningham Falls State Park
14039 Catoctin Hollow Road
Thurmont, MD 21788
(301) 271-7574

Location

Covering 4,946 acres in Frederick County, this park is about 15 miles north of Frederick. Cunningham Falls has 2 separate camping areas: the Manor Area (with 31 campsites) is located off US 15; the William Houck Area (with 148 campsites) is 3 miles west of Thurmont, off MD Route 77, on Catoctin Hollow Road. Cunningham Falls State Park, in the scenic Catoctin Mountains, features shaded glens, mountain streams, winding trails, and a 43-acre lake. About 21 miles of trails of varying difficulty are open for hiking. Cunningham Falls is a 78-foot cascading waterfall in a rocky gorge; it is the highest waterfall in Maryland. A 200-yard-long wheelchair accessible trail begins off MD Route 77.

Facilities & Activities

179 improved campsites*
5 camper ready campsites
dump station
4 camper cabins
picnicking/picnic shelters
food/drinks
camp store
swimming
fishing
boat launch/rental
flatwater canoeing
hiking trail
cross-country skiing
historic interest

———————————
*Reservations: phone park office

Deep Creek Lake State Park

For Information

Deep Creek Lake State Park
Route 2, Box 69-C
Swanton, MD 21561
(301) 387-5563

Location

This park covers 1,818 acres in Garrett County. It's 10 miles northeast of Oakland, on the east side of Deep Creek Lake, 2 miles east of Thayerville, off of US 219. Deep Creek Lake State Park fronts on a 6-square-mile, man-made lake that has about 3,900 acres of water surface and 62 miles of shoreline. About 700 feet of beach have been developed, with stumps and boulders removed and sand added. Water sports of all kinds are popular, and in the winter the park offers 6 miles of snowmobile trails.

Facilities & Activities

112 improved campsites*
dump station
picnicking/picnic shelters
food/drinks
camp store
swimming
fishing
boat launch/rental
flatwater canoeing

The park is located on the east side of Deep Creek Lake—a man-made lake that has about 3,900 acres of water surface and 62 miles of shoreline.

hiking trail
snowmobile trail
campfire program

*Reservations: Memorial Day through Labor Day, phone (301) 387-4111

Elk Neck State Park

For Information

Elk Neck State Park
4395 Turkey Point Road
North East, MD 21901
(410) 287-5333

Location

This park is in Cecil County, 9 miles south of North East, on MD Route 272. If approaching the area on I-95, take exit 100 and head south on MD 272. Elk Neck State Park covers 2,188 acres and presents a great variety of topography, from sandy beaches and marshlands to heavily wooded bluffs rising above the Northeast River. A park naturalist is on duty during the summer months; programs are posted on bulletin boards. Camping and boating are major recreational activities; one camping loop remains open all year.

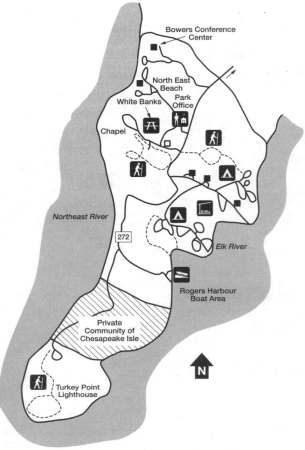

Flatwater canoeing on the Elk River is popular at this park. Camping facilities include 302 campsites; one camping loop remains open all year.

Facilities & Activities

302 improved campsites*
full hookups
dump station
9 cabins
picnicking/picnic shelters
food/drinks
camp store
swimming
fishing
boat launch/rental
flatwater canoeing
hiking trail
cross-country skiing
campfire program
visitor center/historic interest

---

*Reservations: phone park office

Fort Frederick State Park

For Information

Fort Frederick State Park
11100 Ft. Frederick Road
Big Pool, MD 21711
(301) 842-2155

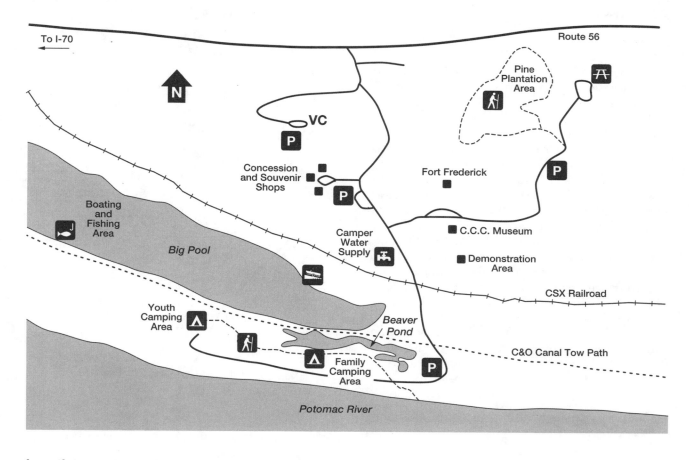

Location

Covering 561 acres in Washington County, this park lies in the historic Cumberland Valley, 16 miles west of Hagerstown. Take exit 12 at I-70 and travel south on Maryland Route 56. Fort Frederick was erected in 1756, during the French and Indian War, and is considered the best-preserved, pre-Revolutionary War stone fort in the country. The fort's stone wall and two barracks have been restored to their 1758 appearance. The historic C & O Canal passes through the park and the towpath is popular for hiking, jogging, and bicycling. The C & O Canal is managed by the National Park Service. There is no boating access onto the Potomac River from Fort Frederick State Park. Boats can be launched from National Park Service ramps a few miles south of the park at McCoy's Ferry or Four Locks. Access onto Big Pool, a 2-mile long section of the C & O Canal, is available from a boat ramp located within the state park.

Facilities & Activities

30 unimproved campsites
picnicking/picnic shelters
food/drinks
camp store
fishing
boat launch/rental
flatwater canoeing
hiking trail
cross-country skiing
campfire program
visitor center/historic interest

Gambrill State Park

For Information

Gambrill State Park
c/o Greenbrier State Park
21843 National Pike
Boonsboro, MD 21713
(301) 791-4767

Location

This park covers 1,137 acres in Frederick County, and is located 6 miles northwest of Frederick on Catoctin Mountain. Take exit 48 off I-70 to US 40 and head north; from US 40, a hard-surfaced road, about a mile in length, leads directly to the park. Three native stone overlooks, strategically located on the 1,600-foot summit of High Knob, midway between the Mason-Dixon Line and the Potomac River, offer excellent and exciting views of the surrounding area. Two separate areas of Gambrill State Park provide recreational facilities and activities: the Rock Run area is located at the park entrance and the High Knob area is located at the top of Catoctin Mountain. The campground is located in the upper portion of the Rock Run area. The High Knob area offers 75-person shelters as well as a lodge-type native stone shelter.

Gambrill State Park comes alive in the spring, with the flowering of many trees and shrubs, highlighted by the blooming of the dogwood trees in late May and the abundance of the beautiful mountain laurel's large white flowers in early June.

Facilities & Activities

35 improved campsites*
dump station
picnicking/picnic shelters
fishing
hiking trail
cross-country skiing
campfire program
visitor center

---

*Reservations: phone park office

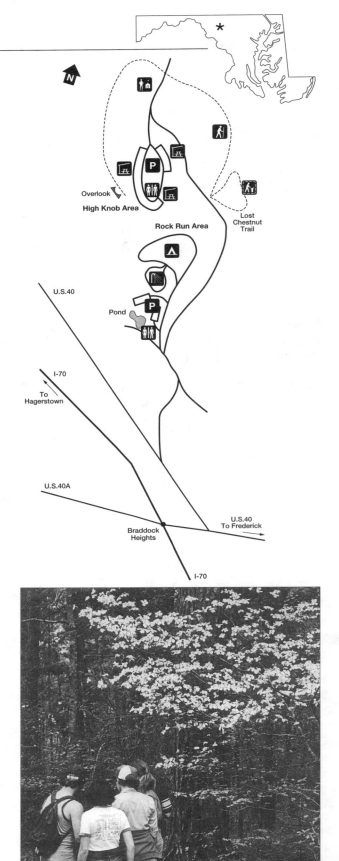

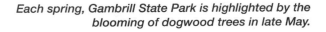

Each spring, Gambrill State Park is highlighted by the blooming of dogwood trees in late May.

Greenbelt Park

For Information

Greenbelt Park
6565 Greenbelt Road
Greenbelt, MD 20770
(301) 344-3948

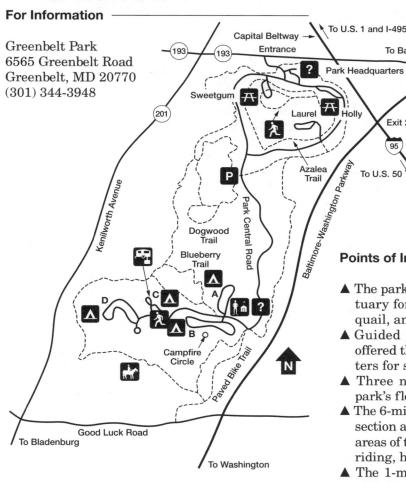

Points of Interest

▲ The park's hardwood forests are a natural sanctuary for raccoons, squirrels, red fox, bobwhite quail, and many other birds.

▲ Guided walks, talks, and evening programs offered throughout the year. Check at headquarters for schedules.

▲ Three nature trails introduce visitors to the park's flora, ecology, and human history.

▲ The 6-mile Bridle Trail circles the park's western section and leads to some of the most picturesque areas of the park. Though primarily for horseback riding, hikers and joggers also use the trail.

▲ The 1-mile Fitness Trail is an exercise course with 20 fitness stations; each station has exercises for different levels of ability and scoring.

Location

Greenbelt Park is 12 miles from downtown Washington and 23 miles from Baltimore. The land of Greenbelt Park was acquired in 1950 by the National Park Service along with the land for the establishment of the Baltimore-Washington Parkway. The parkway was created to provide an uninterrupted and scenic route for passenger vehicles between the two cities. The 1,176-acre Greenbelt Park is surrounded by development; it offers a restive greenspace and retreat from the hectic urban surroundings and a conveniently located campground for visitors to the Nation's Capital. From the Capital Beltway (I-95), take Exit 23 at Kenilworth Avenue (MD 201), proceed south, then left on Greenbelt Road (MD 193) to the park entrance. From the Baltimore-Washington Parkway, exit at Greenbelt Road (MD 193) and west on MD 193 to the park entrance.

General Information

▲ A camping fee is charged, but there is no entry fee.

▲ Park headquarters is located near the park entrance; an information station is also located at the campground entrance. A park brochure, schedule of activities, and information on the various trails are available.

▲ The campground is open year-round for RV and tent camping. Maximum trailer length is 30 feet. All sites are on a first-come, first-served basis. Camping is limited to 7 days from Memorial Day through Labor Day, and 14 days the remainder of the year.

▲ Modern restrooms, drinking water, tables, and fire grills are provided. Utility hookups and showers are not available; the park has a dumping station and water hookup to fill tanks.

▲ Each picnic area has restrooms, water, picnic tables, and fireplaces, in which only charcoal

Greenbelt Park *(continued)*

fires are permitted. Holly and Laurel may be reserved. Sweetgum is available on a first-come, first-served basis.

▲ The Bridle Trail is primarily for horseback riding; horses are not available in the park. Hikers and joggers also use the trail.

▲ All vehicles, including bicycles, are restricted to paved roads. Their use on any trail or off the pavement is strictly prohibited.

▲ The park is closed at dark, although there is a 24-hour access to the park campground.

▲ Bus and subway service to and from Washington DC is available; stations are located within 5 miles of the park. For current information on schedules and fares call (202) 637-7000.

Facilities & Activities

174 RV & tent campsites
sanitary dump
3 picnic areas
3 nature trails
1-mile fitness trail
bicycling
6-mile equestrian trail
ranger-led talks/walks
evening ranger programs

Greenbrier State Park

For Information

Greenbrier State Park
21843 National Pike
Boonsboro, MD 21713
(301) 791-4767

Location

Covering 1,288 acres in Washington County, 10 miles east of Hagerstown, on US 40, this park is easily accessible from I-70 from either the Myersville, Beaver Creek, or Hagerstown interchanges. Greenbrier State Park, nestled in the scenic Appalachian Mountains is located in an area rich in history. Outlines of farms can still be plainly identified by the massive stone fences that once surrounded the homesteads; old foundations and the ruins of log cabins dot the mountainsides. Greenbrier is a multi-use park providing many kinds of recreation; it has a 42-acre, man-made lake and beach, bathhouse, and modern campsites. The Appalachian Trail, which winds from Maine to Georgia, enters the eastern edge of the park on Bartman's Hill, commonly called South Mountain.

Greenbrier State Park *(continued)*

Facilities & Activities

165 improved campsites*
electric hookups
dump station
picnicking
food/drinks
camp store

swimming
fishing
boat launch/rental
flatwater canoeing
hiking trail
cross-country skiing
campfire program
visitor center

*Reservations: phone park office

Hart-Miller Island State Park

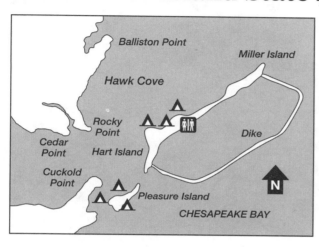

ACCESS BY BOAT ONLY

The western shore of the island has a 3,000-ft-long sandy beach—a great place for parent and child to spend some quality time.

For Information

Hart-Miller Island State Park
c/o Gunpowder Falls State Park
10815 Harford Road
P.O. Box 5032
Glen Arm, MD 21057
(410) 592-2897

Location

Located in Baltimore County waters of the Chesapeake Bay, Hart-Miller Island is located in the Chesapeake Bay near the mouth of Middle River and is accessible only by boat. Originally a part of a peninsula that extended from Edgemere, the two islands, Hart and Miller, were joined on the Bay side by a dike in 1981. The park, which now covers 244 acres, remains in developmental stages as the impoundment is being filled with dredge material from the Baltimore Harbor. The completion of the dike will increase the park size to 1,000 plus acres and will bring new opportunities for land use of the Island.

The western shore of the island offers safe mooring, wading and access to a 3,000-ft-long sandy beach. All campsites are available on a first-come, first-served basis. All sites have a picnic table, lantern post, and campfire grill. Camping is available from May 1 through September 30. Although pets are not allowed on Hart-Miller Island, they are allowed on Pleasure Island. Pleasure Island offers day use and camping opportunities.

Facilities & Activities

22 primitive campsites
restrooms
picnicking
swimming
fishing
boating
hiking trail
park programs

Janes Island State Park

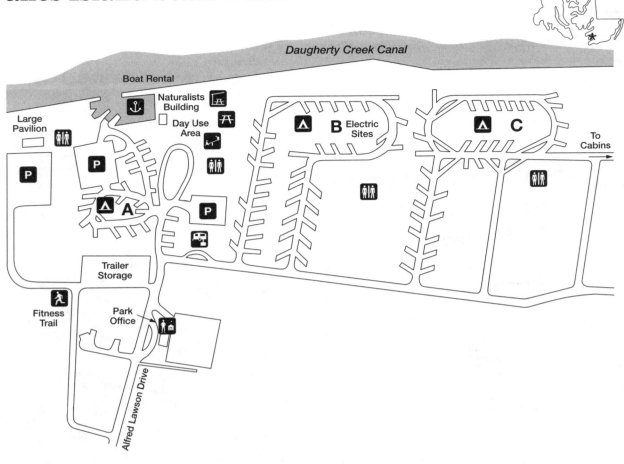

For Information

Janes Island State Park
26280 Alfred Lawson Drive
Crisfield, MD 21817
(410) 968-1565

Location

In Somerset County, this park is reached by US Route 13 to MD Route 413. Continue about 12 miles to Plantation Road then make a right into the park. Janes Island State Park, which covers 3,147 acres, is nearly surrounded by the waters of the Chesapeake Bay and its inlets. The 27-acre mainland portion of the park is accessible by car; the island portion, separated by the Daugherty Creek Canal, is accessible only by boat. The island portion has marsh areas and miles of isolated shoreline; several sand beaches offer excellent swimming. However, jellyfish may be a seasonal problem.

Facilities & Activities

104 improved campsites*
   40 with electric hookups
hot showers
dump station
4 cabins
picnicking/picnic shelters
camp store
swimming beaches on Janes Island
fishing and crabbing
boat launch
25 boat slips
boat rental (row boat/motor boat/canoe);
   April–October
flatwater canoeing/4 canoe trails
self-guided nature trail
1-mile physical fitness trail
naturalist programs
visitor center/historic interest

---

*Reservations: phone park office

Little Bennett Regional Park

For Information

Little Bennett Regional Park
2370 Frederick Rd.
Clarksburg, MD 20871
(301) 972-6581 (park manager)
(301) 972-9222 (campground registration)

Location

Little Bennett Regional Park is located on the east side of I-270 between Washington, DC and Frederick off Frederick Road (MD 355) between Hyattstown and Clarksburg. The park's 3,600 acres are forested and lie among the tributaries of Little Bennett Creek. If you plan a visit to the nation's capital, ask the registration attendant about Metro service; the Metrorail station is reasonably close to the park.

The park hosts a wide variety of special events in the campground. Regularly scheduled movies, concerts, hayrides, and other activities are offered throughout the season. A special attraction at the Hawk's Reach Nature Center (972-9458) is the "Wild Wings" garden planted just for butterflies and hummingbirds. The camping season runs from the first week in April through the last week of October. The campground is open for winter camping on most weekends, from November through March; it is closed on the following holidays: Thanksgiving, Christmas Eve, Christmas Day, New Year's Eve, and New Year's Day.

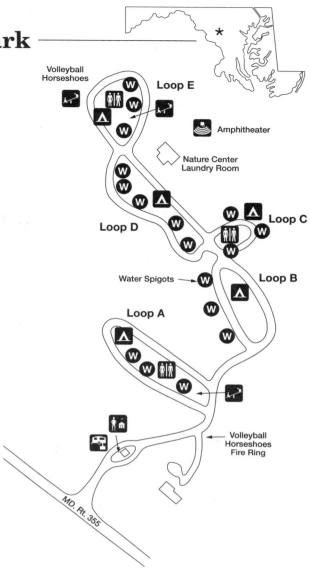

Facilities & Activities

91 campsites (some with electrical hookups)*
flush toilets/showers
dump station
primitive youth group camping area (100 max.)
laundry
camp store
creek fishing
14 miles of equestrian/hiking trails
cross-country ski trails
athletic fields (equipment available)
amphitheater
campfire programs
naturalist led walks/programs
historic sites
Wild Wings garden
Hawk's Reach Nature Center

*Reservations available

Little Bennett Regional Park has 14 miles of hiking trails. The park's 3,600 acres are forested and lie among the tributaries of Little Bennett Creek.

Martinak State Park

For Information

Martinak State Park
137 Deep Shore Road
Denton, MD 21629
(410) 479-1619

Location

Located in Caroline County, at the confluence of the Choptank River and Watts Creek, this park is 2 miles south of Denton, off MD Route 404 on Deep Shore Road. Covering 107 acres, the park is rich in Indian lore, and its high ground suggests that an Indian village might once have been located here. A boat pier and launching ramp make boating and fishing easily accessible after a short run up Watts Creek. Both Choptank River and Watts Creek are tidal waters, and no fishing license is required.

Facilities & Activities

63 improved campsites
dump station
1 cabin

picnicking/picnic shelters
fishing
boat launch
boat rental
flatwater canoeing
hiking trail
campfire program
visitor center

New Germany State Park

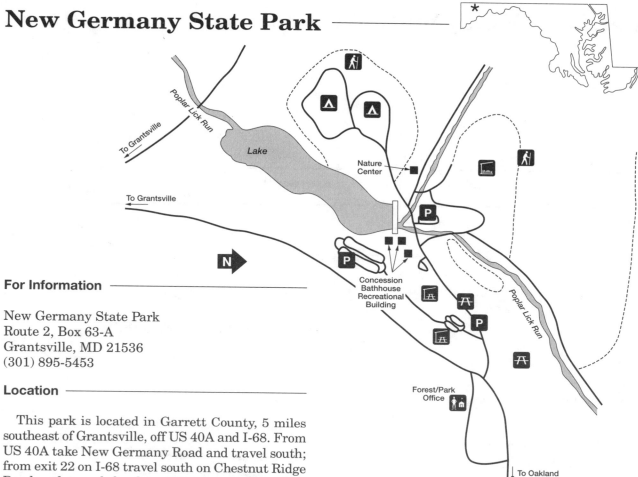

For Information

New Germany State Park
Route 2, Box 63-A
Grantsville, MD 21536
(301) 895-5453

Location

This park is located in Garrett County, 5 miles southeast of Grantsville, off US 40A and I-68. From US 40A take New Germany Road and travel south; from exit 22 on I-68 travel south on Chestnut Ridge Road and turn left when it intersects New Germany Road. New Germany State Park, which covers 455 acres, is built on the site of a once prosperous milling center in the Savage River State Forest; it was noted for its numerous sawmills and a gristmill that supplied local needs. The park features a 13-acre lake and 11 rental cabins. Trails for hiking in summer and cross-counry skiing in winter lead through forest lands typical of western Maryland.

Facilities & Activities

39 improved campsites
dump station
11 cabins
picnicking/picnic shelters
food/drinks
camp store
swimming
fishing
boat launch/rental
flatwater canoeing
hiking trail
cross-country skiing
campfire program
visitor center/historic interest

Trails for cross-country skiing in winter and hiking in summer lead through forest lands at New Germany State Park, typical of western Maryland.

Patapsco Valley State Park

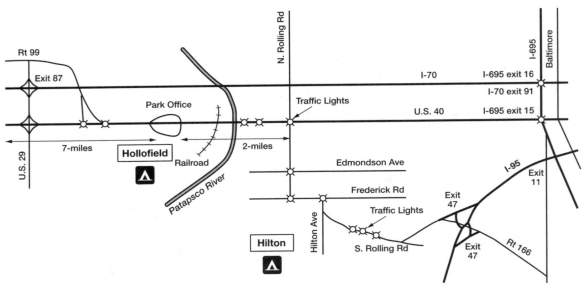

For Information

Patapsco Valley State Park
8020 Baltimore National Pike
Ellicott City, MD 21043
(410) 461-5005

Location

This park spans Baltimore, Howard, Carroll and Anne Arundel Counties, on the western outskirts of Baltimore. The park, covering 12,699 acres, sprawls along the Patapsco River, and offers woods and streams for all kinds of recreation; it begins about 7 miles upstream from the Patapsco River's mouth and extends to Liberty Dam on the North Branch and Sykesville on the South Branch.

Patapsco Valley State Park has 5 separate recreation areas: Glen Artney, Hilton, Hollofield, Pickall, and McKeldin. *Hilton and Hollofield are the only two areas that provide camping.* The Hilton Area is reached from Rolling Road, south of Frederick Road in Catonsville, and the Hollofield Area is adjacent to US 40 near Ellicott City (see vicinity map.) The campground at the Hilton Area is open Friday through Sunday only.

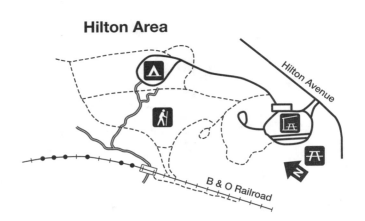

Hilton Area

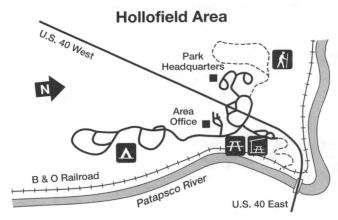

Hollofield Area

Patapsco Valley State Park (continued)

Facilities & Activities

84 improved campsites*
electric hookups at Hollofield Area
Hilton Area campground open Friday–Sunday only
dump station at Hollofield Area
picnicking/picnic shelters
fishing

flatwater/whitewater canoeing
hiking trail
bicycle trail
horseback trail
cross-country skiing
campfire program
historic interest

———
*Reservations: phone park office

Pocomoke River State Park

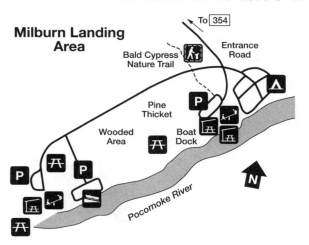

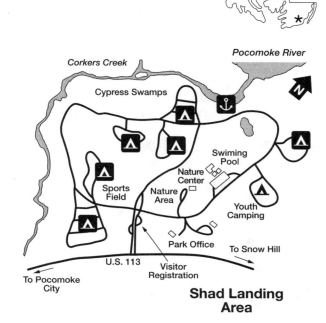

For Information

Pocomoke River State Park
3461 Worcester Highway
Snow Hill, MD 21863
(410) 632-2566

Location

Pocomoke River State Park is located in Worchester County in the Pocomoke State Forest along the banks of the Pocomoke River. The park is divided into 2 sections: Milburn Landing on the north bank of the river, and Shad Landing on the south bank. The 370-acre **Milburn Landing** is located about 8 miles west of Snow Hill via MD Route 12 and MD Route 364. The surrounding creeks, tributaries, and marshlands are inviting for many outdoor activities. The 544-acre **Shad Landing Area** is 4 miles southwest of Snow Hill, off US 113. A large swimming pool is a popular park feature.

The Pocomoke River is a waterway of scenic and historical interest. In 1975, the Milburn Landing and Shad Landing areas were combined and named Pocomoke River State Park. Because of its outstanding qualities, the Pocomoke was the first of Maryland's rivers to be officially classified as scenic.

Facilities & Activities

250 improved campsites*
electric hookups at Shad Landing Area
dump station
picnicking/picnic shelters
food/drinks
camp store
swimming
fishing
boat launch/rental
flatwater canoeing
hiking trail
bicycle trail
campfire program
visitor center

———
*Reservations: Shad Landing Area, May 1–Sept. 30; phone park office

Point Lookout State Park

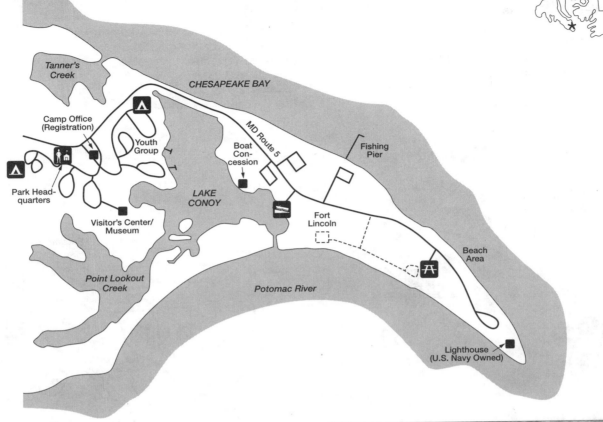

For Information

Point Lookout State Park
P.O. Box 48
Scotland, MD 20687
(301) 872-5688

Location

Covering 525 acres on the southern tip of St. Mary's County at the junction of the Potomac River and the Chesapeake Bay, this park is reached by MD Route 235 and MD 5. Point Lookout is historically important as the site of a Civil War prison housing Confederate soldiers. The park's attractions include beaches, a boat launch area, a 710-foot fishing pier, camping and great fishing. Cruises are available during the summer season to Smith Island. Groups, as well as the general public, can be accommodated; fee required.

Facilities & Activities

143 improved campsites*
full hookups at one loop
dump station
picnicking/camp store
swimming

People always seem to know what to do at the beach—and it doesn't necessarily involve getting wet.

fishing
boat launch/rental
flatwater canoeing
hiking trail
bicycle trail
campfire program
visitor center/historic interest

———
*Reservations: phone park office

Rocky Gap State Park

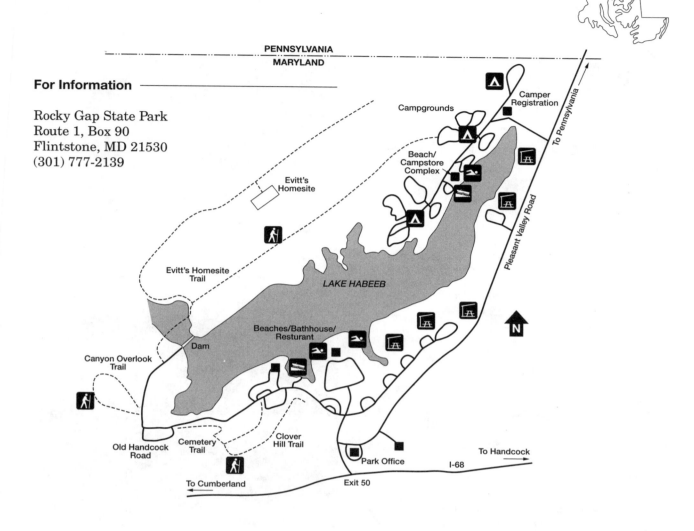

For Information

Rocky Gap State Park
Route 1, Box 90
Flintstone, MD 21530
(301) 777-2139

Location

This park is located in Allegany County, 7 miles northeast of Cumberland on the Pennsylvania state line. Take exit 50 off I-68 and travel north. Rocky Gap Park, a year-round recreational facility, covering 2,983 acres, lies in an area of impressive scenic beauty. Rugged mountains surround it and a splendid mile-long gorge descending to Rocky Gap Run, displays sheer cliffs, overlooks, dense rhododendron, and a hemlock forest. Nestled in a natural saddle created by Evitts Mountain and Martin Mountain, this park offers mountain scenery and interesting hiking trails. Three swimming beaches and a modern bathhouse adjoin a 243-acre lake and a large campground.

Facilities & Activities

278 improved campsites*
electric hookups
dump station
picnicking/picnic shelters
food/drinks
camp store
swimming
fishing
boat launch/rental
flatwater canoeing
hiking trail
campfire program
visitor center/historic interest

———

*Reservations: phone park office

Smallwood State Park

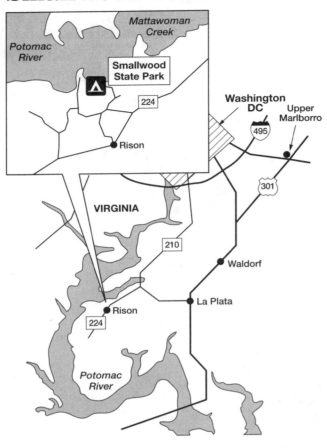

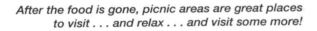

After the food is gone, picnic areas are great places to visit . . . and relax . . . and visit some more!

For Information

Smallwood State Park
Route 1, Box 64
Marbury, MD 20658
(301) 743-7613

Location

Covering 629 acres in Charles County, 4 miles west of Pisgah, off MD 224, Smallwood was the home of General William Smallwood, a Revolutionary War officer who was once governor of Maryland. His house, called Smallwood's Retreat, has been restored and is open to visitors. The park's Sweden Point Marina has become a popular boating area; it is located at the mouth of Mattawoman Creek and gives access to the Potomac River and surrounding tributaries.

Facilities & Activities

16 improved campsites with electric hookups*
picnicking/picnic shelters
fishing
300-foot "T" fishing pier
6 deep-draft boat ramps
marina with meeting room, showers, laundromat
boat rental (row boats/motor boats/paddle
    boats/canoes)
50 boat slips with electricity/water
concession store
flatwater canoeing
hiking trail
cross-country skiing
campfire programs
historic interest

*Reservations: phone (301) 888-1410

South Mountain State Park

Map #1— North Half

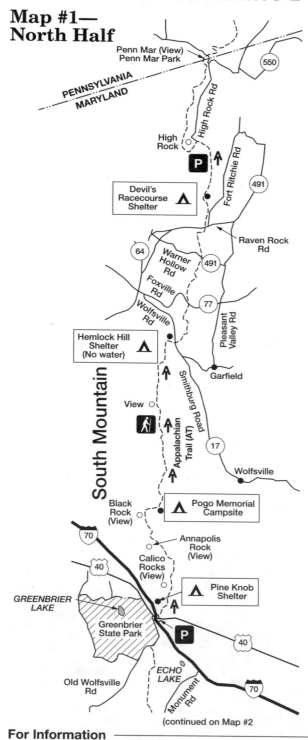

Penn Mar (View)
Penn Mar Park

550

PENNSYLVANIA
MARYLAND

High Rock Rd

High Rock

P

Fort Ritchie Rd

491

Devil's Racecourse Shelter

64

Warner Hollow Rd

491

Raven Rock Rd

Foxville Rd

77

Wolfsville Rd

Pleasant Valley Rd

Hemlock Hill Shelter (No water)

South Mountain

Smithburg Road

Garfield

View

Appalachian Trail (AT)

17

Wolfsville

Black Rock (View)

Pogo Memorial Campsite

Annapolis Rock (View)

Calico Rocks (View)

70

40

Pine Knob Shelter

GREENBRIER LAKE

Greenbrier State Park

P

40

ECHO LAKE

Old Wolfsville Rd

Monument Rd

70

(continued on Map #2)

Map #2—South Half

WASHINGTON MONUMENT STATE PARK

Monument Rd

N

40A

Old National Pike

Dahlgren Camp

Bolivar Rd

Reno Monument Rd

Rocky Run Shelter

Reno Monument Rd

White Rocks (View)

67

Appalachian Trail (AT)

Crampton Gap Shelter

Arnoldtown Rd

Townsend Rd

GATHLAND STATE PARK

Gapland Rd

Crampton Gap

Gapland Rd

South Mountain

Rohrersville Rd.

67

Weverton Cliffs

340

WEST VIRGINIA

Potomac River

C&O Canal

P

MARYLAND

Harper's Ferry National Historical Park

Trail Follows Towpath

VIRGINIA

Potomac River

Harper's Ferry

340

P

Shenandoah River

671

For Information

South Mountain State Park
c/o Greenbrier State Park
21843 National Pike
Boonsboro, MD 21713
(301) 791-4767

South Mountain State Park *(continued)*

Location

On 8,039 acres in Washington and Frederick Counties, South Mountain is a ridge composed largely of resistant quartzite that runs in a general north-south direction from the Pennsylvania border near Pen Mar to the West Virginia border near Weverton and rises from 200 feet above sea level in the south by the Potomac River to nearly 2,000 feet at Pen Mar. South Mountain State Park follows this ridge and includes 40 miles of the 2,050 mile-long Appalachian Trail (AT) which runs from Maine to Georgia. The area provides excellent hiking, primitive camping for trail hikers, and exciting vistas.

About the Trail

Day hikers may begin their excursions at various trailheads located wherever the AT intersects a road. Backpackers are permitted to camp along the AT *only* at the 7 designated camping areas. Echo Lake, an area attached to South Mountain State Park, may be reserved in advance through the park for organized youth groups. The purity of water from unprotected water sources is not guaranteed; to be safe, all water should be purified by boiling or chemically treated before use.

Scenic overlooks are within a short hike of the trailheads on US 40, Weverton Cliff, Gathland State Park, MD 17, Pen Mar Park, and High Rock. There are three state parks adjacent to the trail that runs the length of South Mountain State Park: Greenbrier, Washington Mounument, and Gathland. There is a large developed campground at Greenbrier State Park.

The Potomac Appalachian Trail Club, Inc. has compiled and published a detailed map for the Maryland section of the Appalachian Trail. It is available from the Appalachian Trail Conference, P.O. Box 807, Dept. SD, Harpers Ferry, WV 25425-0807. Anyone hiking the South Mountain section of the AT should obtain an official map. Do not rely on the map provided here because it is for general reference only to show the approximate location of the designated campsites, the scenic overlooks, parking areas, and a few of the major roads that provide access to the trail.

A South Mountain State Park brochure lists the following points of interest along South Mountain:

.2 Pen Mar Park
3.6 High Rock View
5.1 Devils Racecourse shelter*
6.2 MD Route 491
7.0 Warner Hollow Road
8.2 MD Route 77
9.6 MD Route 17

9.7 Hemlock Hill shelter*
14.6 Pogo Memorial campsite*
15.0 Black Rock Cliff View
16.0 Annapolis Rock View
17.4 Pine Knob shelter*
18.2 US Route 40 footbridge
19.6 trail to Greenbrier State Park
21.0 Washington Monument State Park
23.6 US Route 40-A
23.9 Dahlgren Camp*
24.4 Reno Monument Road
25.3 Rocky Run shelter*
27.3 White Rock View
30.3 Cramptons Gap shelter*
30.7 Gathland State Park
33.7 unmarked view
36.6 Weverton Cliff View
37.4 parking for Weverton Cliff
37.9 C & O Canal
41.7 footbridge from canal to Harpers Ferry

*Camping is permitted **only** at these designated sites. Distances are in miles from north to south.

Facilities & Activities

7 designated primitive campsites along the AT
   Devils Racecourse shelter (5.1 mile-marker)
   Hemlock Hill shelter (9.7 mile-marker)
   Pogo Memorial campsite(14.6 mile-marker)
   Pine Knob shelter (17.4 mile-marker)
   Dahlgren Camp (23.9 mile marker)
   Rocky Run shelter (25.3 mile-marker)
   Cramptons Gap shelter (30.3 mile-marker)
picnicking/picnic shelters
hiking trail
cross-country skiing
historic interest

Day hikers may begin their excursion on the 40-mile section of the Appalachian Trail in Maryland at various trailheads, which are located wherever the trail intersects a road.

State Forests (Garrett, Green Ridge, Potomac, Savage River)

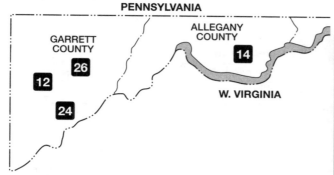

*Numbers correspond to location numbers on region map, page 34

For Information

(12) Garrett State Forest
c/o Potomac State Forest
Route 3, Box 9305
Oakland, MD 21550
(301) 334-2038

(14) Green Ridge State
Forest
HCR #13, Box 50
Flintstone, MD 21530
(301) 777-2345

(24) Potomac State
Forest
Route 3, Box 9305
Oakland, MD 21550
(301) 334-2038

(26) Savage River State
Forest
Route 2, Box 63-A
Grantsville, MD 21536
(301) 895-5759

Fat-tire bicycling has become quite popular in recent years; bicycle trails are located on the Green Ridge and the Savage River state forests.

Locations

(12) Garrett State Forest: Covering 6,781 acres in Garrett County, the forest is 5 miles northwest of Oakland, off US 219. The forest, reached from the Herrington Manor and San Run Roads, contains a diversity of trees, abundant wildlife, and beautiful scenery. In 1906, this forest was given to the state of Maryland and was the beginning of our present public lands system. Within the forest are 2 state parks—Herrington Manor and Swallow Falls. Garrett State Forest and Potomac State Forest are managed together as a single managment unit, and referred to as Potomac-Garrett State Forest. The forest headquarters is located southeast of Oakland in the Potomac State Forest. See Potomac State Forest for directions to the headquarters.

(14) Green Ridge State Forest: Located in eastern Allegany County, about 22 miles east of Cumberland, the state forest headquarters is just south of I-68 at exit 64. This vast forest covers 38,811 acres and stretches across the mountains of Western Maryland and occupies portions of Town Hill, Polish Mountain, and Green Ridge Mountain. Wildlife is plentiful and includes wild turkey, grouse, squirrel, and deer. A boat ramp at Bonds Landing provides easy access to the Potomac River.

(24) Potomac State Forest: Located in southeastern Garrett County, 10,416-acre Potomac State Forest, situated between the towns of Oakland and Westernport and partially bordering the Potomac River, is reached from MD Routes 135 and 560. The Potomac River has its headwaters in this rugged mountain forest where wildlife abounds and there is excellent trout fishing. The forest features the highest point in any Maryland state forest—Backbone Mountain, elevation 3,220 feet.

The Potomac-Garrett State Forest Headquarters is reached by traveling south on MD 560 from Loch Lynn for about 2¼ miles to Bethlehem Road, then following Bethlehem Road for about 3¾ miles to the Potomac Camp Road, and finally following the Potomac Camp Road for about 1¼ miles to the headquarters area.

(26) Savage River State Forest: This is the largest of Maryland's state forests, covering 52,812 acres. In central and eastern Garrett County, generally south of US 40, you can reach the state forest headquarters by taking exit 24 from I-68 and traveling south on New Germany Road past New Germany State Park. Savage River State Forest is a strategic watershed surrounding the Savage River Reservoir. This forest is classified as a northern hardwood forest. About 2,700 acres of the forest have been designated as the Big Savage Wildland. Within the forest are 2 state parks—New Germany and Big Run—and the 350-acre Savage River Reservoir, which has a 17½-mile shoreline.

Facilities & Activities	Garrett State Forest	Green Ridge State Forest	Potomac State Forest	Savage River State Forest
primitive campsites	17	97	22	42
picnicking		•	•	•
picnic shelters			•	•
swimming			•	
fishing	•	•	•	•
boat launch		•		•
flatwater canoeing		•		•
whitewater canoeing				•
shooting range		•		
hiking trail	•	•	•	•
bicycle trail		•		•
horseback trail	•	•	•	•
cross-country skiing	•		•	•
snowmobile trail	•	•	•	•
campfire program		•		•
historic interest	•	•		•
visitor center		•		

Recreation facilities at each of the 4 state forests in Maryland include snowmobile trails. With the exception of Green Ridge State Forest, they all offer cross-country ski trails, as well.

Susquehanna State Park

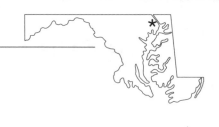

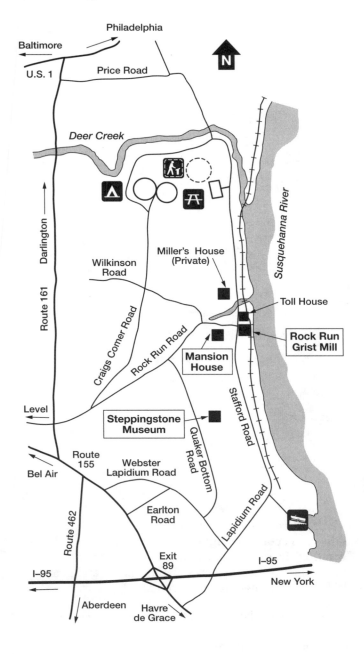

Location

Located in Harford County, 3 miles north of Havre de Grace, off Route 155, the setting for this 2,639-acre park is the Susquehanna River Valley with its varying topography, heavy forest cover, massive rock outcrops, and interesting history. The park's focal point is the river front historic area where Rock Run flows into the Susquehanna River.

Rock Run Grist Mill, an imposing four-story water-powered structure that was built in 1794, houses a collection of milling-related machinery; it is open on weekends and holidays from Memorial Day until the end of September and is operated from 2–4 pm each afternoon. A 19th-century farm is the site for the Steppingstone Museum. The museum offers displays and demonstrations of rural arts and industries around 1900 and is open weekends and holidays, from May to September; there is a small admission fee. The Manor House is open from Memorial Day to Labor Day on weekends and holidays from 10 am to 6 pm. The L-shaped house contains 13 rooms, and was built in 1804 by John Carter.

Facilities & Activities

75 improved campsites*
picnicking
fishing
boat launch
flatwater canoeing
hiking trail
horseback trail
cross-country skiing
campfire program
historic interest

---

*Reservations: weekends and holidays only, Memorial Day thru Labor Day; phone park office

For Information

Susquehanna State Park
c/o Rocks State Park
3318 Rocks Chrome Hill Road
Jarrettsville, MD 21084
(410) 557-7994

Swallow Falls State Park

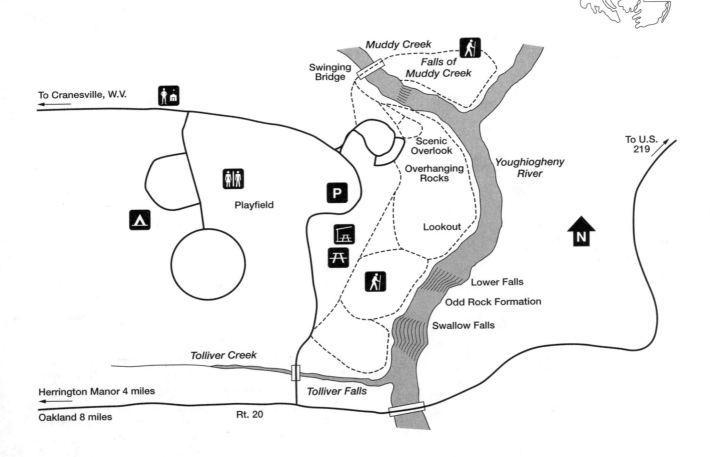

For Information

Swallow Falls State Park
c/o Herrington Manor State Park
Route #5, Box 2180
Oakland, MD 21550
(301) 334-9180

Location

Located in Garrett County, 9 miles northwest of Oakland on County Route 20, this park is 4 miles beyond the entrance to Herrington Manor State Park, and 3 miles east of the West Virginia state line. It covers 257 acres and contains some of Maryland's most beautiful and picturesque scenery. Nestled along the Youghiogheny River between Swallow Falls and Muddy Creek Falls, it is a mountain paradise of scenic beauty, a place of rushing water and towering trees, of cliffs and rocks and wildflowers.

Muddy Creek Falls is a crashing 63-foot water-fall—a spectacular sight. Hiking trails follow the winding river; here in the park is one of Maryland's last virgin forests, 40 acres of giant pines and hemlocks rising to heights of more than 100 feet.

Facilities & Activities

64 improved campsites*
5 camper ready campsites
dump station
picnicking/picnic shelters
fishing
hiking trail
horseback trail
cross-country skiing
campfire program
historic interest

———————————
*Reservations: phone park office

Watkins Regional Park

Western
Branch

Old Maryland
Farm

Garden
Plot Rental

Old
Enterprise
Road

Train

Carousel

Miniature
Golf

Tennis
Court

Softball Fields

Entry
Station

Nature
Center

Practice
Field

Volleyball
Courts

Tennis
Bubble

Football
and Soccer
Field

Watkins Park Drive Route 556

Hiking trails follow the winding river at Swallow Falls State Park and lead to 3 spectacular waterfalls: Muddy Creek Falls, Lower Falls, and Swallow Falls.

For Information

Robert M. Watkins Regional Park
301 Watkins Park Drive
Upper Marlboro, MD 20722
(301) 249-9220
(301) 249-6900 (campground)

Location

This park is located east of Largo. From MD 214 (Central Avenue) take MD 556 (Watkins Park Drive) south for 1 mile to the park entrance. It is situated on 437 well used and preserved acres encompassing a variety of habitat, from wetlands to meadows, to densely shaded forest. Watkins Nature Center (249-6202) nestles in tall trees at the far end of the park. An indoor pond, live animals, and natural history exhibits are featured. Public programs are offered year-round for all ages and interests.

Watkins Regional Park (continued)

Special attractions at the park include the Chesapeake Carousel, with its handcrafted/restored animals, and the Watkins "Daylight Special," a miniature train that winds through scenic woodlands, passing the Old Maryland Farm during its one-mile stretch. A lighted 18-hole minature golf course is hidden in the wooded landscape. All three of these attractions are open from late April to Labor Day.

Facilities & Activities

34 campsites*
flush toilets/showers
dump station

group camping
picnicking/3 group picnic areas
snack bar
antique carousel
miniature train
18-hole miniature golf
nature/hiking trails
5 indoor tennis courts
4 lighted outdoor tennis courts
5 softball fields
3 volleyball courts
football/soccer field
2 basketball courts
garden plot rentals
Old Maryland Farm
Watkins Nature Center

_____

*Reservations available

Watkins Regional Park is a great place to have family reunions, as they have 3 group picnic areas. Special attractions at the park include a handcrafted/restored carousel, a miniature train that winds through the scenic woodlands, and a lighted 18-hole minature golf course.

Youghiogheny River Lake

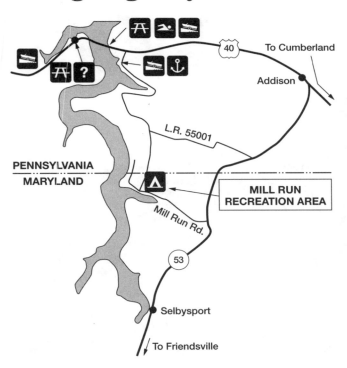

Youghiogheny River Lake spans the Mason-Dixon line between Pennsylvania and Maryland. The size of the marina on US 40 attests to its popularity as a fishing, power boating, and water-skiing lake.

For Information

Youghiogheny River Lake
R.D. #1, Box 17
Confluence, PA 15424
(814) 395-3242

Location

Youghiogheny River Lake lies in the heart of the Laurel Highlands and spans the Mason-Dixon line between Pennsylvania and Maryland. The clean waters, mountains, and steep-sided valleys provide an unsurpassed setting for outdoor recreation opportunities. Boaters consider Youghiogheny River Lake, with its 16-mile length and channels up to one-half mile wide, one of the best power boating and water-skiing lakes in the area. For the fisherman, there are numerous coves and backwater areas along the lake that provide excellent fishing. An especially scenic time for sightseeing at the lake is during the first half of October when fall foliage colors are at their peak.

There are 3 campgrounds at Youghiogheny River Lake; two of them are located in Pennsylvania—Outflow below the dam near Confluence, and Tub Run on the west side of the lake off of PA 281 north of US 40. Recreational facilities located near the US 40 bridge that crosses the lake include marina, boat launches, picnic area, swimming area, and restrooms. *Mill Run is the only recreation area located in Maryland;* it is located on the east side of the lake on Mill Run Road, off of MD 53 between Addison and Selbysport. Mill Run is open year round and is a fee area.

Facilities & Activities for Mill Run Recreation Area

30 campsites
tables/grills
restrooms
dump station
drinking water
playgrounds
swimming
fishing
boating/water-skiing
boat launch
campground programs

Virginia

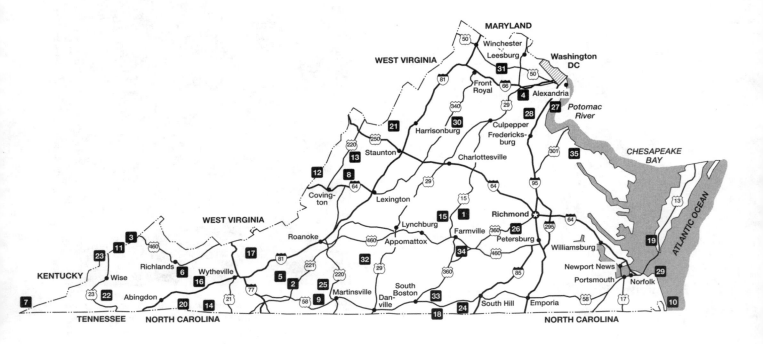

1—Bear Creek Lake State Park, page 73
2—Blue Ridge Parkway, page 74
3—Breaks Interstate Park, page 77
4—Bull Run Regional Park, page 79
5—Claytor Lake State Park, page 80
6—Clinch Mountain Wildlife Management Area, page 81
7—Cumberland Gap National Historical Park, page 82
8—Douthat State Park, page 84
9—Fairy Stone State Park, page 85
10—False Cape State Park, page 86
11—Flannagan (John W.) Dam & Reservoir, page 87
12—Gathright Dam & Lake Moomaw, page 88
13—George Washington National Forest, page 90
14—Grayson Highlands State Park, page 105
15—Holliday Lake State Park, page 106
16—Hungry Mother State Park, page 107
17—Jefferson National Forest, page 108

18—Kerr (John H.) Dam & Reservoir, page 114
19—Kiptopeke State Park, page 115
20—Mount Rogers National Recreation Area, page 116
21—Natural Chimneys Regional Park, page 119
22—Natural Tunnel State Park, page 120
23—North Fork of Pound Lake, page 121
24—Occoneechee State Park, page 122
25—Philpott Lake, page 123
26—Pocahontas State Park, page 124
27—Pohick Bay Regional Park, page 125
28—Prince William Forest Park, page 126
29—Seashore State Park and Natural Area, page 129
30—Shenandoah National Park, page 130
31—Sky Meadows State Park, page 133
32—Smith Mountain Lake State Park, page 134
33—Staunton River State Park, page 135
34—Twin Lakes State Park, page 136
35—Westmoreland State Park, page 137

Bear Creek Lake State Park

For Information

Bear Creek Lake State Park
Route 1, Box 253
Cumberland, VA 23040-9518
(804) 492-4410

Cumberland
State Forest

Running
Cedar Trail

Campground–A
Trail

To 629   666

BEAR CREEK LAKE

Lakeside Trail

Lakeside Trail

Facilities & Activities

45 campsites
   29 with electrical/water hookups
showers
dump station
picnicking/shelters
snack bar
lake swimming & bathhouse
freshwater fishing
boating (non-gasoline powered)
boat ramp
canoe/paddleboat/rowboat rentals
7 miles of hiking trails
interpretive programs

Location

This park is nestled in the heart of Cumberland State Forest; it can be reached by turning off US 60 just east of Cumberland on Route 622. Travel north on Route 622 for 4½ miles, then west on Route 629. Activities revolve around the 40-acre lake. Five trails wander through the hardwood forest and around the lake in this 326.4-acre park; the surrounding Cumberland State Forest has additional hiking trails, including the 16-mile Willis River Trail.

Blue Ridge Parkway

Map #1—Virginia

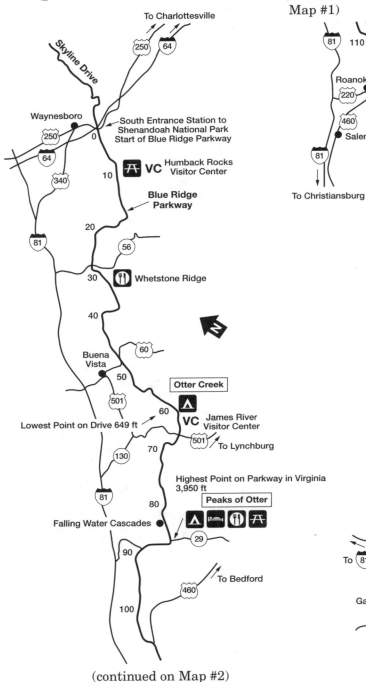

To Charlottesville

Skyline Drive

250   64

Waynesboro

250

64

340

South Entrance Station to
Shenandoah National Park
Start of Blue Ridge Parkway

0

10   VC   Humback Rocks
Visitor Center

**Blue Ridge
Parkway**

20

81

56

30   Whetstone Ridge

40

60

Buena
Vista

50

501

Otter Creek

60

Lowest Point on Drive 649 ft

VC   James River
Visitor Center

501   To Lynchburg

70

130

Highest Point on Parkway in Virginia
3,950 ft

81

80   **Peaks of Otter**

Falling Water Cascades

29

90

To Bedford

460

100

(continued on Map #2)

(continued from
Map #1)

Map #2—Virginia

81   110   Unit Office

Roanoke

220   120   Roanoke Mountain

460

Salem   220

81   130   **Blue Ridge
Parkway**

To Christiansburg   140

Devil's Backbone
2,708 ft

221

150   Smart View

160

8

Rocky Knob
Visitor Center   170   Mabry Mill

VC   58

221   180

Groundhog
Mountain
3,025 ft

58   190

52   VIRGINIA

200   NORTH CAROLINA

77

To   81   58

221   77

Galax   210

89

220   VC   Cumberland Knob
Visitor Center

For Information

Blue Ridge Parkway
400 BB&T Building
One Pack Square
Asheville, NC 28801
(704) 298-0398 Voice Message

Location

From Shenandoah National Park, the Blue Ridge
Parkway follows the Blue Ridge Mountains, eastern rampart of the Appalachians, for 355 miles.
Then, for the remaining 114 miles, it skirts the
southern end of the massive Black Mountains,

weaves through the Craggies, the Pisgahs, and the Balsams, and ends in the Great Smokies. At Mile 0, Rockfish Gap near Waynesboro, Virginia, the northern end of the parkway connects directly to Shenandoah National Park's 105-mile Skyline Drive. The parkway crosses the North Carolina and Virginia state line at Mile 216.9. The southern end of the parkway intersects with US 441 in the Great Smoky Mountains National Park in North Carolina at Mile 469. Elevations range from 649 to 6,053 feet above sea level, with an average elevation of 3,000 feet. Visitors are encouraged to pick up the detailed map/brochure of the park as it displays the mile markers; it will help locate features, facilities, and services.

Points of Interest

▲ Flowering shrubs (azalea, mountain laurel, dog wood, and rhododendron) put on a springtime show that rivals the display of trees in fall. Because of the range in elevation, peak blooming occurs somewhat earlier in Virginia than North Carolina.
▲ Autumn flames brilliant with the reds of sumac, gums and maples, and the bright yellow hues of the sassafras, tulip tree and hickory.
▲ Picturesque log cabins and miles of rail fences emphasize the pioneer culture of the Blue Ridge Highlands. The parkway shops offer a variety of colorful mountain handicrafts that include pottery, weaving, woodcraft, and metalcrafts.
▲ The hiker symbol under an overlook-ahead sign is your invitation to leave your vehicle for a walk through the woods. Some trails are short and take only 10 minutes roundtrip; others take 30 minutes or an hour.

General Information

▲ There is no entry fee to the parkway; camping fees are charged.
▲ Four visitor centers are located along the parkway in Virginia. They sell literature, and provide information, interpretive exhibits, and illustrated programs.
▲ Campfire programs and walks are conducted by park naturalists. These activities are listed on the bulletin boards and in the parkway newspaper, *The Milepost,* available free at any visitor center.
▲ RV and tent campgrounds in Virginia are at Otter Creek (Mile 60.9), Peaks of Otter (86.0), Roanoke Mountain (120.5), and Rocky Knob (167.1).
▲ The 4 campgrounds are open from about May 1 through October or into early November. Winter

camping is occasionally available, weather permitting. Inquire in advance. During the winter, when no fee is charged, services are limited; only chemical toilets and frost free faucets are provided. Each campsite has a table and fireplace; drinking water and comfort stations are provided.
▲ Campsites are available on a first-come, first-served basis. Camping is limited to a total of 14 days between June 1 and Labor Day, and 30 days for the calendar year. Campgrounds have sites that will accommodate trailers up to 30 feet in length. Dump stations are available at all campgrounds; no water or electrical hookups are available.
▲ Limited back country camping is available on a first-come, first-served basis at Rock Castle Gorge near Rocky Knob (Mile 167.1). Permits must be requested in advance. Phone: Rocky Knob at (703) 745-3452.
▲ Lodging is provided along the parkway from May through October at Rocky Knob. Lodging is provided year round at Peaks of Otter. Reservations are advisable. Contact the park for addresses of the concessionaires.
▲ Along the Virginia portion of the parkway are 5 picnic areas with tables, fireplaces, drinking water, trash cans, and comfort stations. Several parking overlooks also have picnic tables.

Miles of rail fences and picturesque log cabins emphasize the pioneer culture of the Blue Ridge Highlands along the 216.9 miles of parkway in Virginia.

Blue Ridge Parkway *(continued)*

▲ The parkway offers hikers of all skill levels the opportunity to explore varied and intriguing trails. Ask for the park brochure that lists the trails by milepost location, mileage, and degree of difficulty.

▲ Each of the 4 campgrounds provide access to hiking trails; some have self-guiding nature trails. The Appalachian Trail roughly parallels the parkway from Mile 0 at Rockfish Gap to Mile 103.

▲ Bicycles may be ridden only on paved road surfaces and parking areas; they may not be ridden on trails or walkways. Bicyclists should be prepared for significant distances between developed areas when traveling along the parkway because camping is permitted only in established campgrounds.

▲ When planning a bicycle trip along the parkway, contact the park for information. A brochure is available that displays the total elevation differential between mileposts.

▲ Limited supplies may be purchased at most parkway gasoline stations; several campgrounds have camp stores. Most services along the parkway are available from May 1 through October. Sections of the parkway may be closed by snow or ice.

▲ The maximum speed limit is 45 miles per hour. Mountainous terrain and sightseeing, however, often require slower speeds. Allow 30 miles per hour when figuring actual travel time.

Facilities & Activities

4 RV & tent campgrounds
   69 sites at Otter Creek
   148 sites at peaks of Otter
   104 sites at Roanoke Mountain
   109 sites at Rocky Knob
sanitary dumps at each campground
8 backcountry campsites at Rock Castle Gorge
2 lodges
5 picnic areas
hiking/backpacking
self-guided nature trails
bicycling
cross-country skiing/snowmobiling
auto tour along the 216.9-mile Virginia portion of
   the parkway
restaurants/coffee shops/snacks
gift and craft shops/camp stores
ranger-led talks/walks
evening campfire programs
museums/exhibits/amphitheaters
4 visitor centers

Mabry Mill is located at mile 176.1 on the parkway. A trail takes you to the gristmill, sawmill, and blacksmith shop; old time skills are demonstrated in summer.

Breaks Interstate Park

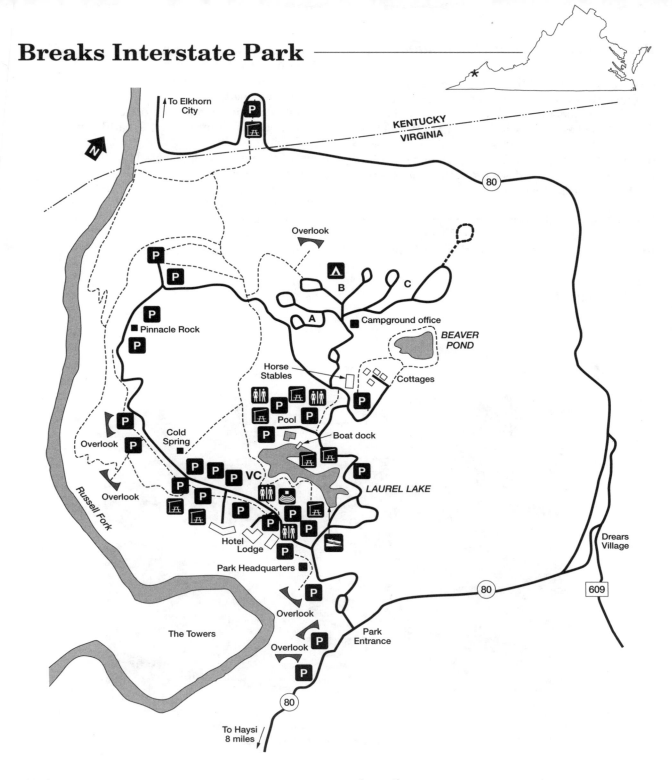

To Elkhorn City

KENTUCKY
VIRGINIA

N

80

Overlook

B

C

A

Campground office

BEAVER POND

Pinnacle Rock

Horse Stables

Cottages

Cold Spring

Pool

Boat dock

Overlook

VC

LAUREL LAKE

Overlook

Russell Fork

Drears Village

Hotel
Lodge

Park Headquarters

80

609

Overlook

The Towers

Overlook

Park Entrance

80

To Haysi
8 miles

For Information

Breaks Interstate Park
P.O. Box 100
Breaks, VA 24607-0100
(703) 865-4413
(703) 865-4414 (motel reservations)

Location

Breaks Interstate Park is located on the Kentucky-Virginia border, 7 miles east of Elkhorn City, KY, and 8 miles north of Haysi, VA, on Route 80. The Russell Fork River has carved the largest canyon east of the Mississippi. Sometimes called the "Grand

Breaks Interstate Park (continued)

Canyon of the South," this craggy, untouched beauty is more than 5 miles long and 1,600 feet deep, guarded by sheer vertical walls most of the way. Some of the best whitewater rafting in the eastern United States occurs at this 4,500-acre park during the first 4 weekends in October, when John Flannagan Reservoir provides whitewater releases into the Russell Fork River.

Facilities & Activities

122 campsites with full and partial hookups
showers
dump station
16-site group camp
4 housekeeping cottages (2-bedroom)
34-unit motor lodge
restaurant/gift shop in lodge
picnicking/shelters
pool concessions/camping supplies
olympic-size swimming pool & bathhouse
freshwater fishing
boating (non-gasoline powered)
boat ramp/dock
paddleboat rentals
12 miles of hiking trails
self-guiding trail
bicycle trails
horse stable/horse & pony rides
interpretive programs
amphitheater
visitor center

This overlook provides a view of the Russell Fork River and an area called "The Towers." It is a good vantage point during the weekends in October when John Flannagan Reservoir provides releases into this river sufficient for whitewater rafting.

Bull Run Regional Park

For Information

Bull Run Regional Park
7700 Bull Run Drive
Centreville, VA 22020
(703) 631-0550

Location

Bull Run Regional Park is located about 30 miles west of Washington, DC, off I-66. Take exit 52 on I-66 near Centreville, travel west on US 29 about 3 miles and turn south on Bull Run Post Office Road (SH 621) to the park entrance. The 1,800-acre park, owned and operated by the Northern Virginia Regional Park Authority (703/352-5900), is open from mid-March through November. In the springtime, acres of bluebells and other wildflowers bloom beside a picturesque, meandering stream. Special programs include summer country music festivals, large crafts shows, and dog shows.

Facilities & Activities

150 tent/RV campsites*
  100 with electricity
restrooms/showers/laundry
dump station

group campsites for youth groups**
picnic tables/grills
rental picnic shelters**
playground
snack bar/camp store
swimming pool (Memorial Day week-end through
  Labor Day)
small stream fishing
canoeing (winter & spring)
boat ramp/jon boat rentals
nature trails/interpretive programs
access to 17-mile Bull Run Occoquan Trail
bridle path and staging area
athletic fields
roller blading
miniature & disc golf
archery/skeet & trap range

*Reservations accepted but not required
**Reservations required (703) 352-5900

Claytor Lake State Park

For Information

Claytor Lake State Park
Route 1, Box 267
Dublin, VA 24084-9607
(703) 674-5492

Location

This state park is located southeast of Dublin and southwest of Radford on the 21-mile long, 4,500-acre, Claytor Lake. From I-81 (exit 101), take Route 660 and travel southeast about 2 miles. The 472-acre park features the only full-service marina in the state park system. The park is home base for the *Pioneer Maid,* a cruise boat offering lunch, dinner, and scenic cruises of Claytor Lake and New River. The visitor center is located in the Historic Howe House, built between 1876 and 1879; it features exhibits on the life of the early settlers of the region, as well as the plant and animal life.

Facilities & Activities

132 campsites
    44 with electrical/water hookups
showers

dump station
12 lakefront cabins (2-bedroom)
picnicking/6 shelters
snack bar
lake swimming & bathhouse
freshwater fishing
boating (motor boats permitted)
boat ramp
rowboat/motor boat rentals
full-service marina
scenic cruises on the *Pioneer Maid*
4 miles of hiking trails
interpretive trail
bridle trails/rental horses
interpretive programs
environmental education center
visitor center

Clinch Mountain Wildlife Management Area

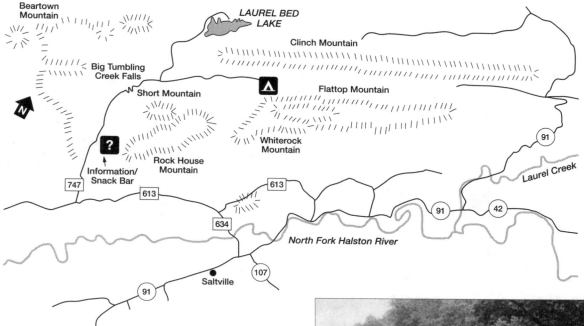

For Information

Clinch Mountain Wildlife Management Area
Route 2, Box 569
Saltville, VA 24370
(703) 783-3422

Location

A 25,000-acre forested area with elevations from 2,200 to 4,600 feet, Clinch Mountain Wildlife Management Area (WMA) includes portions of the North Fork of the Holston and Big Tumbling Creek and its numerous tributaries. At the headwaters of Big Tumbling Creek is the 330-acre man-made Laurel Bed Lake, as well as several beaver ponds. This remote mountain area is popular for the hunter and trapper as well as the angler. The cool waters of the river, creek and lake provide some of the best trout fishing in Virginia.

Clinch Mountain WMA is located northwest of Marion off I-81. From I-81, take either Route 91 or Route 107 exit north to Saltville. At Saltville follow Route 634 to Route 613. Follow Route 613 west for 5 miles to Route 747. Follow this gravel road north to the entrance of Clinch Mountain WMA. Follow signs to the information station, Laurel Bed Lake, Big

This youngster has a reason to be so happy—his parents are doing all the paddling while he fishes.

Tumbling Creek Falls, and the primitive campground. Camping is first-come, first-served; a fee is charged.

Facilities & Activities

20 primitive campsites
  pit toilets
  hand-pumped well
freshwater fishing
boating (non-gasoline powered)
boat ramp
hiking trails

Cumberland Gap
National Historical Park

For Information

Cumberland Gap National Historical Park
P.O. Box 1848
Middlesboro, KY 40965-1848
(606) 248-2817

★ Closed to trailers and vehicles Over 20 ft long

Location

This national historical park is located at the far southeastern corner of Kentucky and straddles the crest of the Cumberland Mountains between Kentucky, Tennessee, and Virginia for more than 20,000 acres. It can be reached by taking US 25E from Kentucky and Tennessee or US 58 from Virginia. This mountain pass, explored by Daniel Boone, developed into a main artery of the great trans-Allegheny migration for settlement of "the Old West." By 1800 over 300,000 people had crossed the gap going west. The gap was an important military objective in the Civil War. US 58 bears the name "Route of the Wilderness Road" and winds past the main camping area. Dense oak-hickory forests predominate throughout the region.

Points of Interest

▲ The Pinnacle Overlook rises almost 1,000 feet above the low point of the pass; from this view of the valley below, one can see why the "gap"

through the long mountain range was so vital to westward expansion.

▲ There are over 50 miles of hiking trails in the park; they range from one mile to the scenic 17-mile Ridge Trail.

▲ A visit to the park wouldn't be complete without a trip to the Hensley Settlement—a community that flourished for nearly 5 decades through the mid 1900s. The settlement is accessible by way of a 4-wheel drive road or a 4-mile hike.

▲ The overlooks and scenic drives near the visitor center provide dramatic views when the fall colors peak around mid-October.

▲ Several park features, like Skylight Cave, Sand Cave, and White Rocks are accessible only by trail. Trail guides and information are available at the visitor center.

General Information

▲ An entrance fee is not charged; there is a charge for camping at the Wilderness Road Campground.

▲ The visitor center is ¼-mile south of Middlesboro on US 25E. Visitors can view a film on the park and a slide program on the Hensley Settlement.

A museum explains the significance of the Gap; crafts and books are available.

▲ Campfire programs, hikes, walks, music and craft demonstrations, and other interpretive activities are scheduled daily from mid-June to Labor Day and on weekends during the spring and fall.

▲ Wilderness Road Campground is located on US 58 in Virginia. Each site has a paved pull-in, picnic table, and grill. There are no RV hookups. The campground is open year-round on a first-come, first-served basis and uses a self-registration system.

▲ Fires should be built only in established fire rings or grills or in portable grills. Firewood may be available near the beginning of "A" loop.

▲ The group campground is open from late spring to late fall. Reservations are required; call the park. There are 13 sites; most sites accommodate 12, but the largest site can accommodate 42 persons.

▲ Backcountry camping is permitted only at the designated locations. Permits are required; for reservations, up to 3 months in advance, contact the visitor center.

▲ There are 5 backcountry campsites:
Gibson Gap—3 groups or 24 persons
Chadwell Gap—4 groups or 32 persons
Martins Fork—8 groups or 64 persons
White Rocks—4 groups or 32 persons
Hensley Horse Camp—20 persons/horses

▲ Camping at Hensley Horse Camp is restricted to horse users and their horses.

▲ The Martins Fork Cabin consists of a one-room primitive cabin with a fireplace and 6 board bunks. It is available for a fee by advance reservation only; reservations can be made up to 3 months in advance.

▲ Horses are permitted on many trails within the park, but not all of them. Check at the visitor center regarding horse entry points, restricted trails, and other regulations. Horses are permitted *only* at Hensley Horse Camp (20 horses max.), Martins Fork Campsite (20 horses max.), and White Rocks Campsite (8 horses max.).

▲ Day hikers should take enough water for the entire trip. Treated water is available at the Hensley Settlement. Water from any other source should be boiled and treated.

▲ Pinnacle Road is closed to trailers and vehicles over 20 feet long. The road can be closed temporarily due to snow.

Facilities & Activities

160 RV & tent campsites
flush toilets & showers
sanitary dump
13 group campsites
5 backcountry campsites
horse camping allowed at 3 backcountry sites
1 backcountry cabin
5 picnic areas
picnic shelter
50 miles of hiking trails
backpacking
self-guided nature trails
horseback riding
ranger-led talks/walks
evening ranger programs/campfire programs
historic buildings/museum/exhibits/amphitheater
living history program/crafts
visitor center

The Hensley Settlement, a community that flourished for nearly 5 decades through the mid-1900s, is accessible by way of a 4-wheel drive road or a 4-mile hike. Two backcountry campsites and a horse camp are nearby.

Douthat State Park

For Information

Douthat State Park
Route 1, Box 212
Millboro, VA 24460-9540
(703) 862-8100

Location

This state park is located north of Clifton Forge off I-64/US 60; take exit 27 and travel north on Route 629 for 7 miles. This 4,493-acre park was named a National Historic Landmark for its blend of recreational offerings in a rustic and preserved natural setting; it has some of Virginia's most outstanding mountain scenery. A restaurant overlooks the water on the trout-stocked 50-acre lake.

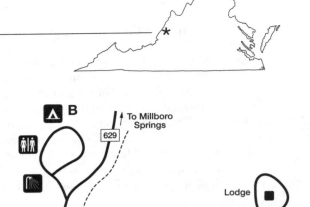

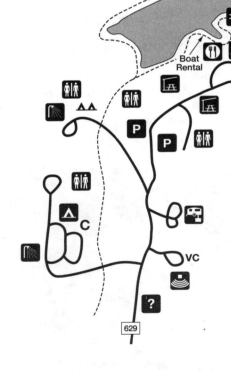

DOUTHAT LAKE

Boat Rental

Cabins
△ 1 Room
○ 1 Bedroom
□ 2 Bdr. Log
◇ 2 Bdr. Block

Facilities & Activities

78 campsites
   25 with electrical/water hookups
showers
dump station
15 group campsites
30 housekeeping cabins (1-room; 1-bedroom;
   2-bedroom)
lodge (12 persons)
picnicking/shelters
snack bar
lake swimming & bathhouse
freshwater fishing
boating (non-gasoline powered)
boat ramp
paddleboat/rowboat rentals
24 hiking trails (36.6 miles)
interpretive trail
store/gift shop
restaurant
interpretive programs
environmental education center
visitor center

Fairy Stone State Park

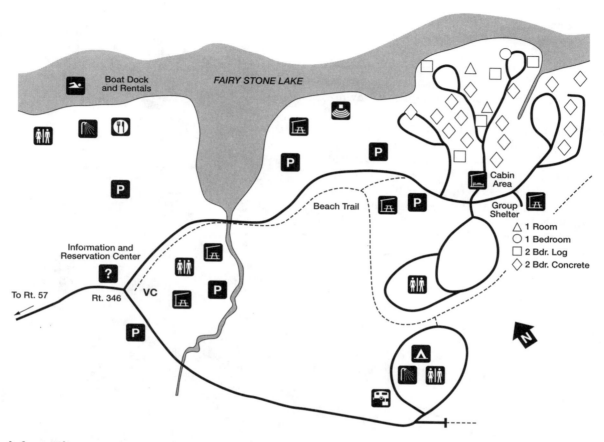

FAIRY STONE LAKE

Boat Dock and Rentals

Beach Trail

Information and Reservation Center

To Rt. 57   Rt. 346   VC

Cabin Area

Group Shelter

△ 1 Room
○ 1 Bedroom
□ 2 Bdr. Log
◇ 2 Bdr. Concrete

N

For Information

Fairy Stone State Park
Route 2, Box 723
Stuart, VA 24171-9588
(703) 930-2424

Location

Located in the foothills of the Blue Ridge Mountains on a 168-acre lake that adjoins Philpott Reservoir, the park is northwest of Martinsville off Route 57. From the Blue Ridge Parkway, take either US 58 or Route 8, then northeast on Route 57. This 4,868-acre park is the home of the mysterious "fairy stones," which are brown staurolite, a combination of silica, iron, and aluminum. Together, these minerals crystalize in twin form, accounting for the cross-like structure. The stones are most commonly shaped like the St. Andrew's and Roman crosses; the most sought after are those in the shape of the Maltese cross.

Facilities & Activities

51 campsites with electrical/water hookups
showers
dump station
4 primitive backcountry campsites
24 housekeeping cabins (1-room; 1-bedroom; 2-bedroom)
picnicking/shelters
snack bar
lake swimming & bathhouse
freshwater fishing
boating (non-gasoline powered)
boat ramp
paddleboat/rowboat rentals
25 miles of hiking trails
2-mile Mountain View bicycle trail
interpretive programs
visitor center

False Cape State Park

For Information

False Cape State Park
4001 Sandpiper Road
Virginia Beach, VA 23456-4325
(804) 426-7128

Location

A mile-wide barrier spit between Back Bay and the Atlantic Ocean, False Cape State Park has 5.9 miles of beach. The park's location allows visitors to observe beaches, dunes, maritime forests of oak and pine, wooded swamps, marshes, and the bay all in one visit. There is no vehicular access to this 4,321-acre park. Access is by foot or bicycle about 5 miles through Back Bay National Wildlife Refuge. The park is also accessible by boat across Back Bay; 3 boat docks are provided. Camping permits are required and are issued from Seashore State Park (see page 129).

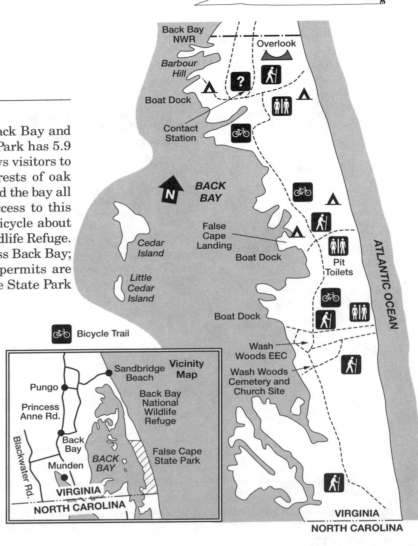

False Cape State Park is 20 miles south of the boardwalk in Virginia Beach. From I-64, take Indian River Road (Route 407) southeast to New Bridge Road. Take New Bridge to Sandbridge Road, then go south on Sandpiper Road. Daytime parking is available at the Back Bay National Wildlife Refuge. Overnight parking is available at the Little Island Recreation Area. Parking fees may be required. The park features an extensive environmental education program, including aquatic classroom adventures on a pontoon boat.

Facilities & Activities

12 hike-in primitive campsites
    pit toilets
    potable water *not* available

ACCESS BY BOAT, FOOT, BICYCLE

freshwater/saltwater fishing
boating (motor boats permitted)
3 boat docks
pontoon boat (The *Osprey*)
7½ miles of trails
hiking/interpretive trails
bicycle trails/rentals
interpretive programs
Wash Woods Environmental Education Center—
    for day visitors or 22 people overnight. Offers kitchen, restrooms, shower, meeting room, library, AV equipment & lab

Flannagan (John W.) Dam & Reservoir

For Information

Resource Manager, Corps of Engineers
John W. Flannagan Dam & Reservoir
Route 1, Box 268
Haysi, VA 24256-9736
(703) 835-9544

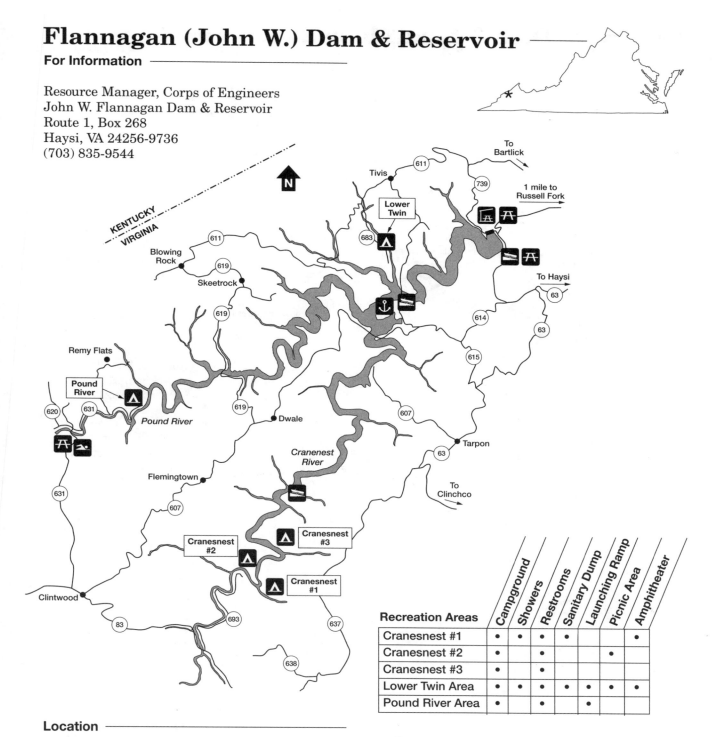

Recreation Areas	Campground	Showers	Restrooms	Sanitary Dump	Launching Ramp	Picnic Area	Amphitheater
Cranesnest #1	•	•	•	•			•
Cranesnest #2	•		•			•	
Cranesnest #3	•		•				
Lower Twin Area	•	•	•	•	•	•	•
Pound River Area	•		•		•		

Location

Located in the Cumberland Mountains, the 1,145-acre John W. Flannagan Reservoir stores the waters of the Cranesnest and Pound Rivers and has almost 40 miles of shoreline. Built primarily for flood control, the lake surface is kept at an elevation of 1,396 feet above sea level for recreation during the summer. During the fall, the lake is lowered 16 feet to hold additional water from winter and spring runoff.

Camping is available in 3 different areas around the lake. Lower Twin Area is located on the northeast side of the lake off SR 80, via 611 and 683. Cranesnest campgrounds #1, #2, and #3 are located along the east side of the Cranesnest River and are accessible from SR 83 east of Clintwood via 693 that parallels the river. The Pound River Area is on the north side of Pound River off SR 83 west of Clintwood, via 631.

Gathright Dam & Lake Moomaw

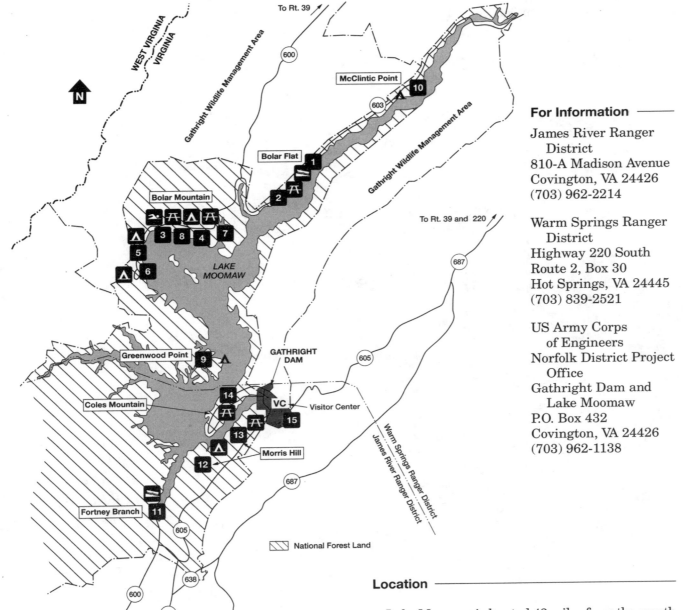

For Information

James River Ranger
  District
810-A Madison Avenue
Covington, VA 24426
(703) 962-2214

Warm Springs Ranger
  District
Highway 220 South
Route 2, Box 30
Hot Springs, VA 24445
(703) 839-2521

US Army Corps
  of Engineers
Norfolk District Project
  Office
Gathright Dam and
  Lake Moomaw
P.O. Box 432
Covington, VA 24426
(703) 962-1138

Location

Lake Moomaw is located 43 miles from the mouth of the Jackson River and 19 miles north of Covington. From the dam the lake extends 12 miles along the Jackson River. At its normal recreational level of 1,582 feet above sea level, the lake covers a surface area of 2,530 acres and has a shoreline of more than 43 miles. Much of the shoreline of Lake Moomaw is adjacent to the Gathright Wildlife Management Area. Construction of the lake and dam was completed in 1981; the area's official name is Gathright Dam and Lake Moomaw.

George Washington National Forest is responsible for resource and recreation management functions; the Corps manages flood control and water quality. The Corps also administers the visitor center above the dam, one picnic area, and a bank fishing area below the dam. Management of the recreation areas is shared by two ranger districts: James River and Warm Springs. To the south, Fortney Branch, Morris Hill, and Coles Mountain are managed by the James River Ranger District. To the north, Bolar Flat, Bolar Mountain, Greenwood Point, and McClintic Point, are managed by the Warm Springs Ranger District.

Directions to Lake Moomaw's Recreational Facilities

South End Recreational Facilities: Take exit 16 from I-64 at Covington and follow US 220 north for 4 miles. Take SR 687 north for 3 miles. Take SR 641 west for about 1 mile. Take SR 666 north for 5 miles. Turn right on SR 605 and proceed 2 miles north to the entrance road to Morris Hill. To reach Coles Mountain, proceed north on SR 605 for another mile, and cross the dam.

North End Recreational Facilities: Take exit 16 at Covington and follow US 220 north for 25 miles to Warm Springs. Then travel 13 miles west on SR 39. Take SR 600 south for 7 miles and follow the signs to Bolar Flat and Bolar Mountain.

Map#/Recreation Areas	Campsites	Trailer Sites	Trailer Dump Station	Drinking Water	Toilets	Showers	Picnicking	Swimming	Boating	Fishing	Hiking Trails
Warm Springs Ranger District											
1 Bolar Flat Marina					F				L/$	L	
2 Bolar Flat Picnic Area				•	F		•			L	
3 Bolar Mountain Beach				•	F	W		$			•
4 Bolar Camping Area #1 (21E,R,$)	42	•	•	•	F	W				L	•
5 Bolar Camping Area #2($)	17	•	•	•	F	W				L	•
6 Bolar Camping Area #3($)	32	•	•	•	F	W				L	•
7 Bolar Mountain Picnic Area #1				•	F		•			L	•
8 Bolar Mountain Picnic Area #2				•	F		•			L	•
9 Greenwood Point*	5				V					L	•
10 McClintic Point**	•				V					L	
James River Ranger District											
11 Fortney Branch Boat Launch				•	RC				L/$	L	•
12 Morris Hill Campground (R,$)	55	•	•	•	F	W					•
13 Morris Hill Picnic Area							•				•
14 Coles Mountain				•	F	W	•	$	L/$	L	•
Corps of Engineers											
15 Visitor Center & Picnic Area				•	F		•				

* = Boat/hike access only; **open Dec.–March only
$ = fee
E = electrical hookups; R = some reservations accepted
Toilets: F = flush; V= vault; RC = recirculating chemical
Showers: W = warm
Boating: L = launch
Fishing: L = lake

George Washington National Forest

For Information

Forest Supervisor
George Washington National Forest
Harrison Plaza, 101 North Main Street
P.O. Box 233
Harrisonburg, VA 22801
(703) 564-8300

Location

The George Washington National Forest extends 140 miles along the Appalachian Mountains and contains nearly one million acres of rugged mountain land in 13 northwestern counties of Virginia and about 100,000 acres in 4 counties in eastern West Virginia. The forest is administrered by six ranger districts. Primary access through the length of the forest is I-81; major highways traversing the forest include US 33, US 250 and I-64/US 60.

About the Forest

The forest has more than 3,500 acres of open water in lakes, ponds and streams. Several rivers, including the South Fork of the Shenandoah River and the Jackson River are popular for canoeing and float fishing. Elevations average between 1,000 and 3,000 feet, with some peaks about 4,000 feet. The average rainfall is 38 inches a year, including an annual average snowfall of 15 to 20 inches a year. In addition to a wide variety of wildflowers, trees, shrubs, ferns and mosses, visitors are likely to encounter abundant wildlife.

The 2,530-acre **Lake Moomaw** is the forest's largest lake and contains the most recently devel-

oped recreation sites on the forest. Morris Hill Recreation Area, located on the James River Ranger District, is at the southern end of the lake; Bolar Mountain and Bolar Flat recreation areas, located on the Warm Springs Ranger District, are on the northwest shore of the lake. Information on Lake Moomaw appears on pages 88–89.

Wilderness Areas

George Washington National Forest contains 6 designated wildernesses totalling just over 32,000 acres. They are Ramseys Draft Wilderness (6,518 acres) located on the Deerfield Ranger District; Rich Hole Wilderness (6,450 acres) located on the James River Ranger District; Rough Mountain Wilderness (9,300 acres) located on the Warm Springs Ranger District; St. Mary's Wilderness (9,835 acres) located on the Pedlar Ranger District; and small portions of Barbour's Creek (20 acres) and Shaver's Run (95 acres). These areas are generally characterized by rugged and remote mountain terrain. They contain no developed facilities and are accessed by a few primitive trails. For more information about the wilderness areas, contact the respective ranger district offices or the forest supervisor's office.

Special Notes

With its mountains and valleys, woodlands and wildlife, the George Washington National Forest offers a variety of outdoor recreation opportunities. Although developed recreation sites are a big attraction, many visitors seek recreation in undeveloped areas. People may camp at undeveloped sites almost anywhere on the forest. No permits are required, and campers at primitive campsites are asked only to follow basic guidelines for outdoor safety, which include care with campfires, litter and waste disposal, and taking proper steps to purify water for drinking.

Most developed camping and picnicking areas are open by mid-spring; all major camping areas are usually open by May 15. Some may have reduced services in the late fall; several areas are open year-round. Check with the district ranger station for dates of operation. Each fee campground has either a self-service registration and fee payment station near the entrance or an entrance station.

Reservations for several developed sites (see facility chart) may be made by calling the National Recreation Reservation System at 1-800-280-CAMP (2267). Reservations for group sites are usually made by calling the district office that manages the area. Most parking spurs and campground area roads are built to handle campers and trailers up to 22 feet in length. The campgrounds at Trout Pond and Bolar Camping Area #1 at Lake Moomaw have electrical sites available.

The **Massanutten Visitor Information Center,** on US 211 between New Market and Luray, is open daily 9 am to 5 pm, April through October. The center is fully staffed and features exhibits, programs, and information about recreation opportunities on the George Washington National Forest. Maps, books, and field guides are available for sale. Three interpretive trails are nearby.

Trails

There are more than 800 miles of trails; most are open to hikers, horses, and pedal-powered bicycles. Mountain biking is an increasingly popular recreational pastime. With over 200 miles of open backcountry trails on the forest, and even more miles of paved, gravel, and dirt roads, bicyclists have ample room to explore. Dry River, Lee, and Pedlar ranger districts have ATV trail systems, ranging in length from 12 to 25 miles. Of the many trails, the following are especially noteworthy:

Wild Oak National Recreation Trail—a 26-mile trail on the Dry River District that follows ridgetops and circles the headwaters of the North River.

Appalachian National Scenic Trail—a 58-mile section crosses on the Pedlar Ranger District.

Shenandoah Mountain Trail (South)—a 23.7-mile remote backcountry trail on the Deerfield Ranger District.

North Mountain Trail—a trail that winds along the Great North Mountain on the Deerfield and James River ranger districts for more than 23 miles.

Allegheny Trail—12 miles pass through the James River Ranger District. When complete, it will extend 330 miles from near the Pennsylvania border in West Virginia, to the Appalachian Trail.

Crabtree Falls Trail—a 3-mile trail on the Pedlar Ranger District, with 4 overlooks; the falls include 5 major cascades and a number of smaller ones that fall a total of 1,200 feet.

Camping is allowed at undeveloped sites almost anywhere in the forest. No permits are required, and campers at primitive campsites are asked only to follow basic guidelines for outdoor safety, which include care with campfires, litter, and waste disposal, and taking proper steps to purify water for drinking.

Southern Ranger Districts (Deerfield, James River, Pedlar, & Warm Springs)

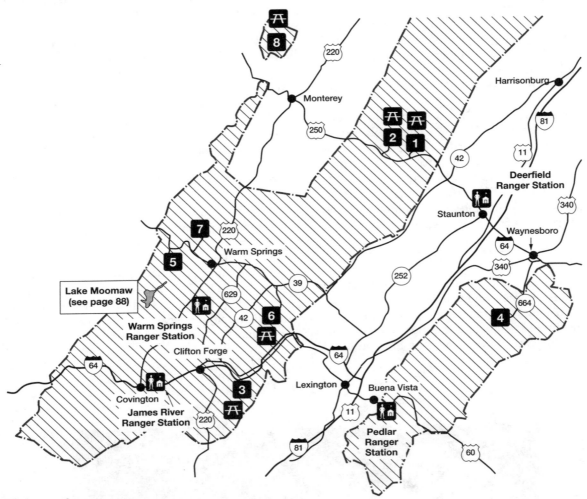

For Information

Deerfield Ranger District
West Beverely Street
Route 6, Box 419
Staunton, VA 24401
(703) 885-8028

James River Ranger District
810-A Madison Avenue
Covington, VA 24426
(703) 962-2214

Pedlar Ranger District
2424 Magnolia Avenue
Buena Vista, VA 24416
(703) 261-6105

Warm Springs Ranger District
Highway 220 South
Route 2, Box 30
Hot Springs, VA 24445
(703) 839-2521 or 839-2442

Location

The Deerfield Ranger District is in the heart of the scenic ridge and valley province of northwestern Virginia's Allegheny Mountains. The James River Ranger District, in the beautiful Allegheny highlands of Virginia, is the southernmost district on the George Washington National Forest. A portion of the Gathright Dam and Lake Moomaw Recreation Area is within the district boundaries. The Pedlar Ranger District is situated in the picturesque Blue Ridge Mountains. Stretching from near Waynesboro to the James River, it surrounds portions of both the Appalachian Trail and the Blue Ridge Parkway. The Warm Springs Ranger District is nestled in Virginia's scenic Allegheny Mountains. A recreational focal point is Lake Moomaw, which is 12 miles long with 43 miles of national forest shoreline.

(continued on page 101)

The beautiful mountain terrain of Chief Logan State Park in southern West Virginia displays a special magnificence in the early morning hours.

Seneca Creek originates on Spruce Mountain and empties into the North Fork at Seneca Rocks. Not only is it a great canoeing stream, but it has the reputation of being one of the best trout streams in West Virginia.

There are numerous ways to experience Shenandoah National Park; some prefer to drive the 105-mile Skyline Drive, others hike, but some prefer to climb.

The New River Gorge National River, located in southern West Virginia, protects 53 miles of the New River as a free-flowing waterway; it is one of the finest whitewater rivers in the eastern United States.

Pinnacle Overlook provides a panoramic view into Tennessee, Kentucky, and Virginia, as well as the Wilderness Road through the Cumberland Gap.

If you love the beach, then the sun, sand, and surf of Assateague Island National Seashore may be for you—for beach-walking, sunbathing, and even "surf watching."

The Mountain Creek Lodge at Pipestem Resort State Park is located in the Bluestone Gorge and accessible only by tramway.

West Virginia's Bluestone Lake area could be called a water-oriented recreation mecca. Nearby are located Bluestone and Pipestem state parks, Bluestone National Scenic River, and the New River Gorge National River, known for its whitewater rafting.

The flowering dogwoods adorn the forests in the spring and give a special touch to the high views of the Blue Ridge Mountains.

The 2,144-mile Appalachian National Scenic Trail winds through the scenic and wooded lands of the Appalachian Mountain. The 40-mile section in Maryland is along the ridge crest of South Mountain; more than one-fourth of the entire Trail lies in Virginia.

Located in the Appalachian Mountains of Maryland, Catoctin Mountain Park is quite scenic during all seasons of the year.

Cunningham Falls, a 78-foot high cascading waterfall is the highest in Maryland; it is accessible from a parking area along MD 77, as well as from hiking trails from Catoctin Mountain Park, and Cunningham Falls State Park.

M. Little

M. Little

A portion of the Great Cypress Swamp lies within Delaware's Trap Pond State Park and holds the northernmost stand of bald cypress trees in the United States.

R. Koesler

Who says that camping is a warm-weather, summer-time only activity? Try it . . . you may like it . . . see, she's even grinning!

In Virginia, the Blue Ridge Parkway extends 216.9 miles along the crests of the Southern Appalachians from the southern end of the Shenandoah National Park to the North Carolina border. Numerous overlooks provide seemingly endless views, even on hazy days.

The canyon at Breaks Interstate Park, at the Kentucky-Virginia border, winds around the Towers, an imposing pyramid of rocks over one-half mile long and one-third mile wide.

These falls at Blackwater Falls State Park are one of the most photographed sites in West Virginia; its amber-colored waters plunge five stories, then twist and tumble through an eight-mile-long gorge.

Cross-country skiing provides the perfect opportunity to see nature at its best; in season, an abundance of trails exist in this region.

Deep Creek State Park in Maryland has developed about 700 feet of beach by removing stumps and boulders and adding sand. Water sports of all kinds are popular.

The John W. Flannagan Dam & Reservoir, located in the Cumberland Mountains of Virginia, has almost 40 miles of shoreline; all types of boats are popular at this lake.

The 2,650-acre lake is the main focus of Stonewall Jackson Lake State Park. The 34-site campground is located on a small peninsula, so everyone has a waterfront view.

This lone fisherman at Westmoreland State Park doesn't appear bothered that the fish aren't biting. The park is located on Virginia's Northern Neck Peninsula and extends about 1$\frac{1}{2}$ miles along the Potomac River.

Shenandoah National Park is a hiker's paradise; it has more than 500 miles of trails that lead to numerous waterfalls, clear rushing streams, old home sites, and scenic vistas hidden below Skyline Drive.

Anglers try their luck along the banks of the Indian River Inlet at Delaware Seashore State Park. This unique park offers what has been termed "a boaters dream"—a full-service, public marina offering year-round access to the Atlantic Ocean and Indian River and Rehoboth Bays.

Grayson Highlands State Park is located near Virginia's highest point, 5,729-foot Mount Rogers; the park provides rugged alpine scenery and panoramic views of the the valleys below.

Southern Ranger Districts (continued from page 92)

Directions to Recreation Areas With Campgrounds

Pedlar Ranger District:

   Sherando Lake—From I-64 at Wayesboro, take SR 624 (exit 96) southwest 2 miles to SR 664. Take SR 664 south about 8 miles to FR 91 (entrance sign). Take FR 91 west about ½ mile to the entrance stations.

Warm Springs Ranger District:

   Blowing Springs—From Warm Springs, take SR 39 west for 9 miles to the campground.

   Hidden Valley—From Warm Springs, take SR 39 west for 3 miles. Turn right and take SR 621 north for 1 mile. Take FR 241 for 1.75 miles to the campground.

Map#/Recreation Areas	Campsites	Trailer Sites	Trailer Dump Station	Drinking Water	Toilets	Showers	Picnicking	Swimming	Boating	Fishing	Hiking Trails
Deerfield Ranger District											
1 Braley Pond				•	V		•			L	•
2 Mountain House				•	V		•			S	•
James River Ranger District											
3 Longdale				•	F	C	•	$		L/S	•
Pedlar Ranger District											
4 Sherando Lake* (G,R,$)	65	•	•	•	F	W	•	$	A/N	L	•
Warm Springs Ranger District											
5 Blowing Springs ($)	23	•	•	•	V		•			S	•
6 Bubbling Springs Picnic Area				•	V		•				
7 Hidden Valley Campground ($)	30	•	•	•	V					S	•
8 Locust Springs Picnic Area				•	V		•				•

*Has visitor center & amphitheater
$ = fee
A = carry down access; N = no motors allowed
G = group camping (125 people max.); R = reserve with ranger district
Toilets: F = flush; V = vault
Showers: C = cold; W = warm
Fishing: L = lake; S = stream

Sherando Lake Recreation Area

Northern Ranger Districts (Dry River & Lee)

For Information

Dry River Ranger District
112 North River Road
Bridgewater, VA 22812
(703) 828-2591

Lee Ranger District
Windsor Knit Road
Route 4, Box 515
Edinburg, VA 22824
(703) 984-4101

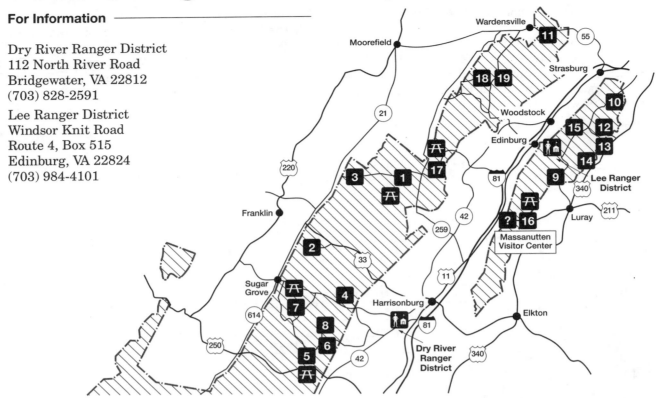

Location

The Dry River Ranger District includes portions of Virginia and West Virginia as it straddles the scenic Shenandoah Mountain. The Lee Ranger District includes portions of two scenic mountain ranges at the north end of the Shenandoah Valley. This northernmost district on the George Washington National Forest includes a scenic portion of West Virginia.

Directions to Recreation Areas With Campgrounds

Dry River Ranger District:

Brandywine—About 2 miles east of Brandywine, WV, and about 26 miles west of Harrisonburg on US 33. The entrance is 4.2 miles west of the Virginia-West Virginia state line.

Camp Run—From Harrisonburg, follow US 33 west to Brandywine, WV. At stop sign in Brandywine, take a right and continue to follow US 33 for another 3.3 miles to the intersection with Route 3 at Oak Flat, WV. Turn right onto Route 3 and follow for 10 miles towards Moorefield, WV to the intersection with Route 3/1 (a gravel/shale road). Turn right onto Route 3/1 and follow for 1.5 miles to the intersection with FR 526, turn right, road dead ends in campground. (Note: access on Route 3/1 and FR 526 may require the use of a higher clearance vehicle.)

Hone Quarry—From Harrisonburg, take SR 42 south to Dayton. Turn right on SR 257 and pro-

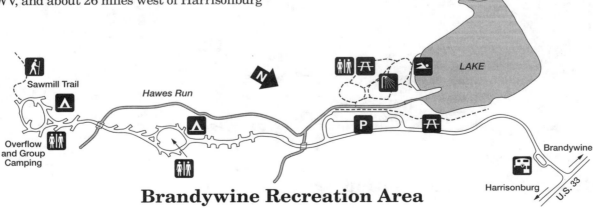

Brandywine Recreation Area

ceed 11 miles west to FR 62 and follow the sign about 3 miles to the campground.

North River Campground—Follow US 250 west from Staunton to Churchville. Continue west on US 250 for 10 miles past Churchville and turn right onto SR 715 (this route turns into FR 96). Follow 715/FR 96 for 8.5 miles to FR 95 and turn right. Follow FR 95 for 2.1 miles to the intersection with FR 95B and turn right. Campground is one mile on the left.

Todd Lake—From Bridgewater, take US 42 about 3 miles south to Mossy Creek. Take SR 747 about 3 miles west to Mt. Solon. Take SR 731 north about 1 mile. Turn left onto SR 730 and follow it about 3 miles to the Stokesville junction. Turn right on SR 718 and follow it about 1 mile to FR 95. Follow FR 95 about 3 miles to the Todd Lake turn-off.

Lee Ranger District:

Camp Roosevelt—From Edinburg, take SR 675 southeast for 9 miles.

Elizabeth Furnace—From Strasburg, take SR 55 east for about 5 miles to Waterlick. Then take SR 678 south for 5 miles.

Hawk—From Strasburg, take SR 55 northwest toward Wardensville, WV, for 16 miles. Turn right on FR 502 for 2 miles, then left on FR 347 for ½ mile.

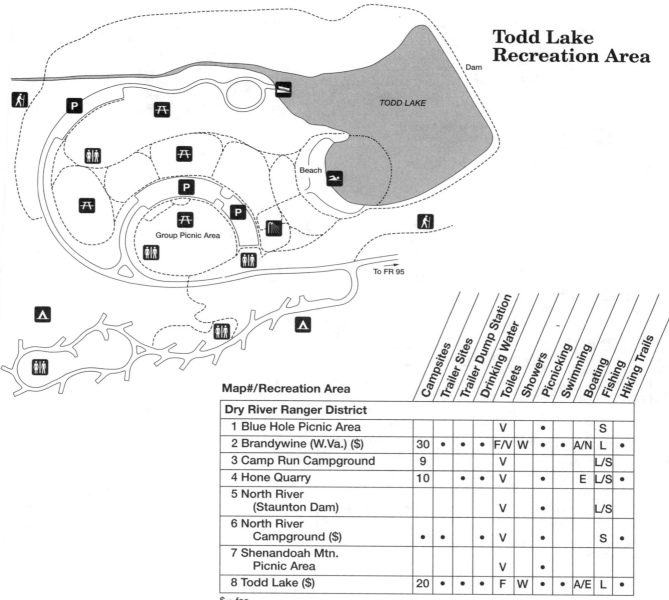

Todd Lake Recreation Area

Map#/Recreation Area	Campsites	Trailer Sites	Trailer Dump Station	Drinking Water	Toilets	Showers	Picnicking	Swimming	Boating	Fishing	Hiking Trails
Dry River Ranger District											
1 Blue Hole Picnic Area					V		•			S	
2 Brandywine (W.Va.) ($)	30	•	•	•	F/V	W	•	•	A/N	L	•
3 Camp Run Campground	9				V					L/S	
4 Hone Quarry	10		•	•	V		•		E	L/S	•
5 North River (Staunton Dam)					V		•			L/S	
6 North River Campground ($)	•	•		•	V		•			S	•
7 Shenandoah Mtn. Picnic Area					V		•				
8 Todd Lake ($)	20	•	•	•	F	W	•	•	A/E	L	•

$ = fee

Toilets: F= flush; V= vault

Showers: C = cold; W = warm

Boating: A = carry down access; E = electric motors only; N = no motors

Fishing: L = lake; S = stream

Northern Ranger Districts *(continued)*

Hazard Mill Campground—From US 340 at Bentonville, take SR 613 northwest for 1 mile; cross the river and turn left on FR 236. Travel along the river for 3 miles to the campground.

Little Fort—From US 11 at Woodstock, travel east on SR 758 for 4 miles.

Elizabeth Furnace Recreation Area

Trout Pond—Take exit 296 from I-81 at Strasburg and take SR 55 west for about 18 miles to Wardensville, WV. Take SR 23/10 south about 6 miles. Take SR 259/5 south for about 6 miles. Take FR 500 for about 1 mile.

Wolf Gap—From Woodstock, take SR 42 west for 5 miles to SR 675 at Columbia Furnace; turn right and travel about 6 miles to the campground.

Trout Pond Recreation Area

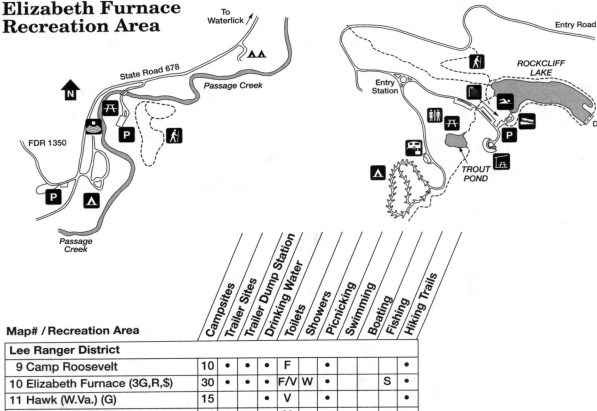

Map# / Recreation Area	Campsites	Trailer Sites	Trailer Dump Station	Drinking Water	Toilets	Showers	Picnicking	Swimming	Boating	Fishing	Hiking Trails
Lee Ranger District											
9 Camp Roosevelt	10	•	•	•	F		•				•
10 Elizabeth Furnace (3G,R,$)	30	•	•	•	F/V	W	•			S	•
11 Hawk (W.Va.) (G)	15			•	V		•				•
12 Hazard Mill Campground**	15			•	V						•
13 Hazard Mill Canoe Camp*	•				V				A	S	
14 High Cliff Canoe Camp*	•				V				A	S	
15 Little Fort	10				V		•				
16 New Market Gap Picnic Area					V		•				•
17 Tomahawk Pond Picnic Area				•	V		•			L	•
18 Trout Pond (W.Va.) (E,R,$)	50	•	•	•	F	W	•	•	L/E	L	•
19 Wolf Gap (W.Va.)	10			•	V		•				•

*Hike in/boat in access on Shenandoah River
**Access by foot only
$ = fee
G = group camping; R = reservations
E = electrical hookups available
Toilets: F = flush; V = vault
Showers: C = cold; W = warm
Boating: A = carry down access; L = launch; E = electric motors only
Fishing: L = lake; S = stream

Grayson Highlands State Park

For Information

Grayson Highlands State Park
Route 2, Box 141
Mouth of Wilson, VA 24363-9533
(703) 579-7092

Location

This park is located near Virginia's highest point, 5,729-foot Mount Rogers and is adjacent to Mount Rogers National Recreation Area. The 4,754-acre park offers rugged alpine scenery and panoramic views of the valleys below. Grayson Highlands State Park is on US 48 midway between Independence and Damascus and is reached from I-81 at exit 45 in Marion, then south on Route 16 to Volney, then west on US 58. The park offers access to the Appalachian Trail and to the Virginia Highlands Horse Trail in the surrounding Jefferson National Forest. The park's visitor center and reconstructed cabins recapture the lives of the hardy pioneers who settled this rugged land.

Facilities & Activities

73 campsites
showers
dump station
24 campsites adjacent to stables for riders
picnicking/shelters
freshwater fishing
9 hiking trails
self-guiding trail
mountain bike trail
2 miles of bridle trails
overnight horse stables
store
interpretive programs
visitor center

Holliday Lake State Park

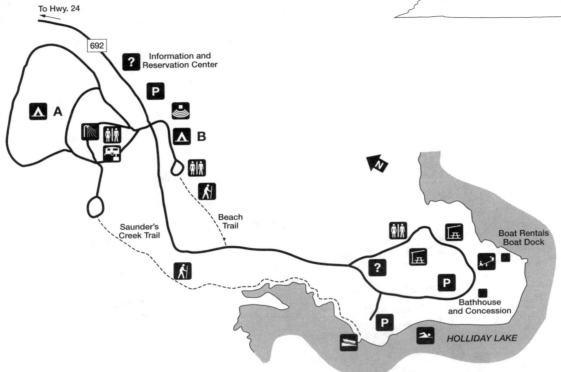

For Information

Holliday Lake State Park
Route 2, Box 622
Appomattox, VA 24522-9209
(804) 248-6308

Location

Located deep within the Appomattox-Buckingham State Forest, Holliday Lake State Park boasts scenic rolling hills and a 113-acre lake; activities at the park focuses on the lake. Access to this 250-acre park is via Route 24 between US 460 at Appomattox and US 60 at Mt. Rush. From Route 24, the park is about 7 miles southeast via Routes 626, 640, and 692. Appomattox Courthouse National Park, the surrender site that ended the Civil War, is located off Route 24 east of Appomattox—just minutes from the state park.

Facilities & Activities

48 campsites
showers
dump station
picnicking/shelters
snack bar
lake swimming & bathhouse

Paddleboats are available for rent at many parks; some differ in style from these, but all provide a means of traveling on the water by using quite a bit of leg-power.

freshwater fishing
boating (non-gasoline powered)
boat ramp
paddleboat/rowboat rentals
3 hiking trails
interpretive programs
visitor center

Hungry Mother State Park

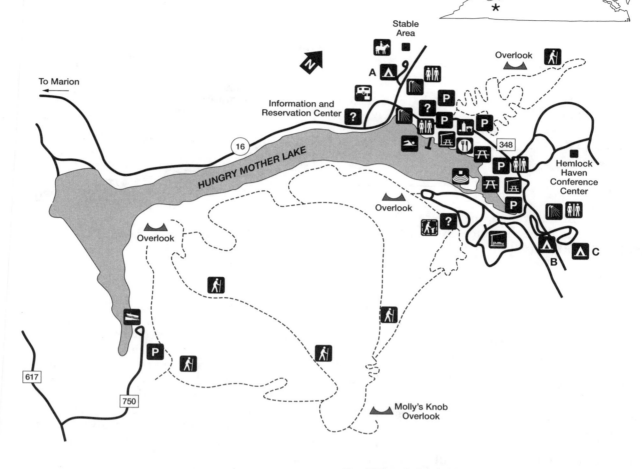

For Information

Hungry Mother State Park
Route 5, Box 109
Marion, VA 24354-9323
(703) 783-3422

Location

This state park is known for its beautiful woodlands and placid 108-acre lake in the heart of the mountains. The lake has a reputation for having the best northern pike fishing in the state. This 2,200-acre park is located north of I-81 at Marion. Take exit 47 from I-81, travel about 1 mile on Route 11 toward Marion, then turn right on Route 16 north and travel 4 miles to the park. Hungry Mother is the site of the state park system's first conference center—Hemlock Haven. This 35-acre complex includes cabins, meeting rooms, swimming pool, sports complex, and picnic area.

Facilities & Activities

43 campsites
   32 with electrical/water hookups
showers
dump station
20 housekeeping cabins (1-room; 1-bedroom;
   2-bedroom)
Hemlock Haven Conference Center
picnicking/shelters
lake swimming & bathhouse
freshwater fishing
handicapped accessible fishing pier
boating (non-gasoline powered)
boat ramp
paddleboat/rowboat rentals
12+ miles of trails
hiking/interpretive trails
bridle trails
horse stable/rental horses
restaurant/snack bar
interpretive programs
visitor center

Jefferson National Forest

For Information

Forest Supervisor
Jefferson National Forest
5162 Valleypointe Parkway
Roanoke, VA 24019
(703) 265-6054

Location

In west central Virginia, the Jefferson National Forest extends from the James River southwesterly for 218 miles to within 50 miles of the western tip of the state. The 690,000-acre forest lies within and parallels the Valley and Ridge Provinces of the Blue Ridge Mountains in the southern Appalachians. Primary access through the length of the forest is I-81. With the exception of I-77, which bisects the forest, almost all travelways in a north-south direction are winding two-lane roads.

About the Forest

Elevations range from 600 feet on the James River in the northeast corner of the forest, to 5,729 feet on the top of Mount Rogers, the highest point in the state. The maximum rainfall occurs during the summer, although the precipitation is well distributed throughout the year without distinct dry or wet periods. Snow is common in the winter with up to 30 inches in the mountains. Thunderstorms occur on the average of 32 to 50 days each year, generally between May and September.

The forest cover is mainly Appalachian mixed hardwoods interspersed with conifers. There is a profusion of color throughout the year in the valleys and mountains. Except for the very middle of winter, there are always some wild plants blooming, or showing their fall or spring colors. The diversity of vegetation and elevation provides a variety of wildlife habitat equal to any in the Middle Atlantic states.

Mount Rogers National Recreation Area is a 118,000-acre part of the Jefferson National Forest, which has been dedicated by Congress to be managed for outdoor recreation. The area features the greatest variety of outdoor recreation oppontunities on the forest. Information on Mount Rogers National Recreation Area appears on pages 116–118. The Mount Rogers Visitor Center/Ranger Station is located on State Route 16, 7 miles southeast of Marion.

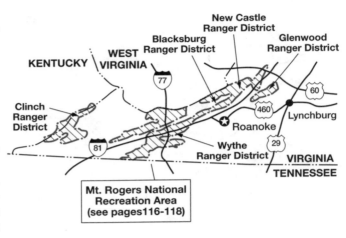

Mt. Rogers National Recreation Area (see pages116-118)

Special Notes

Jefferson National Forest offers visitors a variety of outdoor recreation experiences. Many of the developed campgrounds have both single and double family camping units; several campgrounds offer group sites. Some of the picnic areas have shelters and can accommodate large numbers. The summer recreation season, when all facilities are open, runs from May through September.

Some camping facilities are also open during hunting and fishing seasons. Hunting and fishing on the Jefferson are regulated by Virginia game laws. Various licensing permits are required and can be purchased at county clerks offices and many sporting goods stores.

Camping is encouraged throughout the general forest area except where posted otherwise, such as in day-use areas or some areas of concentrated use. Primitive camping in the general forest area outside of developed sites has always been a popular activity on national forests. Campers are encouraged to practice *no trace camping* techniques, which leave the area in the same natural condition in which it was found.

Horses are not permitted in campgrounds; however, several districts provide special camping areas for visitors who bring horses. Campfires must be confined to fireplaces when they are provided. Trailers up to 22 feet can be accommodated at specified areas. No water or electrical hookups are provided, but central dumping stations are often available for trailers. A daily occupancy fee is charged at most campgrounds (see facility chart).

Jefferson National Forest (continued)

Typical facilities at national forest campgrounds are tent pads, cooking grills, picnic tables and toilets. Some campgrounds have warm water showers and special attractions such as fishing lakes and beaches, outdoor amphitheaters, nature trails, and naturalist programs.

Trails

There are 950 miles of hiking and riding trails on the Jefferson National Forest. Of these, the following are especially noteworthy:

Appalachian National Scenic Trail—300 miles of this 2,000-mile hiking trail pass through the Jefferson.

Cascades National Recreation Trail—a particularly scenic 4-mile round trip hike to a 70-ft waterfall.

Mount Rogers National Recreation Trail—a scenic 4-mile hike from the Fairwood Valley to the Appalachian Trail near Mt. Rogers, the highest point in Virginia.

Virginia Highlands Horse Trail—a 68-mile trail designed for horseback riding and wagon trains. A corral and primitive camping area are available for those who trailer horses.

A special area for hikers and horsebackers is the **Pine Mountain High Country** adjacent to Mt. Rogers. Closed to motor vehicles, the 5,000-acres of open grassy meadows, huge rock outcrops, fields of flowering rhododendron and drainages lined with blueberries is a favorite place for visitors to southwest Virginia.

James River Face Wilderness—on the northeast end of the forest is an 8,703-acre area set aside and managed for its wilderness characteristics. Closed to any kind of vehicular use, the area is accessible only by foot trail.

Blacksburg Ranger District and Wythe Ranger District

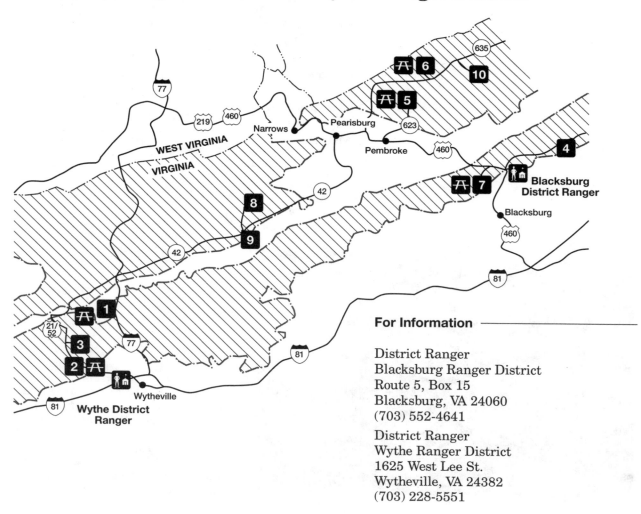

For Information

District Ranger
Blacksburg Ranger District
Route 5, Box 15
Blacksburg, VA 24060
(703) 552-4641

District Ranger
Wythe Ranger District
1625 West Lee St.
Wytheville, VA 24382
(703) 228-5551

Blacksburg Ranger District and Wythe Ranger District (continued)

Location

The Blacksburg Ranger District of the Jefferson National Forest is northwest of Roanoke along the West Virginia/Virginia border. The Blacksburg Ranger Station is on US 460 three miles northwest of Blacksburg. Wythe Ranger District is north of Wytheville; the ranger station is on US 11 west of Wytheville.

Directions to Recreation Areas With Campgrounds

Caldwell Fields—From Blacksburg, travel 6.6 miles north on US 460; then right on VA 621 for 8.7 miles.

Stony Fork—From Wytheville, travel 6.9 miles north on I-77; then left on VA 717 for 4 miles.

Walnut Flats—From Pearisburg, travel 12 miles southwest on US 100; then right on US 42 for 12 miles; right on VA 606 for 1 mile; right on FS 201 for 3 miles.

White Pine Horse Camp—From Pearisburg, travel 12 miles southwest on US 100; then right on US 42 for 12 miles; right on VA 606 for 1 mile; right on FS 201 for 3 miles.

White Rocks—From Pembroke, travel 3 miles west on US 460; then right on VA 635 for 17 miles; right on VA 613 for 0.8 mile; left on FS 645 for 1 mile.

Map#/Recreation Areas	Campsites	Drinking Water	Sanitary Facilities	Trailer Dump Station	Picnicking	Fishing	Hiking Trails	Horse Trails
Wythe Ranger District								
1 Big Bend			•		•			
2 Dark Horse Hollow		•	•		•	•		
3 Stony Fork (F,S,$)	53	•	•	•		•	•	
Blacksburg Ranger District								
4 Caldwell Fields (G,$)	•		•		•	•	•	•
5 Cascades		•	•		•	•	•	
6 Interior		•	•		•	•		
7 Pandapas Pond					•	•	•	•
8 Walnut Flats	7	•	•			•	•	•
9 White Pine Horse Camp	5		•			•	•	•
10 White Rocks (F)	49	•	•	•		•	•	

$ = fee area
G = has 2 group areas
F = flush toilets
S = showers (warm)

Four recreation areas in the Blacksburg Ranger District indicate access to horse trails: Caldwell Fields, Pandapas Pond, Walnut Flats, and White Pine Horse Camp. Horses are not permitted in campgrounds; however, White Pine Horse Camp does provide a special camping area for visitors who bring horses.

Clinch Ranger District

For Information

District Ranger
Clinch Ranger District
Route 3, Box 820
Wise, VA 24293
(703) 328-2931

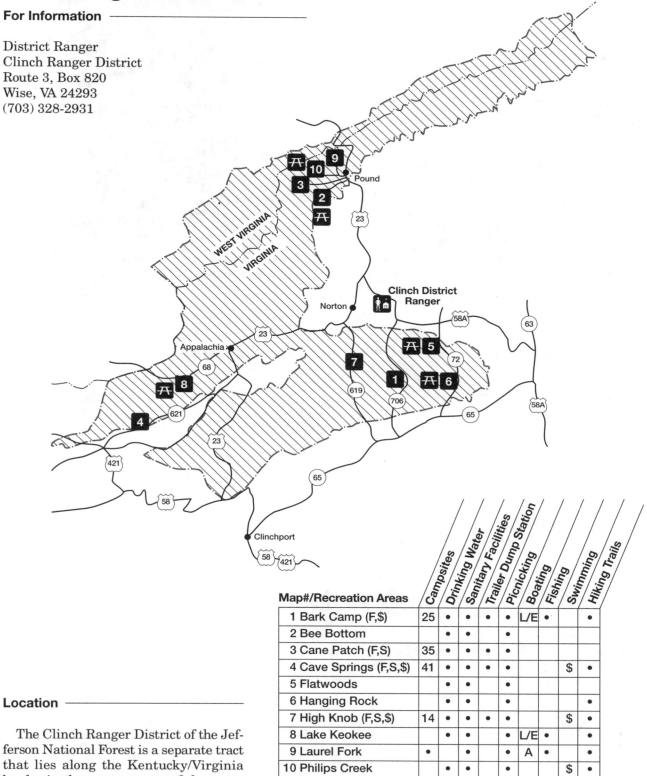

Location

The Clinch Ranger District of the Jefferson National Forest is a separate tract that lies along the Kentucky/Virginia border in the western part of the state; Norton is the largest city in the area. The Clinch Ranger Station is on SR 646, across from Clinch Valley College.

Map#/Recreation Areas	Campsites	Drinking Water	Sanitary Facilities	Trailer Dump Station	Picnicking	Boating	Fishing	Swimming	Hiking Trails
1 Bark Camp (F,$)	25	•	•	•	•	L/E	•		•
2 Bee Bottom		•	•		•				
3 Cane Patch (F,S)	35	•	•	•	•				
4 Cave Springs (F,S,$)	41	•	•		•			$	•
5 Flatwoods		•	•		•				
6 Hanging Rock		•	•		•				•
7 High Knob (F,S,$)	14	•	•	•	•			$	•
8 Lake Keokee		•	•		•	L/E	•		•
9 Laurel Fork	•		•		•	A	•		•
10 Philips Creek		•	•		•			$	•

$ = fee area
F = flush toilets
S = showers (warm)
Boating : L = launch ramp; A = carry down access;
              E = electric motors only

Clinch Ranger District *(continued)*

Directions to Recreation Areas With Campgrounds

Bark Camp—From Norton, travel 6.3 miles east on US 58A; then right on VA 706 for 4.1 miles; left on VA 699 for 0.3 mile; right on VA 822 for 1.7 miles.

Cane Patch—From US 23 at Pound, travel 6.2 miles west on VA 671.

Cave Springs—From Big Stone Gap, travel 2.5 miles west on US 58A; then right on VA 621 for 6.1 miles; right on FS 107 for 0.4 mile.

High Knob—From Norton, travel 3.7 miles south on VA 619; then left on FS 238 for 1.6 miles.

Laurel Fork—From US 23 at Pound, travel 1 mile west on VA 630 to boat launch ramp; then take a 1.3-mile boat ride or a 2-mile hike from parking area.

Chili for breakfast? Surely not! On second thought, with snow on the ground, maybe that's not such a bad idea!

Glenwood Ranger District and New Castle Ranger District

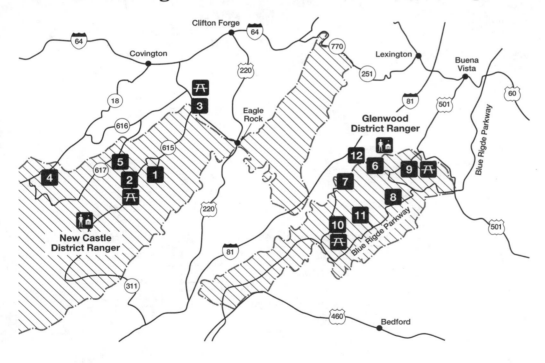

For Information

District Ranger
Glenwood Ranger District
P.O. Box 10
Natural Bridge Station, VA 24579
(703) 291-2189

District Ranger
New Castle Ranger District
Box 246
New Castle, VA 24127
(703) 864-5195

Glenwood Ranger District and New Castle Ranger District (continued)

Location

Glenwood Ranger District is the most eastern tract of the Jefferson National Forest. Glenwood Ranger Station is on SR 130, 1½ miles east of Natural Bridge. New Castle Ranger District is to the west and north; the ranger station is 2 miles east of New Castle on SR 615.

Directions to Recreation Areas With Campgrounds

Cave Mountain Lake—From Glasgow, travel 1.5 miles northwest on VA 130; then left on VA 759 for 3.2 miles; right on VA 781 for 1.6 miles; right on FS 780 for 1 mile.

Colon Hollow Shelter—Take exit 168 from I-81 north of Buchanan; then travel south on VA 614 for 2.9 miles; left on FS 59 for 2.4 miles; 0.1 mile on Trail 14.

Craig Creek—From New Castle, travel 10.5 miles northeast on VA 615; then right on VA 704 for 0.5 mile; right on FS 5058 for 0.2 mile.

Hopper Creek—From Glasgow, travel 1.5 miles northwest on VA 130; then left on VA 759 for 4.7 miles.

North Creek—Take exit 168 on I-81 north of Buchanan; then travel south on VA 614 for 2.9 miles; left on FS 59 for 2.4 miles.

Smith Tract—From Glasgow, travel 1.5 miles northwest on VA 130; left on VA 759 for 2 miles; right on VA 781 for 0.7 miles; right on VA 790 for 3 miles.

Steel Bridge—From New Castle, travel 16 miles northwest on VA 311; right on VA 18 for 3.5 miles.

The Pines—From New Castle, travel 5 miles northeast on VA 615; left on VA 611 for 4.9 miles; right on VA 617 for 5.5 miles.

Map#/Recreation Areas	Campsites	Drinking Water	Sanitary Facilities	Trailer Dump Station	Picnicking	Boating	Fishing	Hiking Trails	Horse Trails
Newcastle Ranger District									
1 Craig Creek (H)	•		•		•		•	•	•
2 Fenwick Mines			•		•			•	
3 Roaring Run Furnace			•		•		•	•	
4 Steel Bridge ($)	20	•	•				•		
5 The Pines (G,H,$)	17	•	•				•	•	•
Glenwood Ranger District									
6 Cave Mtn. Lake (SW$,F,S,$)	42	•	•	•	•		•		
7 Colon Hollow Shelter	•		•		•		•	•	
8 Hopper Creek	•	•	•		•				
9 Locher Tract					•	A	•	•	•
10 Middle Creek		•	•		•		•	•	
11 North Creek ($)	15	•	•	•			•	•	
12 Smith Tract	•				•	A	•		

$ = fee area; A = carry down access
SW = has swimming
F = flush toilets; S = showers (warm)
G = 4 group sites
H = horse camping

With 950 miles of hiking and riding trails in the Jefferson National Forest, you can be certain that some of them cross streams. Be prepared and be careful!

Kerr (John H.) Dam & Reservoir

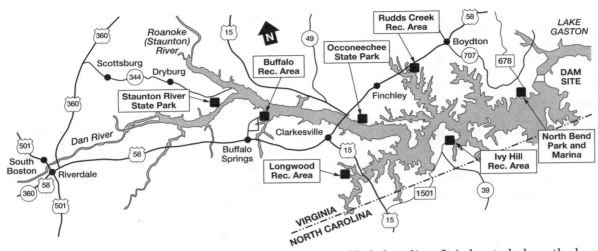

For Information

Resource Manager, Corps of Engineers
John H. Kerr Dam & Reservoir
Route 1, Box 76
Boydton, VA 23917
(804) 738-6662
(804) 738-6371, continuous 24-hour service for
 current and predicted water level elevations

Location

This 50,000-acre lake, one of the largest man-made lakes in the East, extends 39 miles up the Roanoke River along 800 miles of wooded, cove-studded shoreline. It is located along the border of Virginia and North Carolina; from Petersburg, travel southwest via I-85 or US 1, then west on US 58. In Virginia, it is not unusual to hear the reservoir called Buggs Island Lake—its original name. Buggs Island is a 169-acre island located just downstream of the dam.

There are 28 recreation areas located around the lake, with 15 of them offering tent and trailer camping; 7 are in Virginia and 8 are in North Carolina. The map of this park shows the location of only the 7 recreation areas that offer camping facilities in Virginia. Contact the office of the resource manager for the map that displays, in more detail, all of the roads and recreation areas surrounding Kerr Reservoir.

Recreation Areas	Tent & Trailer Camping	Flush Toilets	Hot Water Shower	Hook-Ups	Sanitary Dump	Group Camping
Buffalo Recreation Area	15	•				•
Ivy Hill Recreation Area	25				•	
Longwood Public Use Area	55	•	•	•	•	
North Bend Park & Marina	246	•	•	•	•	•
Occoneechee State Park	85	•	•	•	•	
Rudds Creek Recreation Area	103	•	•		•	
Staunton River State Park*	46	•	•		•	•

Picnic areas and boat ramps are provided at all recreation areas.
*Staunton River State Park has overnight cabins

Seven recreation areas offer tent and trailer camping around the Virginia portion of John H. Kerr Reservoir. This US 58 bridge is visible from the boat ramps at Occoneechee State Park.

Kiptopeke State Park

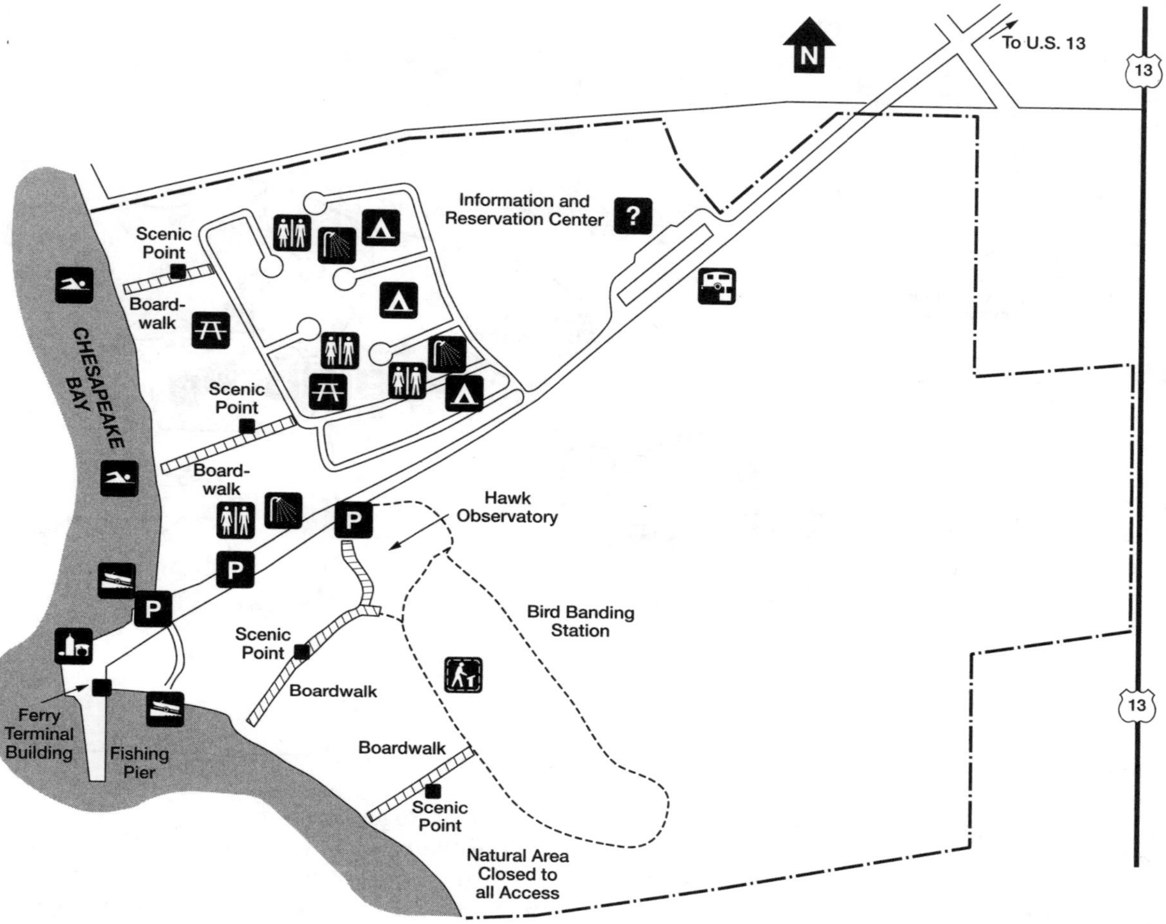

N

To U.S. 13

13

CHESAPEAKE BAY

Scenic Point

Boardwalk

Scenic Point

Boardwalk

Information and Reservation Center

?

Hawk Observatory

Bird Banding Station

P

P

P

Scenic Point

Boardwalk

Ferry Terminal Building

Fishing Pier

Boardwalk

Scenic Point

Natural Area Closed to all Access

13

For Information

Kiptopeke State Park
3540 Kiptopeke Drive
Cape Charles, VA 23310
(804) 331-2267

Location

Located on the Eastern Shore, Kiptopeke State Park offers recreational access to the Chesapeake Bay and the chance to explore a unique coastal habitat featuring a major flyway for migratory birds. It is Virginia's newest state park and is also a park under development. This 375-acre park has a beach frontage along the Chesapeake Bay of 4,276 feet. The northern beach features a beach and lifeguarded swimming area from Memorial Day to Labor Day; the southern beach is great for surf fishing and beach combing. A row of 9 surplus World War II concrete ships form a breakwater about 1,500 feet from the shore; they offer some of Virginia's finest fishing.

Facilities & Activities

121 campsites
   94 with electrical/water/sewage hookups
   27 with no hookups
showers
dump station
picnicking
vending machines
bay swimming & bathhouse
saltwater fishing
lighted fishing pier
boating (motor boats permitted)
boat ramp
interpretive trail
hiking
boardwalks
interpretive programs

Mount Rogers National Recreation Area

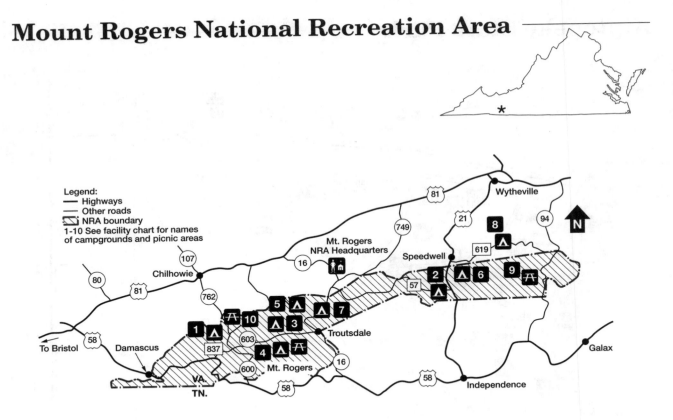

For Information

Mount Rogers National Recreation Area
Route 1, Box 303
Marion, VA 24354
(703) 783-5196

Location

Mount Rogers National Recreation Area, on the Jefferson National Forest, is located in Virginia's beautiful Blue Ridge Mountains. It includes Mt. Rogers, the highest peak in Virginia, and the Crest Zone, an area with elevations over 4,000 feet, large rock formations, and a mixture of mountain "balds" and spruce-fir forests. At 5,729 feet, Mount Rogers is one of the highest peaks east of the Mississippi. Nearby to the southeast is 5,560-foot Whitetop Mountain, and to the east, 5,526-foot Pine Mountain, all part of the 118,000-acre Mount Rogers National Recreation Area. The 60-mile long recreation area starts at the New River near Ivanhoe and parallels the south side of I-81 to the Tennessee-North Carolina line west of Damascus. Major access off the interstate to the high country is VA 16 south from Marion and VA 600 south from Chilhowie. US 21 and US 58 also provide access.

Points of Interest

▲ Mount Rogers has over 350 miles of trails, including the 67-mile long Virginia Highlands Horse Trail and 60 miles of the Appalachian Trail.
▲ Two wilderness areas have been designated on the national recreation area; these areas will remain in their current condition. Some folks say that Lewis Fork Wilderness is the most spectacular of the wilderness areas in Virginia .
▲ Old stone bridges, rail fences, mills, stone iron furnaces, and farmsteads abound in a landscape of intermingled fields and forests.
▲ About 150 ponies roam freely in the high country, and round-ups are held in the spring and fall.
▲ In June, acres of deep-pink rhododendron adorn the landscape at Rhododendron Gap, between Mount Rogers and Pine Mountain.

General Information

▲ There is no entrance fee to the national recreation area but 5 of the 9 campgrounds charge a camping fee. Beartree also charges a day-use fee.
▲ Mount Rogers NRA Headquarters is located on VA 16, 7 miles southeast of Marion. Individual pamphlets are available on topics such as circuit

hikes, cross-country skiing, high country trails, horseback riding, recreation areas, and wilderness areas. Maps are available for purchase.

▲ Camping at most recreation areas is on a first-come, first-served basis. However, group campsites at Beartree must be reserved (1-800-280-2267 or (703) 783-5196) and sites on Cottontail Loop at Grindstone can be reserved (1-800-280-2267). There is a 14-day occupancy limit.

▲ Camping facilities vary but most include a paved or gravel parking spur, picnic table, and fireplace. Some have tent pads. (See facility chart for other facilities provided.)

▲ All campgrounds are open year-round except the following: Beartree, mid-March through December 1; Grindstone, May through November; Hurricane, March through October.

▲ Trailer space is available at all campgrounds. However, there is a walk-in/hike-in camping area at Raven Cliff in addition to the horse camp.

▲ Horse camping facilities are at Fox Creek Trailhead, Hussy Mountain Horse Camp, and Raven Cliff Horse Camp. Stream water and either a corral or hitching rails are available. Fox Creek does not have drinking water. Horses are not allowed on the Appalachian Trail.

▲ Camping in the backcountry outside of developed sites is allowed; it has always been a popular activity in national forests. Campers are encouraged to practice no trace camping techniques. Permits are not required.

▲ Day-use areas are open from dawn to dusk. Several picnic areas have shelters; those at Beartree require a fee and are by reservation only.

▲ Numerous trails offer hikers the opportunity to climb mountain ridges and peaks, to wander down streams and gorges, and to roam through a variety of forest habitats. Brochures are available that describe circuit hikes and other trails.

▲ Off-road-vehicle (ORV) use is allowed on designated trails. The Feathercamp Motorcycle Trails are located in the southwestern portion of Mount Rogers NRA. Ask for the brochure at park headquarters.

▲ A 3-mile jeep trail up the north side of Pine Mountain to the crest zone leads to the Scales, a favorite spot for hunters.

▲ The two wilderness areas on the national recreation area are Lewis Fork and Little Dry Run. The 5,730-acre Lewis Fork Wilderness Area includes Mount Rogers summit, and portions of the Appalachian Trail and the Virginia Highlands Horse Trail. It is reached from Elk Garden Gap on VA 600.

▲ The 3,400-acres of Little Dry Run are moderately steep with elevations ranging from 2,440 to 3,614 feet. It is located 4 miles south of Speedwell with easy access off US 21.

▲ A third wilderness area, Little Wilson Creek, is within the jurisdiction of the Mount Rogers NRA. Adjacent to Grayson Highlands State Park and about 4½ miles south of Troutsdale, it contains 3,855 acres with elevations ranging from 3,280 feet to 4,857 feet. Wilson Creek is a native trout stream.

Facilities & Activities

RV & tent campsites at 6 recreation areas
group campground at Beartree
3 horse camping facilities
backcountry camping
7 picnic areas
swimming at Beartree & Grindstone
bathhouse at Beartree
canoeing/non-motorized boating at Beartree
fishing/hunting
hiking/backpacking
nature trail at Grindstone
ORV trails
mountain biking
3-mile jeep trail
60 miles of Appalachian Trail
67-mile Virginia Highlands Horse Trail
150 miles of trails open to horses
cross-country skiing/snowshoeing
historical/cultural sites
headquarters/visitor center

Including the 67-mile Virginia Highlands Horse Trail, Mount Rogers NRA has 150 miles of trails open to horses.

Mount Rogers National Recreation Area
(continued)

Directions to Recreation Areas With Campgrounds

Beartree—From Damascus, travel east for 7.5 miles on US 58; then left on FS 837.

Comers Rock—From Wytheville, travel 17 miles south on US 21; then right on FS 57.

Fox Creek Horse Camp—From Troutsdale, travel west on VA 603 for 4 miles.

Grindstone—From Troutsdale, travel west on VA 603 for 6 miles.

Hurricane—From Marion, travel south on VA 16 for 15 miles; then right on VA 650 for 1.5 miles.

Hussy Mountain Horse Camp—From Speedwell, travel south on US 21 for 3.3 miles; then left on FS 14 for 2 miles.

Raccoon Branch—From Marion, travel south on VA 16 for 1.2 miles.

Raven Cliff—Off VA 619, 6.5 miles east of Speedwell and 2 miles east of Cripple Creek Community.

Raven Cliff Horse Camp—1 mi. east of Raven Cliff Campground, just south of FS 642.

Map#/Recreation Areas	Campsites	Drinking Water	Sanitary Facilities	Trailer Dump Station	Picnicking	Fishing	Swimming	Hiking Trails	Horse Trails
1 Beartree (A,F,G,R,S,$)	80	•	•	•	•	•	•	•	
2 Comers Rock	10	•	•		•	•		•	
3 Fox Creek Picnic Area			•		•	•		•	
3 Fox Creek Horse Camp	•		•			•		•	•
4 Grindstone (F,R,S,$)	100	•	•	•		•	•	•	
5 Hurricane (F,S,$)	29	•	•			•		•	•
6 Hussy Mtn. Horse Camp (G)	•	•	•		•	•		•	•
7 Raccoon Branch (F,$)	20	•	•	•		•		•	
8 Raven Cliff ($)	20	•	•	•	•	•		•	•
8 Raven Cliff Horse Camp	•	•	•			•		•	•
9 Shepherds Corner			•		•				
10 Skulls Gap			•		•			•	

$ = fee area
A = carry down boating access
F = flush toilets
G = group campsites
R = reservations: required for group campsites at Beartree (1-800-283-2267 or (703) 783-5196); may be made for campsites in Cottontail Loop at Grindstone, June–Sept. (1-800-283-2267)
S = showers (warm)

Camping in the backcountry outside of developed sites is allowed; it has always been a popular activity in national forests. Lewis Fork and Little Dry Run wilderness areas are also available for backcountry camping.

Natural Chimneys Regional Park

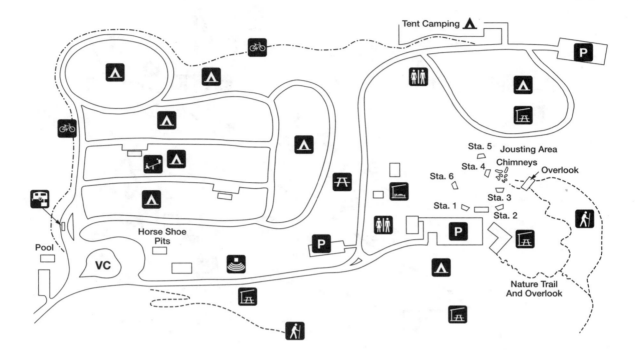

For Information

Natural Chimneys Regional Park
Route 1, Box 286
Mt. Solon, VA 22843
(703) 350-2510

Location

Natural Chimneys Regional Park is located southwest of Harrisonburg off I-81. Take exit 240 south of Harrisonburg and travel on SR 257 across US 11 to Bridgewater. Turn left on SR 42, then right on SR 747 to Mt. Solon. At Mt. Solon, turn right on SR 731 and travel the 1 mile to the park. The 134-acre park, owned and operated by the Upper Valley Regional Park Authority (703-249-5729), is open March 1 through mid-November. Seven chimneys, made of layers of limestone and ranging in height from 65 to 120 feet, are the focal point of the park. Special activities include gospel singing in June and August, and the annual jousting tournament. Natural Chimneys has been designated the National Jousting Hall of Fame. First held in 1821, the tournament is the oldest continuously-held sporting event in North America.

Facilities & Activities

120 campsites with water/electricity*
40 walk-in primitive tent sites
restrooms/showers/laundry
dump station
picnic tables/fire rings
4 picnic shelters
2 playgrounds
athletic fields
camp store
pool and river swimming
self guided tour of the chimneys
nature/hiking/bicycle trails
visitor center

---

*Reservations accepted but not required. However, they are necessary for the annual jousting tournaments, July 4th, Memorial Day, and Labor Day to ensure a campsite.

Natural Tunnel State Park

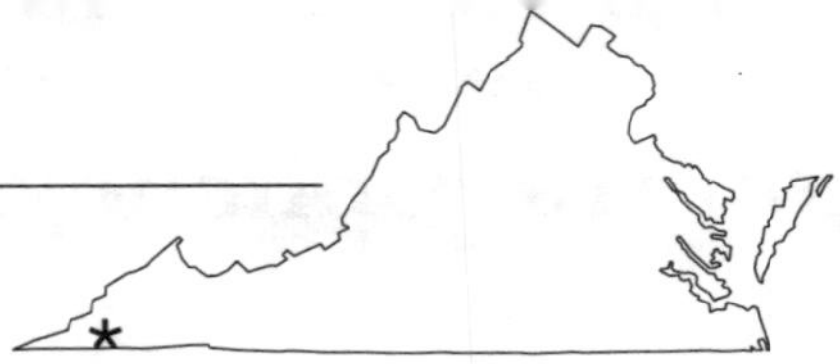

For Information

Natural Tunnel State Park
Route 3, Box 250
Duffield, VA 24244-9361
(703) 940-2674

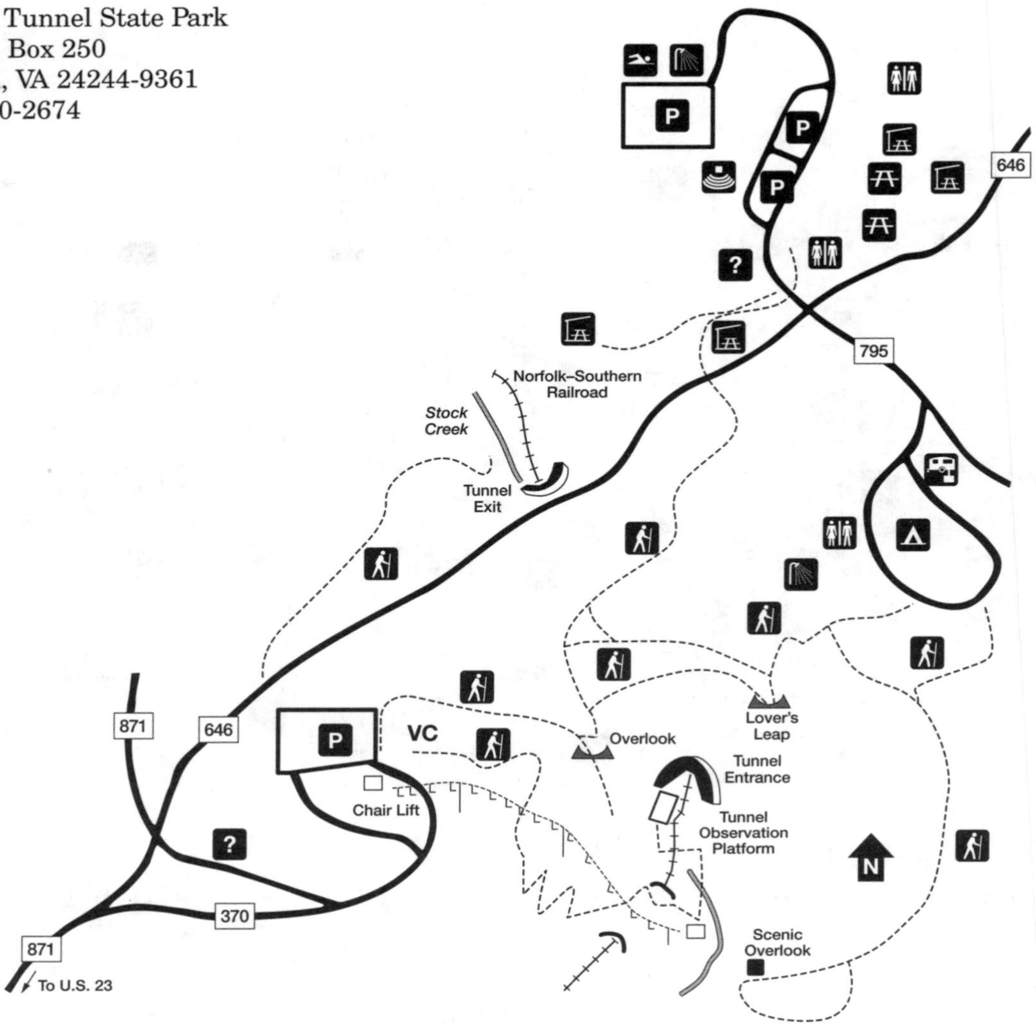

Norfolk–Southern Railroad

Stock Creek

Tunnel Exit

646

795

871

646

VC

871

370

To U.S. 23

Chair Lift

Overlook

Lover's Leap

Tunnel Entrance

Tunnel Observation Platform

N

Scenic Overlook

Location

Natural Tunnel, called the "Eighth Wonder of the World" by William Jennings Bryan, is over 850 feet long and as high as a 10-story building. The tunnel, carved through a limestone ridge over thousands of centuries, is the focal point of the 649-acre Natural Tunnel State Park. The park is about 14 miles northwest of Weber City via US 23/58/421, then 1 mile east on Route 871 to the park entrance. Access to the Natural Tunnel is available via a 536-foot-long chairlift, which descends 230 feet, or via Tunnel Trail, which begins at the visitor center and ends at an observation platform located at the mouth of the tunnel. A 2,000-seat amphitheater, located near the picnic area, attracts local and regional productions, traveling troupes, and other entertainment.

Facilities & Activities

29 campsites
showers
dump station
picnicking/shelters
snack bar
swimming pool & bathhouse
freshwater fishing
7 hiking trails
boardwalk/observation deck
chairlift
2,000-seat amphitheater
interpretive programs
visitor center

North Fork of Pound Lake

For Information

Resource Manager, Corps of Engineers
North Fork of Pound Lake
Route 1, Box 369
Pound, VA 24279
(703) 796-5775

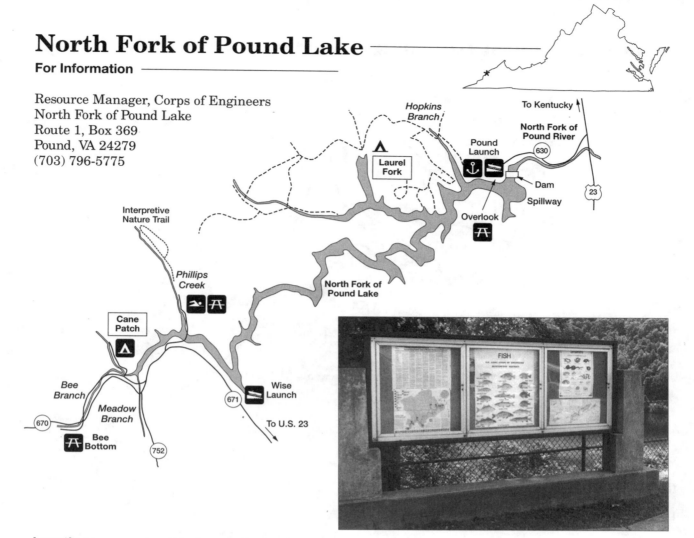

North Fork of Pound Lake has this informative display at the Overlook Area.

Location

The lake, nestled in the hills of southwestern Virginia just west of the town of Pound, was formed by the building of a dam on the North Fork of Pound River. Built for flood control, the lake level is kept 10 feet lower during the late fall through early summer to allow for additional water storage if necessary. The North Fork area is generally a region of steep ridges and rounded knobs interspersed with winding stream valleys. Within the lake area are 5 main ravines; the small streams within these ravines are very clear.

Overlook Area and Pound Launch, located on the north shore of the lake near the dam, are day-use areas with picnic tables, restrooms, hiking trails, launch ramp, and marina. Laurel Fork is a primitive camping area accessible only by boat or foot trail. It is an excellent base camp for hikers who wish to explore the upper reaches of Pine Mountain. A campground is located at Cane Patch and is a fee area. Phillips Creek, a day-use area, has a sandy swimming beach, bathhouse, picnic shelters, and

Recreation Areas	Campground	Restrooms	Showers	Sanitary Dump	Picnic Area
Bee Bottom Picnic Area		•			•
Cane Patch Campground	35	•	•	•	•
Laurel Fork Primitive Area	•	•			•
Overlook Area		•			•
Phillips Creek Day Use Area		•	•		•
Pound Launch Area					•

nature trails; campers at Cane Patch are within walking distance of Phillips Creek. Cane Patch, Bee Bottom and Phillips Creek are all accessible from US 23 at Pound, via Route 671.

Occoneechee State Park

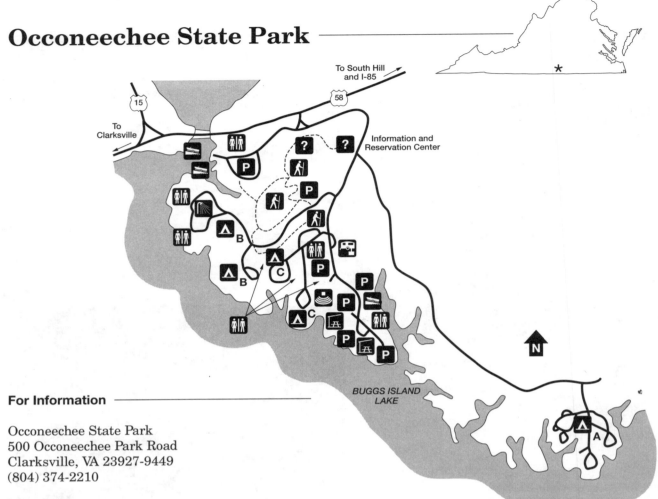

For Information

Occoneechee State Park
500 Occoneechee Park Road
Clarksville, VA 23927-9449
(804) 374-2210

Location

Occoneechee State Park is located 1½ miles east of Clarksville on US 58 near the US 15 intersection. This 2,690-acre park is named for the Occoneechee Indians, pronounced O-ko-nee-chee; it is on Virginia's largest lake, the 48,000-acre John H. Kerr Reservoir, better known as Buggs Island Lake. The main attraction of this park is boating and fishing; swimming from the shoreline is not permitted due to steep drop-offs and heavy boating traffic. Buggs Island Lake and connecting Lake Gaston are famous for the number and size of fish found there.

Facilities & Activities

85 campsites
   76 with electrical/water hookups
showers
dump station
picnicking/shelters
vending machines
freshwater fishing
boating (motor boats permitted)
2 boat ramps

Although Occoneechee State Park has 2 boat ramps, there is sometimes a wait to launch into the Kerr Reservoir, also known as Buggs Island Lake.

4 hiking trails
interpretive trail
interpretive programs

Philpott Lake

For Information

Resource Manager, Corps of Engineers
Philpott Lake
Route 6, Box 140
Bassett, VA 24055
(703) 629-2703

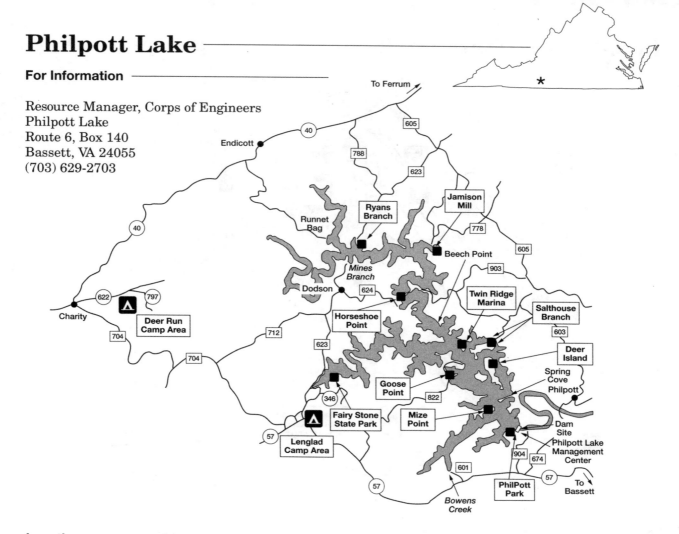

Location

Philpott Lake, nestled in the rugged foothills of the Blue Ridge mountains, encompasses 3,000 acres, stretches 15 miles, and has a 100-mile shoreline. Its clear waters are within sight of the crest of the Blue Ridge Mountains. The lake, constructed on the Smith River for flood control and hydroelectric power generation, takes it name from the nearby downstream village of Philpott. The project adjoins Fairy Stone State Park, which is so named because of the lucky or fairy stones found in the region. Philpott Lake is south of Roanoke and west of US 220; the Blue Ridge Parkway is to the west.

Seventeen recreation areas are located around Philpott Lake; 12 of them have campgrounds. Two of the camping areas are available by water only and one campground is for group camping only. The map of this park highlights the 12 recreation areas that offer camping facilities. Contact the office of the resource manager for the map that displays, in more detail, all of the roads and recreation areas surrounding Philpott Lake.

Recreation Areas	Campground	Flush Toilets	Hot Water Showers	Sanitary Dump	Hook-Ups	Swimming Area	Picnic Area	Boat Launch
Deer Island Camp Area*	•							
Deer Run Camp Area †	•	•	•	•		•		
Fairy Stone State Park †	•	•	•	•	•	•	•	
Goose Point	•	•	•	•		•	•	•
Horseshoe Point	•	•	•	•		•	•	•
Jamison Mill	•	•	•	•		•	•	•
Lenglad Camp Area	•	•	•	•				
Mize Point Camp Area*	•							
Philpott Park & Overlook**		•				•	•	•
Ryans Branch	•					•	•	•
Salthouse Branch	•	•	•	•		•	•	•
Twin Ridge Marina, Inc.	•	•		•	•	•	•	•

*Accessible by water only
**Group camping by reservation only
†Fairy Stone and Deer Run have overnight cabins

Pocahontas State Park

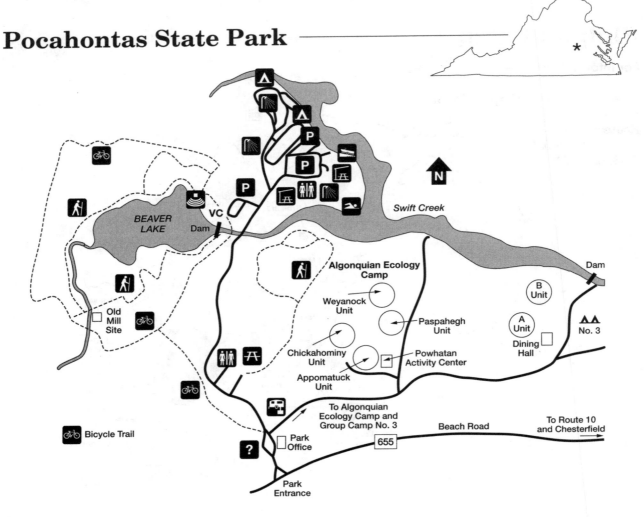

BEAVER LAKE

Dam

VC

Old Mill Site

Bicycle Trail

Swift Creek

N

Algonquian Ecology Camp

Weyanock Unit

Paspahegh Unit

Chickahominy Unit

Appomatuck Unit

Powhatan Activity Center

B Unit

A Unit

Dining Hall

Dam

No. 3

To Algonquian Ecology Camp and Group Camp No. 3

Beach Road

To Route 10 and Chesterfield

655

Park Office

?

Park Entrance

For Information

Pocahontas State Park
10301 State Park Road
Chesterfield, VA 23838-4713
(804) 796-4255

Location

Pocahontas State Park, located just 20 miles south from downtown Richmond is the largest of the state parks, with 7,604 acres and 2 small lakes. The park was once part of the Pocahontas State Forest, but as of 1989, the entire area is now operated as Pocahontas State Park. The park's Algonquian Ecology Camp is available to groups for day and overnight use for environmental education. The modern swimming complex, with over 17,500 square feet of swimming area, is the largest in Virginia. Swimming and wading is not allowed in either lake. Non-motorized boating is allowed on Swift Creek Lake (150 acres), but not on Beaver Lake (24 acres). The park entrance is on Route 655 (Beach Road), accessible from Route 10. Route 10 is accessible from I-95 via several routes: take exit 61 and travel west on Route 10; take the Route 288 exit and travel west; or take exit 67 and travel west on Route 150.

Facilities & Activities

34 campsites
showers
dump station
7 group campsites
group cabin facilities for 16–112 people with
    dining halls
picnicking/shelters
snack bar
swimming pool & bathhouse
freshwater fishing
boating (non-gasoline powered)
boat ramp
canoe/paddleboat/rowboat rentals
5 miles of hiking trails
5-mile bicycle trail/rentals
interpretive programs
visitor center

Pohick Bay Regional Park

For Information

Pohick Bay Regional Park
6501 Pohick Bay Drive
Lorton, VA 22079
(703) 339-6104

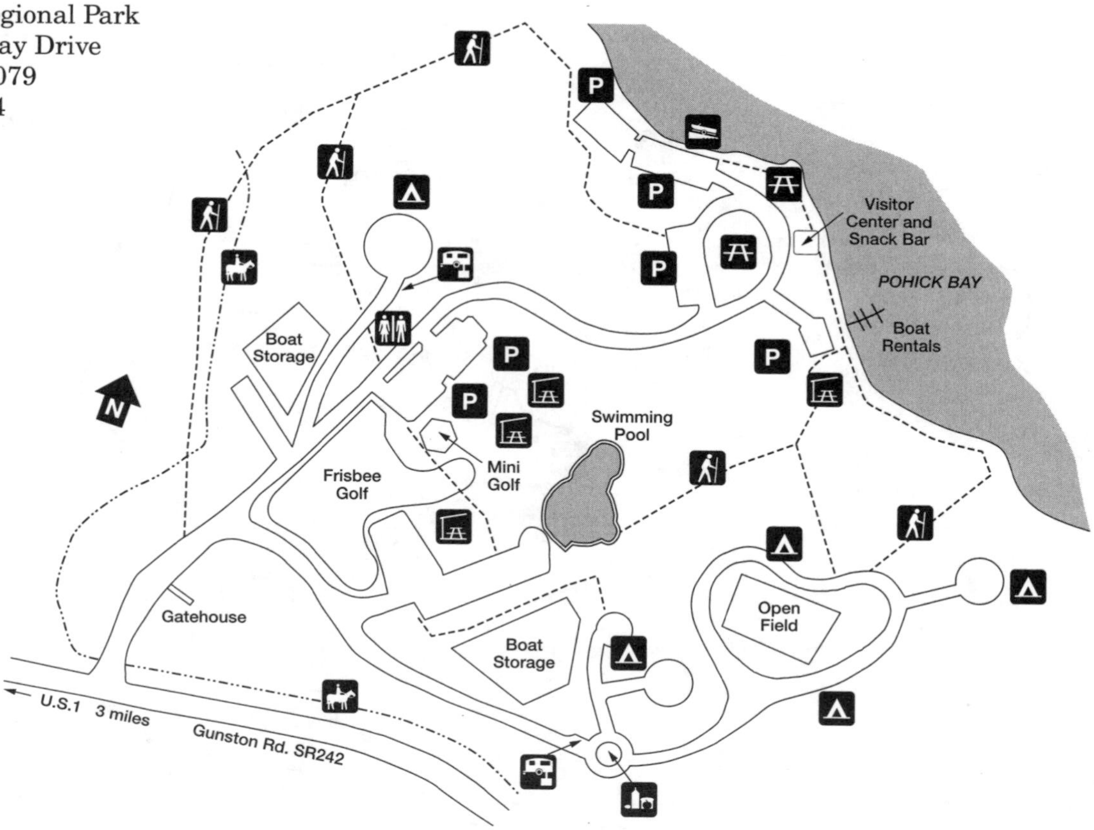

Location

Pohick Bay Regional Park is located about 25 miles south of Washington, D.C., off I-95. Take exit 163 on I-95 at Lorton, travel east on Lorton Road, then right on Armistead Road to light, then right on US 1 to 3rd light, then left on Gunston Road about 4 miles. The 1,000-acre park, owned and operated by the Northern Virginia Regional Park Authority (703-352-5900), is open all year. The Indians called this land "Pohick," the Algonquin word for the "water place." Today, Pohick Bay is still the water place—it occupies a spectacular bayside setting on a bluff on the historic Mason Neck peninsula and has direct boat access to the Potomac River. Mason Neck shelters a profusion of wildlife, especially bald eagles.

Facilities & Activities

150 tent/RV campsites*
   100 with electricity
restrooms/showers/laundry
dump station
group campsites for youth groups**
picnic tables/grills
rental picnic shelters**
playground
snack bar/camp store
swimming pool (Memorial Day week-end through Labor Day)
fishing
boat ramp/marina
sail/pedal/jon boat rentals
marsh canoe trips
boating, sailing, water skiing, wind surfing
RV & boat storage
nature/hiking trails
horse trails
minature & disc golf
18-hole golf course/driving range

*No reservations accepted; first-come, first-served
**Reservations required (703) 352-5900

Prince William Forest Park

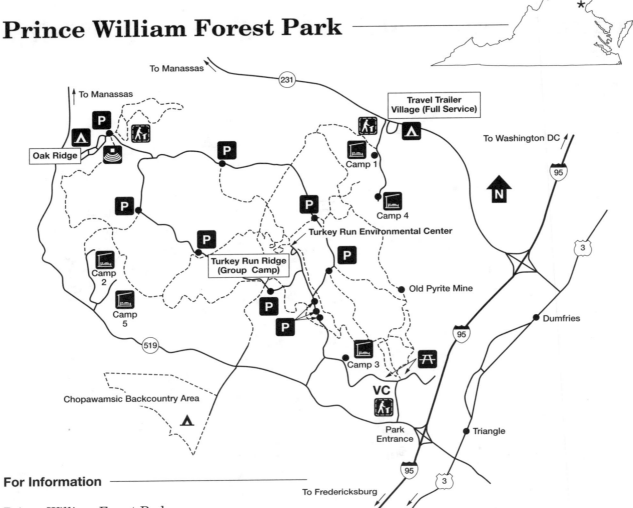

For Information

Prince William Forest Park
P.O. Box 209
Triangle, VA 22172-0209
(703) 221-7181

Location

This park is about 32 miles south of Washington, DC. The park spans 2 physiogeographic provinces; rock outcroppings mark the end of the Atlantic Coastal Plain and the beginning of the Piedmont forest. What once were intensively farmed fields is today a land reclaimed by nature. This 17,410-acre park is a woodland outdoor recreation area that serves to protect the North and South Branches of the Quantico Creek. During the 1930s when the park was designated as Chopawamsic Recreation Demonstration Area, the Civilian Conservation Corps (CCC) built 5 fully equipped cabin camps; many of these buildings are still in use today. The main entrance is west on VA 619, just ¼-mile beyond I-95, Exit 150-B. The visitor center is less than 1 mile from the main entrance. Campers arriving in an RV or travel trailer and desiring hookups, take

the Dumfries/Manassas Exit 152 from I-95 and travel northwest on VA 234 for 2½ miles to the Travel Trailer Village.

Points of Interest

▲ The Piedmont forest of the Quantico Creek watershed, most of which lies within the park's boundaries, serves as a sanctuary for plants and animals in rapidly developing Northern Virginia.

▲ Wildlife abounds in the park. The twilight hours of early morning and evening are best for seeing deer, squirrels, wild turkeys, beaver, or other creatures of the forest. Migratory birds are best seen during the spring and fall.

▲ Park naturalists offer a regular series of walks, talks, and hikes on the weekends and evening campfire programs during the weekends between Memorial Day and Labor Day. Check the park activity schedule.

▲ The Scenic Drive from Pine Grove picnic area to the beginning of the Scenic Loop is 2 miles; the

Scenic Loop is approximately 7½ miles around. Many of the hiking trails are accessible from parking areas along these roads.

▲ Trails totaling more than 37 miles wind through the park and provide a variety of opportunities for nature study, and physical challenge. The 10 major trails are color-blazed.

General Information

▲ An entry fee is charged; it is valid for 7 consecutive days. Campground fees are also charged; there is no fee for backcountry camping.

▲ The visitor center offers information services, interpretitive exhibits, and slide and video programs. Books, maps, and other materials are also for sale. The center is open daily from 8:30 am to 5:00 pm.

▲ Oak Ridge Campground is for tents and RV's shorter than 18 feet. The combined length of a vehicle and trailer should not exceed 30 feet. Each site has a paved parking slip, campfire grill, and picnic table. The campground has water and restrooms; there are no hookups or showers.

▲ Oak Ridge Campground is first-come, first-served, on a self-registration system. Maximum camping limit is 14 consecutive days; 28 camping days are allowed per calendar year.

▲ The Travel Trailer Village, operated by a NPS concessionaire, has sites for RV's and trailers only, with full services available. It also has showers, a coin-operated laundry, dump station, and a swimming pool. Phone (703) 221-2474 for information and reservations.

▲ For organized groups, 2 types of camping are available: cabin camps and tenting areas. Turkey Run Ridge Campground is a 6-site tent camping facility for groups of 6 or more; sites vary in size and can accommodate from 25 to 40 persons. Reservations are required. Phone: (703) 221-7181.

▲ Five cabin camps are available for organized groups; their capacities range from 115 to 211 campers. The camps have sleeping cabins, a central kitchen and dining hall, restrooms, and showers. They are available for spring, summer, and fall use; only Cabin Camp 5 is heated and open year-round, making it available for winter camping. Reservations are required. Phone: (703) 221-4706.

▲ Camping in the 400-acre Chopawamsic (Chop-ah-wahm-zik) backcountry area is by permit only. Located just south of the main park, it is open from February through mid-October. Sites are ½ to 2 miles from the nearest parking area. Two types of camping are available: designated primitive campsites and cross-country primitive camping.

▲ Designated primitive campsites are identified by a post marker and accessible from the circuit trail. There is a maximum of 4 people per site;

Camping in the 400-acre Chopawamsic backcountry area is by permit only. Designated primitive campsites and cross-country primitive camping are available; sites are ½ to 2 miles from the nearest parking area.

Prince William Forest Park   127

campfires are prohibited. All stream and lake waters are considered unsafe for consumption. Campers with a cross-country permit may camp anywhere, but are subject to certain conditions, such as a 3-day limit at any one site.

▲ Both picnic areas have tables, cooking grills, water, and restrooms. Pine Grove has a shelter for use on a first-come, first-served basis.

▲ Winter is an excellent time to hike in the park, for the lack of leaves affords longer views along ridges and in ravines. Snowfall offers opportunities for cross-country skiing and snowshoeing.

▲ Bicycle riding is permitted on all paved roads and designated unpaved roads; bicycles are not permitted on pedestrian trails. Portions of the Scenic Drive and Scenic Loop are quite steep and may not be suitable for youngsters and novices.

▲ Within the park's boundaries are some 15 miles of stream and 3 impoundments which are open to public fishing. A Virginia fishing license is required. Ask for a list of state and park fishing regulations at the visitor center. Hunting is prohibited.

▲ Wood fires are permitted only at established picnic areas and campgrounds, and then only in the grills that are provided. Firewood is provided at the campground but not at the picnic areas. Gathering of dead and downed wood is not permitted.

▲ Pets must be on a leash at all times; they are also not allowed within the Chopawamsic Backcountry Area, Turkey Run Ridge, or the cabin camps.

▲ The Turkey Run Environmental Center can be used by area educators as a resource lab to study the Piedmont forest environment. Phone (701) 221-7181.

▲ The park is closed at dusk except for campers.

Facilities & Activities —————————————

80 RV & tent campsites at Oak Ridge
79 RV & trailer sites with full hookups at Travel Trailer Village
6 group sites for tents at Turkey Run Ridge
5 cabin camps for groups
10 designated backcountry campsites
cross-country backcountry camping
2 large picnic areas
fishing
hiking/backpacking
self-guided nature trails
bicycling
cross-country skiing/showshoeing
scenic auto tour route
ranger-led talks/walks/demonstrations
amphitheater/evening ranger programs
visitor center/exhibits

Winter is an excellent time to hike in the park, for the lack of leaves affords longer views along ridges and in ravines. Snowfall at Prince William Forest Park offers opportunities for cross-country skiing and snowshoeing.

Seashore State Park and Natural Area

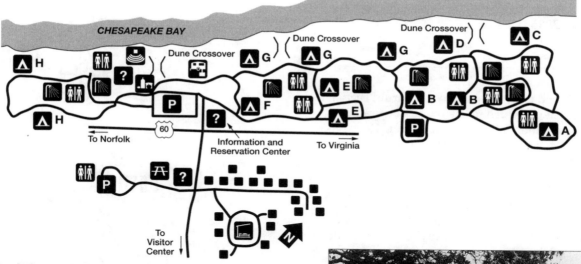

For Information

Seashore State Park and Natural Area
2500 Shore Drive
Virginia Beach, VA 23451-1415
(804) 481-2131

Location

Seashore State Park and Natural Area is just north of the public beach in Virginia Beach. To get there, take exit 282 off I-64 and travel east on US 13; then turn right onto US 60 to Cape Henry. With 1¼-miles of beach, this 2,770-acre park offers an opportunity to explore a unique habitat featuring lagoons, large cypress trees, and rare plants. In 1965, the park's natural area was included in the National Register of Natural Landmarks because of its distinction as the northernmost location on the East Coast where subtropical and temperate plants grow and thrive together. Only registered overnight guests are allowed on the bayfront during the summer months.

The 9 hiking trails at Seashore State Park offer an opportunity to explore a unique habitat featuring lagoons, large cypress trees, and rare plants.

Facilities & Activities

235 campsites
showers
dump station
group campsites
20 housekeeping cabins (2-bedroom)
picnicking/shelter
snack bar

saltwater fishing
boating (motor boats permitted)
boat ramps
9 hiking trails (19 miles)
bicycle trail/rentals
store
interpretive programs
environmental education center
visitor center

Shenandoah National Park

For Information

Shenandoah National Park
Route 4, Box 348
Luray, VA 22835
(703) 999-3500

Location

This national park lies astride a beautiful section of the Blue Ridge, which forms the eastern rampart of the Appalachian Mountains between Pennsylvania and Georgia. In the valley to the west is the Shenandoah River and to the east is the rolling Piedmont country. Skyline Drive, a 105-mile winding road runs along the Blue Ridge through the length of this 195,000-acre park, providing vistas of the spectacular landscape; it connects directly with the 469-mile Blue Ridge Parkway. Concrete mile markers have been placed on the right side of the drive as you head south. They are numbered from north to south. Visitors are encouraged to pick up the detailed map/brochure of the park as it displays the mile markers every 5 miles; it will help locate features, facilities, and services. There are 4 entrances to Skyline Drive: Front Royal (North), via US 340 and VA 55; Thornton Gap, via US 211; Swift Run Gap, via US 33; and Rockfish (South), via I-64 and US 250.

Points of Interest

▲ Numerous overlooks along the 105-mile Skyline Drive provide panoramic views of the ridges and valleys, hills and hollows, laced with sparkling streams and waterfalls.

▲ More than 95% of the park is covered by forests with about 100 species of trees. The largest open area is Big Meadows; here, the abundance of wildflowers, strawberries, and blueberries attract both wildlife and humans.

▲ The park is a place of changing scenes and changing moods. Many wildflowers come into bloom during April and May; pink azalea blooms in late May followed by mountain laurel.

▲ Fall is the season of brilliant colors and clear, crisp days. Some color change begins in late September but October is the month of prime leaf color; it is usually at its peak the second or third week of October.

▲ With more than 500 miles of trails, the park is a hiker's paradise; they lead to numerous waterfalls, clear rushing streams, old home sites, and scenic vistas hidden below Skyline Drive.

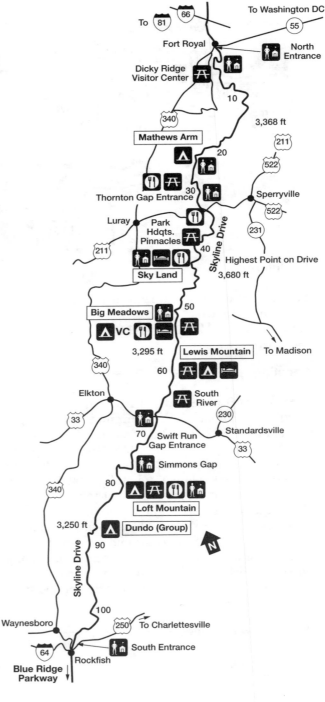

▲ Self-guided nature trails, with signs or leaflets, are at 5 locations: Dickey Ridge, Mathews Arm, Skyland, Big Meadows, and Loft Mountain.

▲ A fee is collected for entry into the park. Entrance stations are located at the 4 access points to Skyline Drive. The entrance permit is good for 7 consecutive days. Camping fees are charged at the 5 campgrounds.

▲ There are 2 visitor centers that sell literature and provide information, interpretive exhibits, and illustrated programs:
—Dickey Ridge Visitor Center (Mile 4.6) is open from about April 1 to November 1.
—Byrd Visitor Center at Big Meadows (Mile 51) is open daily from early spring through fall and on an intermittent schedule during the winter.

▲ Naturalist-led evening programs and campfire talks, hikes, and demonstrations, are offered at several locations. Check bulletin boards for dates and times. The *Shenandoah Overlook,* a free park newspaper available at visitor contact stations, also has the schedule.

▲ Park headquarters is 4 miles west of Thornton Gap and 4 miles east of Luray on US 211. Information and backcountry permits may be obtained here; publications on the park are on sale.

▲ RV and tent campgrounds are at Mathews Arm (Mile 22.2), Big Meadows (51), Lewis Mountain (57.5), and Loft Mountain (79.5). A 14-day limit is in effect from June 1 to October 31. All campgrounds provide drinking water and flush toilets; hook-ups for electricity, water, and sewage are not provided. With the exception of Lewis Mountain, each campground has a sanitary dump.

▲ All campgrounds, except Big Meadows, are open from May through October on a first-come, first-served basis. Big Meadows, open from early spring through late fall, is on the MISTIX reservation system from June through October; the rest of the camping season its sites are on a first-come, first-served basis.

▲ A campground for non-profit organized youth groups is at Dundo (Mile 83.7); it is open from mid-May through October. Reservations are accepted; call the park. Seven sites are available; a maximum of 20 persons per site is permitted.

▲ Backcountry camping is allowed all year throughout much of the park on a first-come, first-served basis. The limit of stay for any one campsite is 2 days; there is no limit on the total length of stay. A backcountry permit is required and may be obtained during daylight hours only at entrance stations, visitor centers, and park headquarters, or by mail.

▲ Backcountry camping is literally "out of sight." Make camp at least 250 yards away from any paved road, half a mile from any developed park area, out of sight of any hiking trail or any other camping party, and at least 25 feet from any stream. Wood fires are not permitted; backpacker stoves should be used.

▲ The Potomac Appalachian Trail Club operates 6 trail cabins in the backcountry and maintains 7 huts for Appalachian Trail hikers. The cabins are fully equipped; some will accommodate as many as 11 persons. A fee of $1 per night is charged for the huts. For reservations, information, and maps, phone: (202) 638-5306.

▲ Do not plan to bed down in one of the other trail shelters. They are for emergency use only—for first-aid or protection in a severe storm.

▲ Hiking trails vary in length from less than a mile to a 95-mile segment of the Appalachian Trail. Many of the trailheads are located on Skyline Drive and in the developed area. Detailed hiking maps may be obtained at park headquarters, visitor centers, and entrance stations.

▲ Horseback riders and cross-country skiers follow old roads. All back-country users should come prepared for severe weather in the winter.

▲ To prevent bears from being attracted to campsites, food should be properly stored while camping in the backcountry or in the campgrounds.

▲ Overnight lodging and restaurants are at Skyland Lodge (Mileposts 41–43) and at Big Meadows Lodge (51.2) plus rental cottages at Lewis Mountain (57.5).

▲ Lodges, campstores, dining facilities, waysides, gift shops, gas stations, showers, washers, dryers, and stables are operated under contract with the National Park Service by a concessionaire. For information and reservations, phone: 1-800-999-4714.

▲ There are seven picnic areas with tables, fireplaces, water fountains and comfort stations. Locations: Dickey Ridge (Mile 4.6), Elkwallow (24.1), Pinnacles (36.7), Big Meadows (51), Lewis Mountain (57.5), South River (62.8), and Loft Mountain (79.5). Water is not available during wintertime weather. Dundo is open to picnicking November through March.

▲ Fishing for native brook trout provides a challenge. A Virginia license is required; a 5-day license is available at a park concession facility. The season runs from early April to mid-October. Some streams are closed to fishing; obtain a current list of open streams at one of the visitor centers or at park headquarters.

▲ Guided horseback trips are available from Skyland Lodge from April through October. Pony

Shenandoah National park (continued)

rides are also available for children. Reservations are recommended.

▲ Skyline Drive is a narrow, mountainous road providing beautiful vistas. The speed limit of 35 miles per hour allows a casual opportunity to enjoy the sights.

▲ Mountain weather is quite changeable. Come prepared for cold, wet conditions at any season. Summer days may be warm, but nights are cool. Fog may occur at any time.

▲ Most facilities close about November 1, but Skyline Drive remains open. The drive is closed during and after periods of bad wather, because of the buildup of ice and snow on the road.

Facilities & Activities

4 RV & tent campgrounds
   186 sites at Mathews Arm (closed for 1996)
   227 sites at Big Meadows
   31 sites at Lewis Mountain
   221 sites at Loft Mountain
sanitary dumps at 3 campgrounds
group campground at Dundo
backcountry camping
lodges/cabins/cottages
7 picnic areas
fishing
hiking/backpacking
5 self-guided nature trails
bicyclying
mountain/rock climbing
guided horseback trips
horse-drawn wagon ride
cross-country skiing
auto tour along the 105-mile Skyline Drive
restaurants/coffee shops/snacks
gift and craft shops/camp stores
ranger-led talks/walks
evening campfire programs
museum/exhibits/amphitheater
2 visitor centers

With more than 500 miles of trails, Shenandoah National Park is a hiker's paradise; they lead to numerous waterfalls, clear rushing streams, old home sites, and scenic vistas hidden below Skyline Drive.

Sky Meadows State Park

For Information

Sky Meadows State Park
Route 1, Box 540
Delaplane, VA 22025-9508
(703) 592-3556

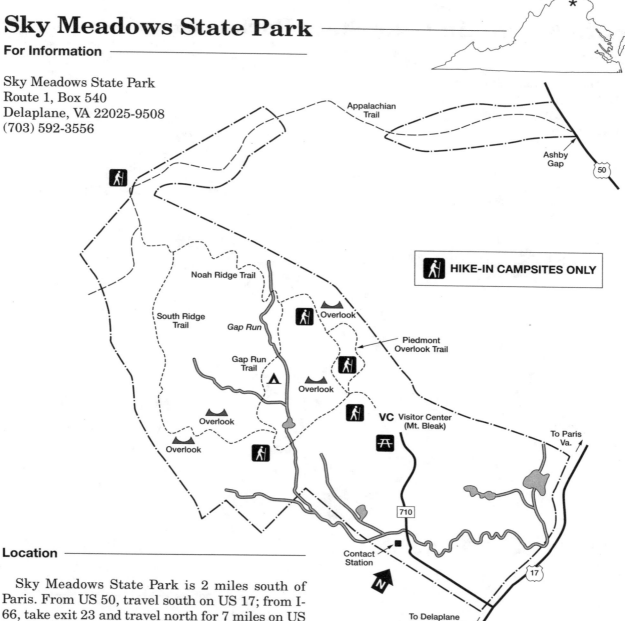

Appalachian Trail

Ashby Gap

50

HIKE-IN CAMPSITES ONLY

Noah Ridge Trail

South Ridge Trail

Gap Run

Overlook

Piedmont Overlook Trail

Gap Run Trail

Overlook

Overlook

Overlook

VC Visitor Center (Mt. Bleak)

To Paris Va.

710

Contact Station

To Delaplane and Warrenton, Va.

17

N

Location

Sky Meadows State Park is 2 miles south of Paris. From US 50, travel south on US 17; from I-66, take exit 23 and travel north for 7 miles on US 17. The park entrance is at Route 710. Located on the eastern side of the Blue Ridge Mountains, this 1,862-acre park has rolling pastures and woodlands, and scenic vistas. A 486-acre tract to the east of US 17 has been developed into an equestrian staging and bridle trails area. The park offers access to the Appalachian Trail; it is a 3-day hike to Harper's Ferry, WV, and 2 days to Shenandoah National Park.

Facilities & Activities

12 primitive hike-in campsites
   pit toilets
   non-potable water
   trail shelter

picnicking
   drinking water
   modern restrooms
freshwater fishing
6 hiking trails
access to the Appalachian Trail
1-mile nature trail
5 miles of bridle trails
11-stall horse barn with corral
interpretive programs
visitor center

Smith Mountain Lake State Park

For Information

Smith Mountain Lake State Park
Route 1, Box 41
Huddleston, VA 24104-9547
(703) 297-6066

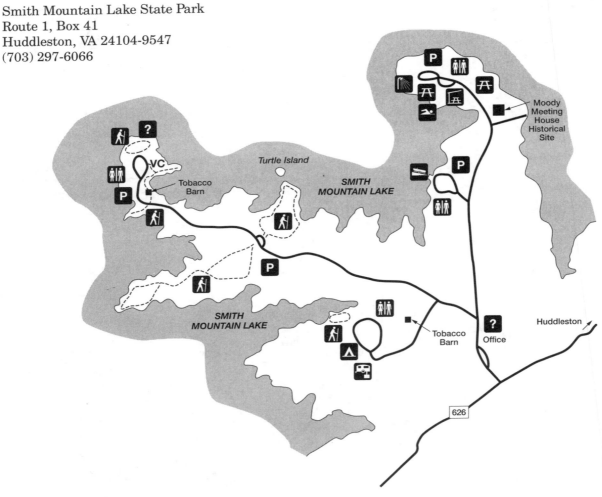

Location

This state park is located on the north shore of Smith Mountain Lake, about 40 miles from both Lynchburg and Roanoke. From US 460 at Bedford, travel south on either Route 122 or Route 43. If on Route 122, turn left on Route 608, then right on Route 626; if on Route 43, turn right on Route 626. This 1,506-acre park includes 16 miles of lake frontage and has access to a 20,000-acre lake, the second largest body of water in the state. The 500-foot-long beach is Smith Mountain Lake's only public swimming beach. The visitor center features exhibits on the history and folklore of the area and the lake's aquatic environment.

Facilities & Activities

50 primitive campsites
   pit toilets
   central water supply
dump station
picnicking/shelter
   drinking water
   modern restrooms
snack bar
lake swimming & bathhouse
freshwater fishing
boating (motor boats permitted)
boat ramp
paddleboat rentals
5 hiking trails
interpretive programs
visitor center

Staunton River State Park

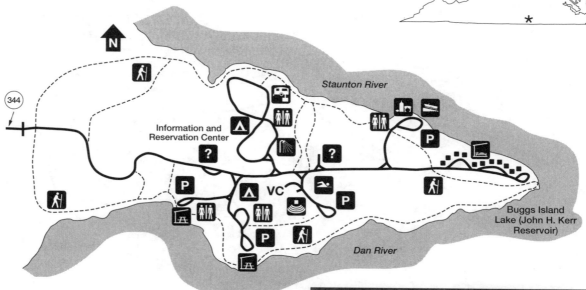

For Information

Staunton River State Park
Route 2, Box 295
Scottsburg, VA 24589-9636
(804) 572-4623

Location

Staunton River State Park is located 18 miles east of South Boston on a lengthy shoreline on the 48,000-acre Kerr Reservoir, also known as Buggs Island Lake. To reach the park from South Boston, travel northeast on US 360 to Route 344; turn right and follow Route 344 for 10 miles to the park. The park takes its name from the river that borders this 1,597-acre park. From 1933 to 1935 a unit of the Civilian Conservation Corps (CCC) built most of the buildings and facilities that are still seen today at the park. Buggs Island Lake was formed with the construction of the Kerr Dam in 1952. Over 150 acres of the original park were flooded, leaving some structures completely underwater.

Most of the buildings and facilities that are still seen today at Staunton River State Park were built by the Civilian Conservation Corps (CCC). This swimming pool was probably one of their projects.

Facilities & Activities

46 campsites
showers
dump station
group camping
7 housekeeping cabins (1-room, 1-bedroom;
    2-bedroom)
picnicking/shelters

snack bar
swimming pool & bathhouse
freshwater fishing
boating (motor and non-motorized)
boat ramp/dock
canoe/paddleboat/rowboat rentals
6 hiking trails
store
interpretive programs
visitor center

Twin Lakes State Park

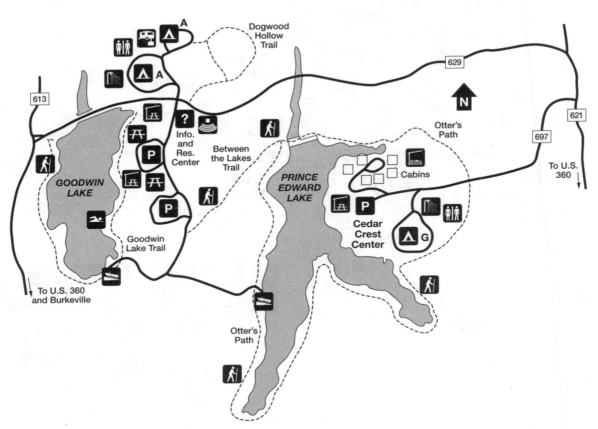

Dogwood Hollow Trail

Info. and Res. Center

Between the Lakes Trail

GOODWIN LAKE

Goodwin Lake Trail

PRINCE EDWARD LAKE

Otter's Path

Cedar Crest Center

Cabins

To U.S. 360

To U.S. 360 and Burkeville

Otter's Path

For Information

Twin Lakes State Park
Route 2, Box 70
Green Bay, VA 23942-9544
(804) 392-3435
(804) 767-2398 Cedar Crest Conference Center

Location

Twin Lakes State Park is located southeast of Farmville in the heart of Prince Edward-Gallion State Forest. From Burkeville, travel 5 miles southwest on US 360 to Route 613; go north on Route 613, then east on Route 629. Two parks, Goodwin Lake and Prince Edward Lake, were founded in 1939, and until the 1960's were run as 2 separate parks. As a result, Twin Lakes State Park has virtually 2 complete sets of facilities. The parks merged in 1976 and were renamed Twin Lakes State Park in 1986. Cedar Crest Conference Center, located on the east side of Prince Edward Lake, is available for family reunions, business meetings, receptions, etc. on a reservation basis.

Facilities & Activities

33 campsites
showers
dump station
Cedar Crest Center (90-person capacity)
    cabins, lodge, 20 campsites, pavilion, shelters,
    gazebo, swimming beach
picnicking/shelters
snack bar
lake swimming & bathhouse
freshwater fishing
boating (non-gasoline powered)
boat ramps
paddleboat/rowboat rentals
6 miles of hiking trails
bicycle trails/rentals
interpretive programs

Westmoreland State Park

For Information

Westmoreland State Park
Route 1, Box 600
Montross, VA 22520-9717
(804) 493-8821

Location

Located on the Northern Neck Peninsula, this park extends about 1½ miles along the Potomac River. The park is 6 miles northwest of Montross on Route 347, just off Route 3. Route 3 is accessible south from US 301 or north from US 360. The park was built in the 1930s by the Civilian Conservation Corps (CCC); its 1,299 acres neighbor the former homes of both George Washington and Robert E. Lee. The park's Horsehead Cliffs provide visitors with a spectacular view of the Potomac River.

Facilities & Activities

118 campsites
   40 with electrical/water hookups
showers
dump station
20 group campsites
24 housekeeping cabins (1-room; 1-bedroom;
   2-bedroom)
6 overnight cabins
picnicking/shelters
snack bar
swimming pool & bathhouse
saltwater fishing
boating (motor boats permitted)
boathouse (gas/ice/bait/fishing supplies)
boat ramp

Westmoreland State Park extends about 1 1/2 miles along the Potomac River. The river is not conducive to swimming, so the park's facilities include a swimming pool and bathhouse.

paddleboat/rowboat rentals
7 hiking trails (6.1 miles)
camp store/restaurant
interpretive programs
visitor center

West Virginia

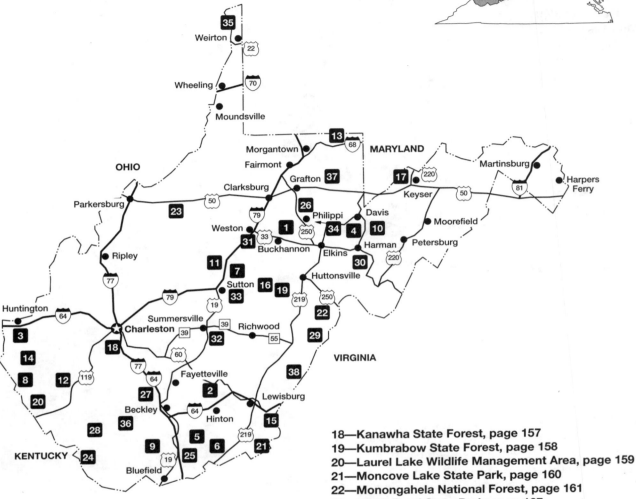

1—Audra State Park, page 139
2—Babcock State Park, page 140
3—Beech Fork State Park, page 142
4—Blackwater Falls State Park, page 143
5—Bluestone State Park, page 144
6—Bluestone Lake Wildlife Managment Area,
    page 145
7—Burnsville Lake, page 146
8—Cabwaylingo State Forest, page 147
9—Camp Creek State Park, page 148
10—Canaan Valley Resort State Park, page 149
11—Cedar Creek State Park, page 150
12—Chief Logan State Park, page 151
13—Coopers Rock State Forest, page 152
14—East Lynn Lake, page 153
15—Greenbrier State Forest, page 154
16—Holly River State Park, page 155
17—Jennings Randolph Lake, page 156

18—Kanawha State Forest, page 157
19—Kumbrabow State Forest, page 158
20—Laurel Lake Wildlife Management Area, page 159
21—Moncove Lake State Park, page 160
22—Monongahela National Forest, page 161
23—North Bend State Park, page 167
24—Panther State Forest, page 168
25—Pipestem Resort State Park, page 169
26—Pleasant Creek Wildlife Management Area,
    page 170
27—Plum Orchard Lake Wildlife Managment Area,
    page 171
28—R. D. Bailey Lake, page 172
29—Seneca State Forest, page 173
30—Spruce Knob-Seneca Rocks National Recreation
    Area, page 174
31—Stonewall Jackson Lake State Park, page 177
32—Summersville Lake, page 178
33—Sutton Lake, page 179
34—Teter Creek Lake Wildlife Management Area,
    page 180
35—Tomlinson Run State Park, page 181
36—Twin Falls Resort State Park, page 182
37—Tygart Lake State Park, page 183
38—Watoga State Park, page 184

Audra State Park

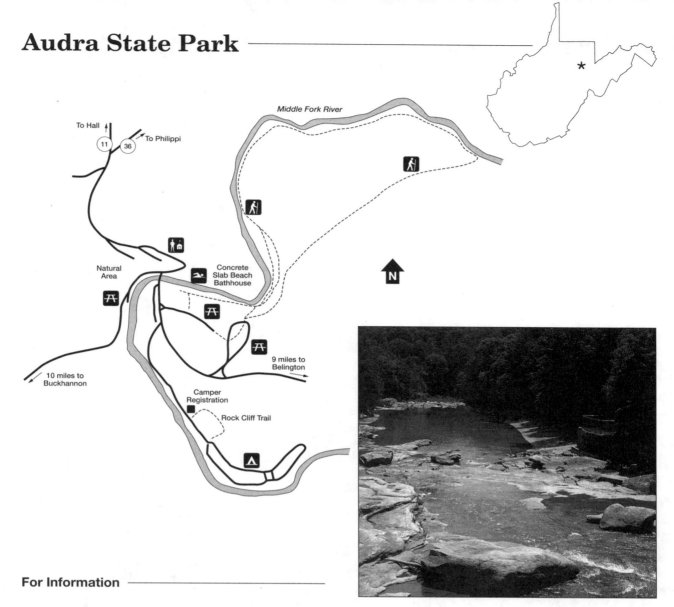

The Middle Fork River is the focus of Audra State Park; visitors swim off the concrete slab beach and hike the river through varied rock formations.

For Information

Audra State Park
Route 4, Box 564
Buckhannon, WV 26201
(304) 457-1162

Location

To reach Audra State Park travel north from Buckhannon on US 119 for about 12 miles, then east through Volga on County Road 11 for about 5 miles. This 355-acre park is nestled in forests and rhododendron thickets along the Middle Fork River; it gets its name from the Lithuanian word meaning "thunderstorm." Rains and snowmelt runoff thunders through the river's cataracts in spring. With riverside camping, river beach swimming and hiking trails through varied rock formations, the river is the focus of this park.

Facilities & Activities

65 tent/trailer sites
flush toilets/hot showers
dump station
picnicking
playground
game courts
snack bar
river swimming
concrete slab beach
bathhouse
hiking trails

Babcock State Park

For Information

Babcock State Park
HC 35, Box 150
Clifftop, WV 25831-9801
(304) 438-3004 (office)
(304) 438-3003 (cabins)

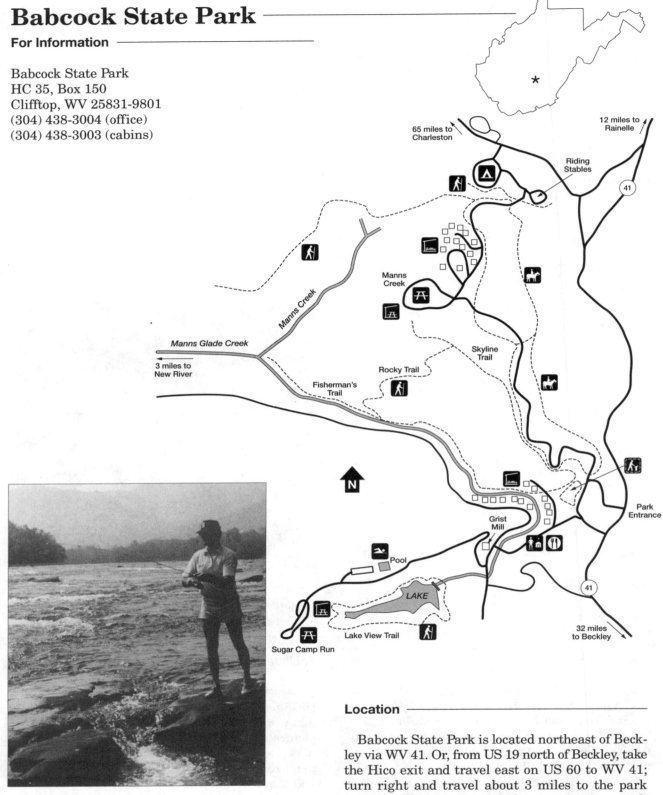

65 miles to
Charleston

12 miles to
Rainelle

Riding
Stables

41

Manns
Creek

Manns Creek

Manns Glade Creek

3 miles to
New River

Skyline
Trail

Rocky Trail

Fisherman's
Trail

N

Park
Entrance

Grist
Mill

Pool

LAKE

41

Lake View Trail

Sugar Camp Run

32 miles
to Beckley

A fisherman tries his luck in the boulder-strewn New River Gorge National River, adjacent to Babcock State Park's west boundary.

Location

Babcock State Park is located northeast of Beckley via WV 41. Or, from US 19 north of Beckley, take the Hico exit and travel east on US 60 to WV 41; turn right and travel about 3 miles to the park entrance. This 4,127-acre park is serene, yet rugged, with waterfalls, a fast flowing trout stream in a boulder-strewn canyon, and mountainous vistas. Whitewater rafting is popular on the New River Gorge

National River, adjacent to the park's west boundary. A reconstructed grist mill, located on Glade Creek, offers freshly-ground cornmeal, buckwheat, and whole wheat flour to park guests.

Facilities & Activities

51 tent/trailer sites
   27 sites with electric hookups
flush toilets/hot showers
dump station
18 standard cabins
6 economy cabins
picnicking
playground
refreshments
swimming pool
tennis/game courts
lake/stream fishing
boating/boat dock
canoe/paddleboat/rowboat rentals
20 miles of hiking trails
cross-country ski trails
horseback riding/bridle trails
rental horses/riding stables
restaurant
seasonal nature/recreation program
fully operable grist mill

Babcock State Park has an extensive trail system—20 miles of hiking trails, cross-country ski trails, and horseback riding trails. There are riding stables, and horses may be rented. Visitors to the park from late spring through early summer are treated to the colorful display of the two varieties of rhododendron, with which the park abounds.

Beech Fork State Park

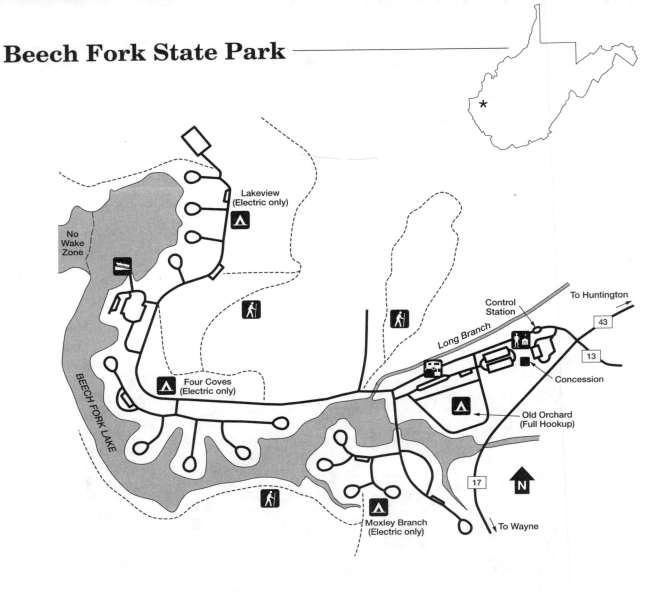

For Information

Beech Fork State Park
5601 Long Branch Road
Barboursville, WV 25504
(304) 522-0303

Location

Beech Fork State Park is located 8 miles southeast of Huntington; from I-64, take exit 11 onto Hughes Branch Road and travel south. Located at the upper end of Beech Fork Lake, this 3,981-acre park is surrounded by an additional 10,000 acres of public hunting land. In the summertime, the lake covers 760 acres and extends for 8 miles up Beech Fork. There is a 10-horsepower limit on all motors operated on the lake.

Facilities & Activities

275 tent/trailer sites with electric hookups
   49 sites with full hookups
flush toilets/hot showers
dump station
picnicking/shelters
playground
refreshments
tennis/game courts
lake fishing/fishing pier
boat launch ramp
boating/boat rentals
hiking/fitness trails
store
seasonal nature/recreation program
visitor center

Blackwater Falls State Park

For Information

Blackwater Falls State Park
Drawer 490
Davis, WV 26260
(304) 259-5216

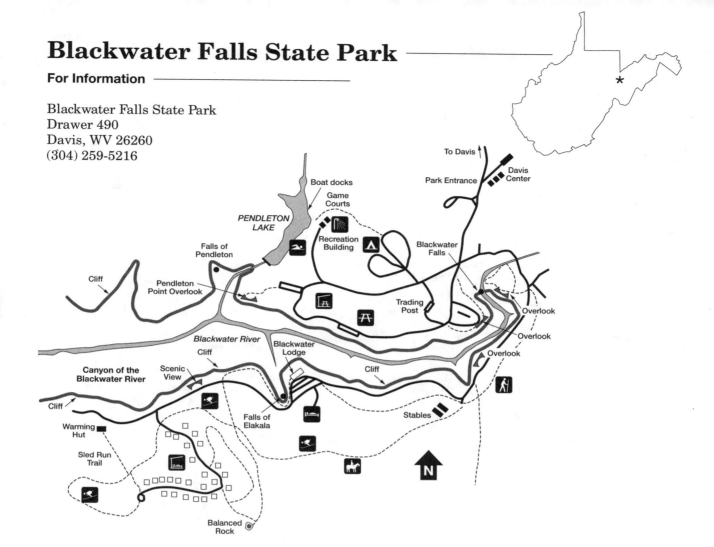

Location

This state park is located in the scenic, mountainous Potomac Highlands area. When approaching the park from the north, travel south on WV 32 from US 219 at Thomas; from the south, travel north on WV 32 from US 33 at Harman. The park is named for the falls of the Blackwater River, whose waters plunge 5 stories, then tumble through an 8-mile-long gorge. Numerous observation points provide panoramic views of the half-mile wide canyon. The extensive network of cross-country ski trails and the four-season nature/recreation program make this 1,688-acre park a popular year-round attraction.

Facilities & Activities

65 tent/trailer sites
   30 sites with electric hookups
flush toilets/hot showers
dump station
25 modern cabins
55-room lodge
conference facilities
picnicking
playground
snack bar
lake swimming
tennis/game courts
boating/boat docks
paddleboat/rowboat rentals
hiking trails
Nordic Ski Center
cross-country ski trails/guided tours/rentals
sled runs with rope tows
rental sleds/toboggans
horseback riding/bridle trails
rental horses/riding stables
restaurant
year-round nature/recreation program
nature center

Bluestone State Park

For Information

Bluestone State Park
Box 3, Athens Star Route
Hinton, WV 25951
(304) 466-2805

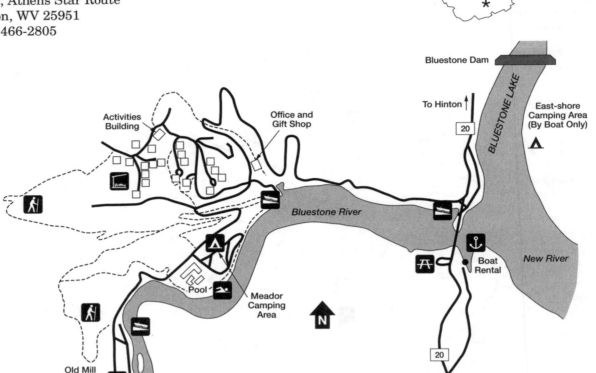

Location

Bluestone State Park is adjacent to the nearly 2,000-acre Bluestone Lake, the state's third largest body of water. The park is accessible by several major highways. From I-64, take exit 139 (Sandstone/Hinton) and travel south on WV 20 for 15 miles to the park; from I-77, take exit 14 (Athens Road) to WV 20 and travel north for 22 miles. The park encompasses 2,155 acres of rugged, heavily forested, mountainous terrain. Due to the proximity of Bluestone Lake, water-related activities are an important facet of the park's recreational program.

Facilities & Activities

32 tent/trailer sites at Meador Campground
   22 sites with electric hookups
   flush toilets/hot showers

   dump station
47 tent/trailer sites at Old Mill Campground
   flush toilets/cold showers
50 primitive sites at East Shore Camping Area
   accessible only by boat
   pit toilets, no drinking water
25 modern cabins
picnicking
playground
game courts
refreshments
swimming pool
lake fishing
boating/launch ramps
marina
canoe/rowboat/motor boat rentals
hiking trails
seasonal nature/recreation program

Bluestone Lake Wildlife Management Area

For Information

Bluestone Lake Wildlife Management Area
HC-65, Box 91
Indian Mills, WV 24935
(304) 466-3398

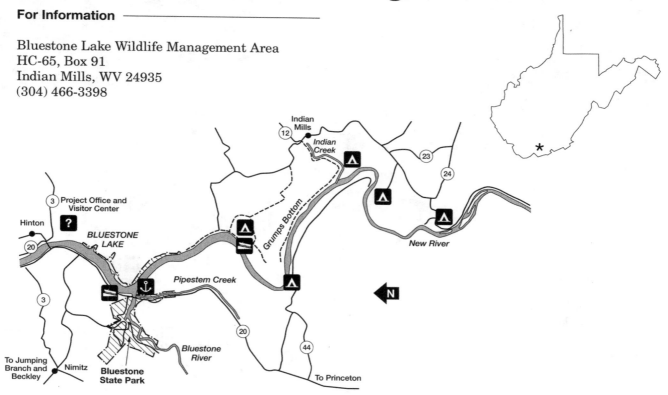

Location

This wildlife management area is located south of Hinton along the banks of Bluestone Lake and the New River; in the northern portion, WV 20 parallels the area along the west bank. Topography in this 17,632-acre WMA ranges from flat bottomlands to rolling uplands, steep mountains and cliffs; New River divides the area. Designated primitive campsites are available along the river; some are available only by boat, others by boat or vehicle. Five of the larger camping areas available by vehicle include: Bertha, Bull Falls, Indian Creek, Cedar Branch, and Shanklins Ferry. Contact either the Bluestone Lake WMA at Indian Mills, or the US Army Corps of Engineers' Bluestone Lake Project Office and Visitor Center at Hinton for a map showing the campground locations.

Facilities & Activities

300 primitive campsites
pit toilets
picnic tables
fishing
boating/boat launch
hiking trails
horseback riding

From this fishing platform near the launch ramp at the state park, the Hwy. 20 river bridge and Bluestone Lake are visible; portions of the WMA lie on either side of the lake.

Burnsville Lake

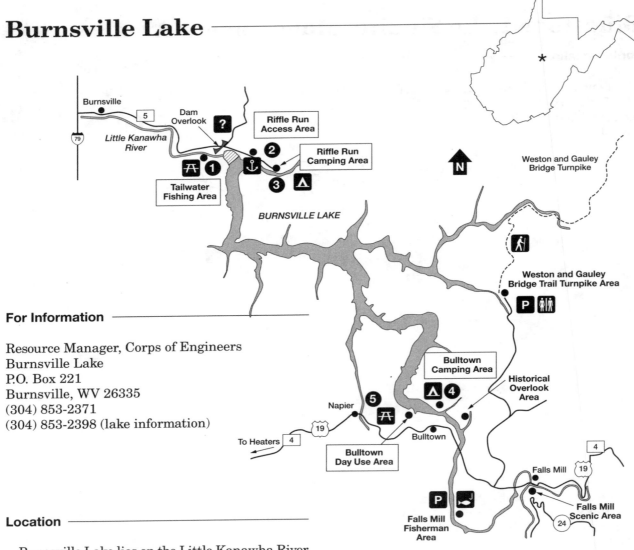

For Information

Resource Manager, Corps of Engineers
Burnsville Lake
P.O. Box 221
Burnsville, WV 26335
(304) 853-2371
(304) 853-2398 (lake information)

Location

Burnsville Lake lies on the Little Kanawha River in the quiet countryside of Braxton County between I-79, which passes through Burnsville 3 miles below the dam, and scenic Falls Mill on winding US 19, nine miles above the dam. Flood control has priority. Beginning about April 1, the lake is raised 13 feet to elevation 789, providing 968 surface acres for the summer season. After October 1 each year, a gradual drop of 13 feet provides additional storage space for flood runoff. Whenever necessary, the Corps may store excess runoff up to the maximum elevation of 825.

Nine recreation areas offer a variety of facilities; two of the areas offer camping. Riffle Run Camping Area is reached by taking exit 79 off I-79 at Burnsville. Bulltown Camping Area is northwest of Falls Mill off Millstone Run Road from US 19. As part of the Burnsville Lake development, the Corps set aside several log structures, common to a traditional Appalachian farm, for reassembly in the Bulltown Historic Area.

Facilities & Activities	(1) Tailwater Fishing Area	(2) Riffle Run Access Area	(3) Riffle Run Camping Area	(4) Bulltown Camping Area	(5) Bulltown Day Use Area
campsites			54	204	
restrooms	•	•	•	•	•
showers			•	•	
sanitary dump			•	•	
picnic area	•	•			•
swimming					•
fishing	•				
marina		•			
launching ramp		•		•	•

Cabwaylingo State Forest

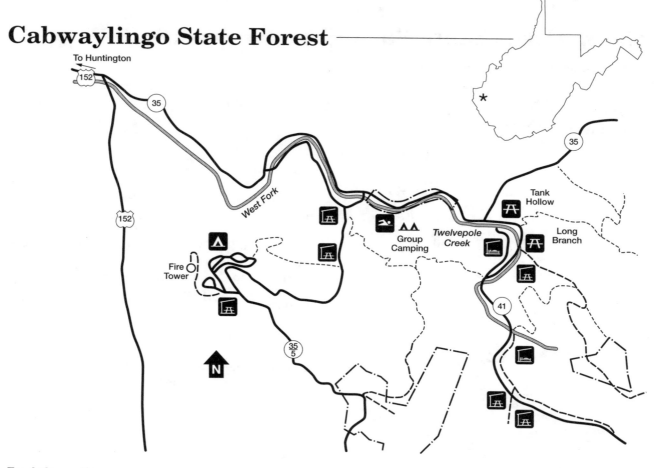

To Huntington

West Fork

Fire Tower

Group Camping

Twelvepole Creek

Tank Hollow

Long Branch

N

For Information

Cabwaylingo State Forest
Route 1, Box 85
Dunlow, WV 25511
(304) 385-4255

Location

To reach Cabwaylingo State Forest, travel 4 miles south of Dunlow on US 152, then east on WV 35. Although its name sounds like an Indian word, this 8,123-acre state forest is actually named for the 4-county area it serves: CABell, WAYne, LINcoln, and MinGO. Visitors may choose from among 3 types of accommodations: standard cabins, camping, or a group camp. Terrain is hilly to steep with gentle slopes in bottomlands and ridgetops. The West Fork of Twelve Pole Creek provides trout fishing.

Facilities & Activities

34 tent/trailer sites
hot showers
pit toilets
dump station
group camp (capacity 100)

The campground at Cabwaylingo State Forest has several picnic shelters like the one pictured here. They're neat!

13 standard cabins
picnicking
playground
swimming pool
fishing
hiking trails

Camp Creek State Park

For Information

Camp Creek State Park
P.O. Box 119
Camp Creek, WV 25820
(304) 425-9481

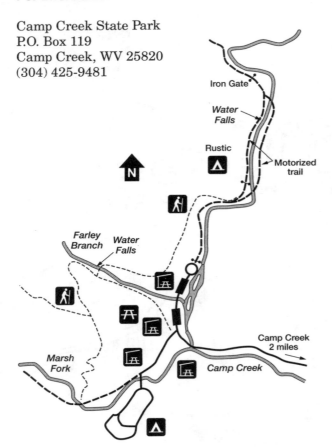

Location

Camp Creek State Park is located south of Beckley just off US 19. From I-77, take exit 20 onto US 19 and travel west to Camp Creek; turn right and continue for 2 miles to the park entrance. This 500-acre park is adjacent to 5,300 acres of state forest lands. Camp Creek, from which the forest gets its name, is one of the best of the stocked trout streams in the area.

Facilities & Activities

25 tent/trailer sites with electric hookups
    flush toilets/hot showers
12 rustic tent/trailer sites
    pit toilets
dump station
picnicking/sheters
playground
game courts
stream fishing
hiking trails

Opportunities for hiking abound at Camp Creek. The 500-acre state park is adjacent to 5,300 acres of state forest lands.

Canaan Valley Resort State Park

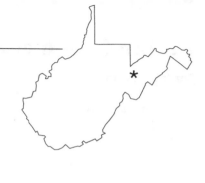

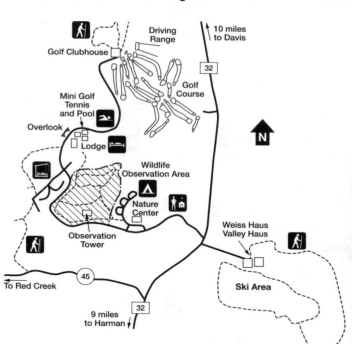

This four-season resort state park has 34 tent/trailer sites with full hookups.

For Information

Canaan Valley Resort State Park
Route 1, Box 330
Davis, WV 26260
(304) 866-4121

Location

Canaan Valley (pronounced Kah-nane') is located in the central Appalachian Mountains and is the highest valley east of the Mississippi River at 3,200 feet. Surrounding mountain peaks rise above 4,200 feet, offering spectacular, rugged scenery. This 6,015-acre park is located 10 miles south of Davis on WV 32. When approaching the park from the north, travel south on WV 32 from US 219 at Thomas; from the south, travel north on WV 32 from US 33 at Harman. One of West Virginia's finest four-season recreation and convention centers, Canaan Valley is the park system's major winter sports area.

Facilities & Activities

34 tent/trailer sites with full hookups
flush toilets/hot showers
dump station
15 modern cabins
250-room lodge
conference facilities
restaurant/snack bar
18-hole golf course/pro shop
indoor & outdoor swimming pools
lighted tennis courts/minature golf
playground
fitness center with saunas and hot tub
fishing
hiking trails
7.9-mile portion of Allegheny Trail
bicycling/bicycle rentals
ski resort
downhill skiing/year-round chairlifts
18 miles of cross-country ski trails
alpine/cross-country ski rentals
ice skating/skate rentals
year-round nature/recreation program

Cedar Creek State Park

For Information

Cedar Creek State Park
Route 1, Box 9
Glenville, WV 26351
(304) 462-7158

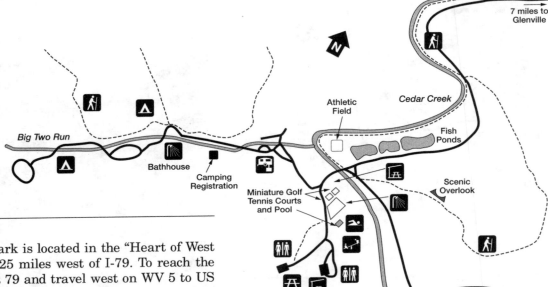

Location

This state park is located in the "Heart of West Virginia" just 25 miles west of I-79. To reach the park, take exit 79 and travel west on WV 5 to US 33/119, turn left and continue 3 miles southwest of Glenville to WV 31, turn left and follow signs to the park entrance. This 2,443-acre park includes a meandering brook and fishing ponds in a pastoral setting of rolling hills and flat valleys. The park features a reconstructed one-room schoolhouse, which was erected as a testimonial to the early years of education.

Facilities & Activities

46 tent/trailer sites
  35 sites with electric hookups
flush toilets/hot showers
dump station
1 group campsite
picnicking/shelter
playground
athletic field
refreshments
swimming pool
tennis courts/miniature golf
stream fishing
boat rentals
hiking trails
bicycling
camp store
seasonal nature/recreation program
historical landmarks

This state park has 3 fishing ponds; boats are available for rental.

Chief Logan State Park

For Information

Chief Logan State Park
Logan, WV 25601
(304) 792-7125
(304) 752-0253 ("Aracoma Story")

Location

Chief Logan State Park is located 4 miles north of Logan on US 119 and WV 10. The park encompasses 3,303 acres of beautiful mountain terrain and is home to a variety of summer musicals, including "The Aracoma Story," a historical drama based on a local Indian legend. The drama is presented every summer at the park's amphitheater with local talent providing the nucleus of the cast. In spring, the many miles of hiking trails are surrounded by colorful wildflowers, among them the delicate Guyandotte Beauty, a rare endangered species.

Facilities & Activities

25 tent/trailer sites
  14 sites with full hookups
flush toilets/hot showers
dump station
picnicking/shelters
playground
game courts
refreshments
swimming pool/water slide/bathhouse
lighted tennis courts/minature golf
lake fishing
hiking/fitness trails
interpretive trail
restaurant
summer musicals/amphitheater

This water slide at Chief Logan, used by young and old alike, is so much fun!!

Coopers Rock State Forest

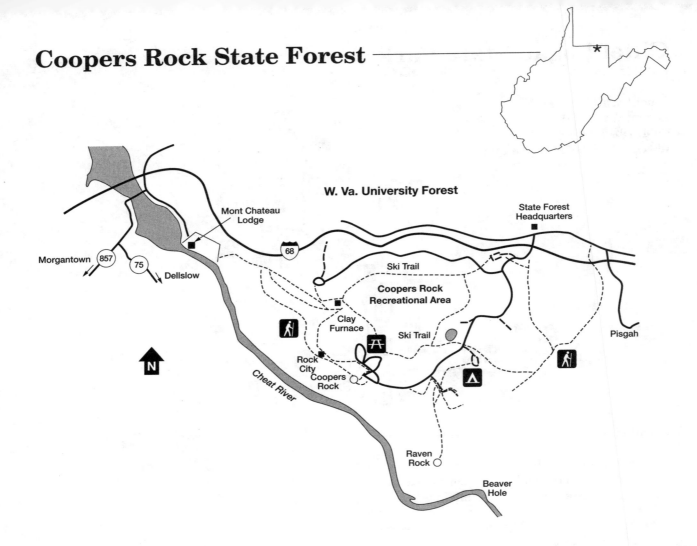

For Information

Coopers Rock State Forest
Route 1, Box 270
Bruceton Mills, WV 26525
(304) 594-1561

Location

Coopers Rock State Forest is located on I-68, about 13 miles east of Morgantown and 8 miles west of Bruceton Mills; it is the largest state forest, providing 12,713 acres for recreation. The forest is bisected by I-68: the side north of I-68, known as the WVU Forest, is leased by the West Virginia University Division of Forestry for forestry research, teaching, and demonstration; the main recreation area is to the south of I-68. Forested mountainous terrain with gently sloping areas on ridgetops, scenic overlooks and unusual rock formations are special aspects of this forest. The historic Henry Clay Iron Furnace, used for the making of iron products in the early 1800s, is located within the forest boundaries. The most popular destination within the forest is to the Main Overlook to view the beautiful 1,200 foot-deep and 1 mile-wide Cheat River gorge.

Facilities & Activities

24 tent/trailer sites
flush toilets/hot showers
picnicking
playground
fishing
23 miles of hiking trails
rock climbing
cross-country ski trails
trading post/snack bar

East Lynn Lake

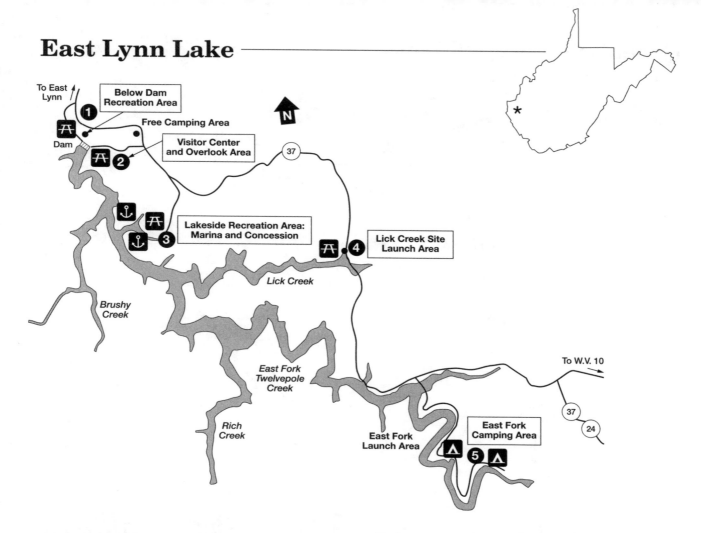

For Information

Resource Manager, Corps of Engineers
East Lynn Lake
East Lynn, WV 25512
(304) 849-2355

Location

This lake was primarily constructed for flood control and fish and wildlife conservation, as well as for general recreation. It is 12 miles long and located on the East Fork of Twelvepole Creek, some 10 miles north of Wayne. During the warmer months, April through October, the lake level is maintained at elevation 662 feet above sea level. From November through March, the level is kept 6 feet lower to provide additional storage area for any excess rainfall.

The East Fork Camping Area is 17 miles southeast of Wayne off of WV 37, then 2 miles on East

Fork access road. The Environmental Center has exhibits and programs; it is located in the Overlook Area near the dam. The Lakeside Marina offers boat and motor repairs, equipment and dock space rentals, fuel, fishing supplies, and a snack bar.

Facilities & Activities	(1) Below Dam	(2) Visitor Center	(3) Lakeside	(4) Lick Creek	(5) East Fork
campsites					172
restrooms	•	•	•	•	•
drinking water	•	•	•	•	•
sanitary dump					•
picnic table/fireplaces	•	•	•	•	•
playground	•		•		•
foot trails		•	•	•	•
launching ramp			•	•	•
marina			•		

Greenbrier State Forest

For Information

Greenbrier State Forest
HC-30, Box 154
Caldwell, WV 24925-9709
(304) 536-1944

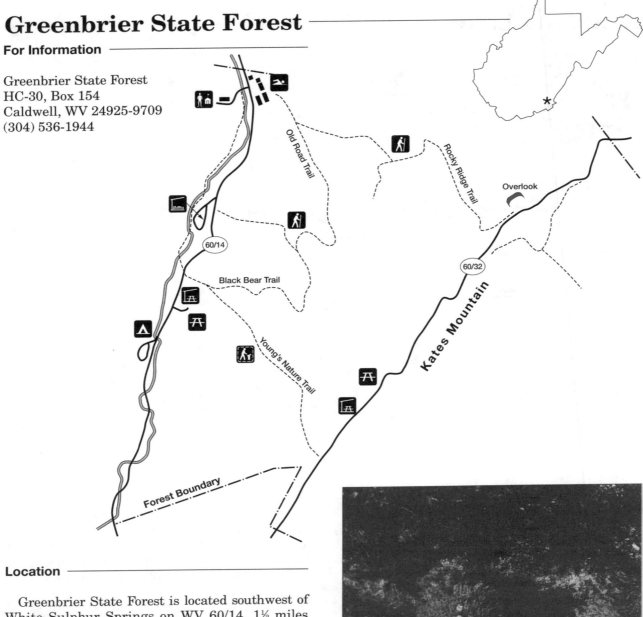

Location

Greenbrier State Forest is located southwest of White Sulphur Springs on WV 60/14, 1½ miles south of exit 175 from I-64. This 5,130-acre state forest offers some of the quaintest guest cabins in the state. Mountainous terrain, covered with mature hardwood forests, is dominated by 3,388-ft Kates Mountain. History buffs will be fascinated by the many quaint antebellum homes in virtually unchanged settings in nearby Lewisburg.

Like other state forests, this campground has hiking trails, but it also has a fitness trail.

Facilities & Activities

16 campsites with electric hookups
flush toilets/hot showers
12 standard cabins
picnicking
playground
game courts

swimming pool
hiking/fitness trails
gift shop
seasonal nature/recreation program

Holly River State Park

For Information

Holly River State Park
P.O. Box 70
Hacker Valley, WV 26222
(304) 493-6353

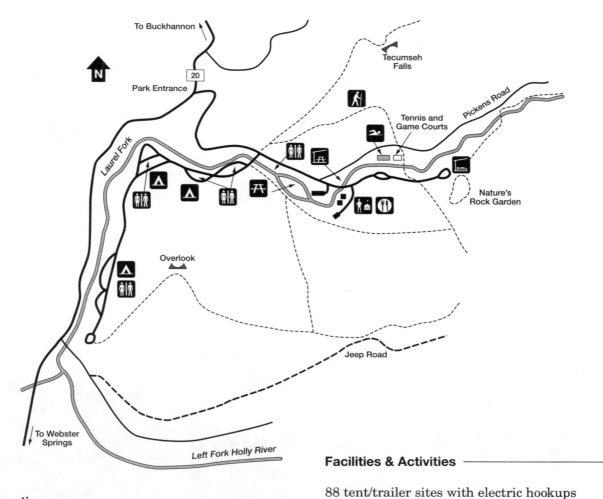

Location

Located on WV 20, 32 miles south of Buckhannon and 20 miles north of Webster Springs, this 8,292-acre park is east of I-79; there are several points of access to WV 20 from I-79. The park is nestled in a narrow valley and surrounded by heavily forested mountains, some reaching heights of over 2,800 feet. The area is known for its heavy rainfall that provides for the lush forest growth and wide range of flora. This rainfall also accounts for the cool streams that course through the boulder-strewn beds of Left Fork and Laurel Fork, tributaries of the river for which the park is named.

Facilities & Activities

88 tent/trailer sites with electric hookups
flush toilets/hot showers
dump station
1 group campsite
9 standard cabins
picnicking/shelter
playground
refreshments
swimming pool
tennis/game courts
stream fishing
hiking trails—overnight backpacking available
groceries
restaurant
seasonal nature/recreation program

Jennings Randolph Lake

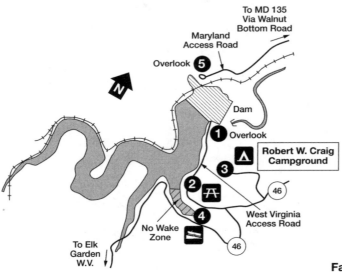

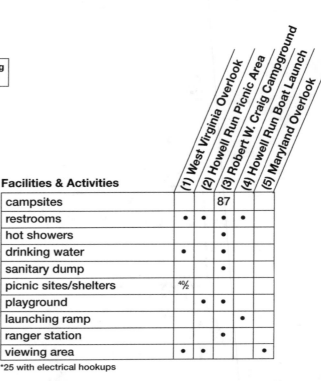

For Information

Resource Manager, Corps of Engineers
Jennings Randolph Lake
P.O. Box 247
Elk Garden, WV 26717
(301) 355-2346

Location

    Jennings Randolph Lake is located on the North Branch Potomac River about 8 miles upstream of Bloomington, Maryland and about 5 miles north of Elk Garden, West Virginia. The full recreation lake has a surface area of 952 acres, a shoreline of 13.6 miles, and extends upstream from the dam a distance of 5.5 miles. The lake is one-half mile wide at its widest point. The project covers an area of 2,700 acres in Maryland, and 1,800 acres in West Virginia.

    The recreation areas in West Virginia include a scenic overlook, picnic area, boat launch, and the Robert W. Craig Campground; these areas are all accessible from WV 46. The overlook area contains a two-tier visitor center; it is also the site of the Waffle Rock—a unique geological feature with a geometrical pattern resembling that of a waffle. The campground is situated on a high ridge overlooking the dam site; a ¾-mile long interpretive trails has been developed in the area to provide campers with a leisurely walk through the surrounding woods.

Facilities & Activities	(1) West Virginia Overlook	(2) Howell Run Picnic Area	(3) Robert W. Craig Campground	(4) Howell Run Boat Launch	(5) Maryland Overlook
campsites			87		
restrooms	•	•	•	•	
hot showers			•		
drinking water	•		•		
sanitary dump			•		
picnic sites/shelters	⁴⁰⁄₂				
playground		•	•		
launching ramp				•	
ranger station			•		
viewing area	•	•			•

*25 with electrical hookups

Jennings Randolph Lake is situated along the border of Maryland and West Virginia. The boat launch is accessible from WV 46.

Kanawha State Forest

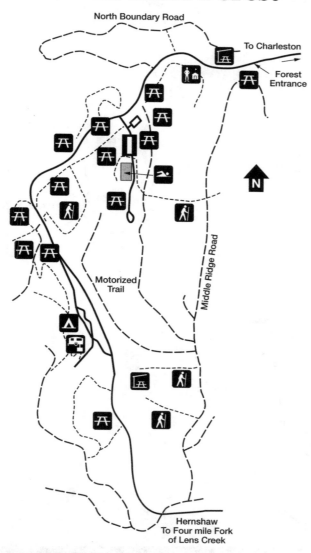

For Information

Kanawha State Forest
Route 2, Box 285
Charleston, WV 25314
(304) 346-5654

Location

Kanawha State Forest is located 11 miles south of Charleston; from exit 58-A off I-64, follow WV 214 to the second traffic light. Take a left and follow Kanawha State Forest signs. Terrain ranges from stream bottoms to moderate slopes covered with mixed hardwoods. Its close proximity to Charleston and the heavily populated Kanawha Valley has made this state forest a recreational haven. Some of the state's most used picnic areas are here, along with significant hiking and cross-country skiing opportunities. This 9,302-acre state forest is the location of the "Spotted Salamander" trail—a paved, level trail with Braille interpretive nature stations designed for both blind and wheelchair-bound visitors.

Facilities & Activities

46 tent/trailer sites
  25 with electric/water hookups
  21 rustic
flush toilets/hot showers
dump station
group campsites
picnicking
playground
swimming pool
fishing
shooting range
hiking trails
cross-country ski trails
horseback riding
snack bar/commissary

The campground at Kanawha State Forest has 21 rustic campsites; it also has 25 campsites with hookups.

Kumbrabow State Forest

For Information

Kumbrabow State Forest
P.O. Box 65
Huttonsville, WV 26273
(304) 335-2219

Location

Kumbrabow State Forest is located south of Elkins; from US 219 just south of Elkwater travel west for 4 miles. Or, from WV 15 at Monterville, travel north for about 4 miles. This 9,474-acre state forest is primarily forested mountainous terrain. If you shy away from developed areas and seek out rugged, wild country, then Kumbrabow is for you. The forest was named for three prominent families who were instrumental in its early development—KUMp, BRAdy and BOWers.

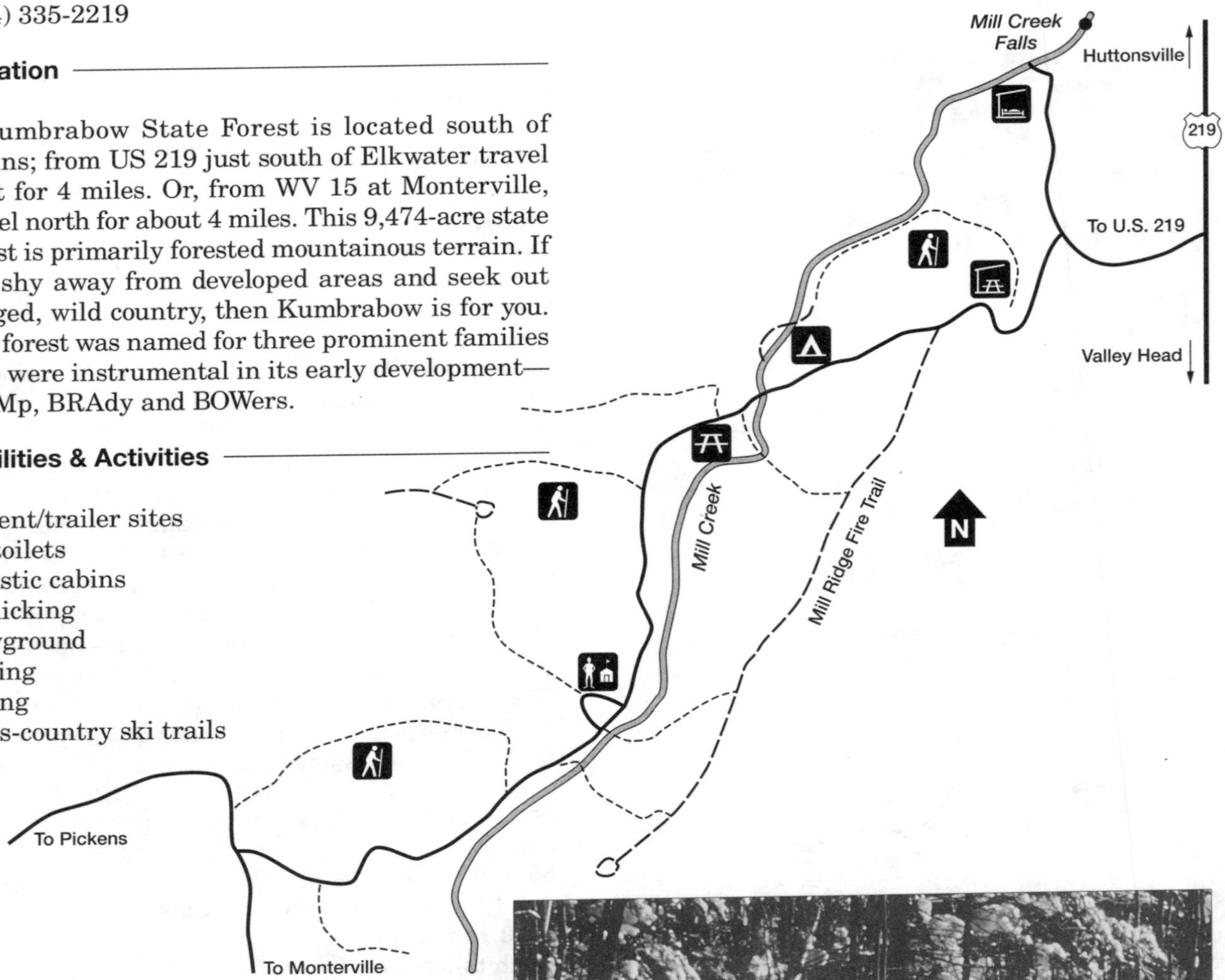

Facilities & Activities

13 tent/trailer sites
pit toilets
5 rustic cabins
picnicking
playground
fishing
hiking
cross-country ski trails

Dense forests in a mountainous terrain provide a true wilderness experience at Kumbrabow. When the snow falls, hiking gives way to cross-country skiing.

Laurel Lake Wildlife Management Area

For Information

Laurel Lake Wildlife Management Area
Route 1, Box 626
Lenore, WV 25676
(304) 475-2823

This charming bridge across Laurel Fork almost seems out of place, because the WMA comprises such rugged terrain.

Location

Laurel Lake Wildlife Management Area is located off WV 65, 12 miles northeast from Lenore with access via County Road 3/5. This 12,854-acre WMA comprises rugged terrain with steep slopes, and narrow ridges and valleys. The heart of this area is a narrow valley cradled by hills up to 1,700 feet above sea level supporting deciduous forests. Only electric motors may be used on the 29-acre lake. A 40 × 70-ft filtered swimming pool is located near the lake.

Facilities & Activities

25 tent/trailer sites
flush toilets/hot showers
fireplace or grill
picnic tables
trailer dump
playground/game courts
swimming pool
fishing
boating/boat launch/rentals
skeet range
hiking trails

Moncove Lake State Park

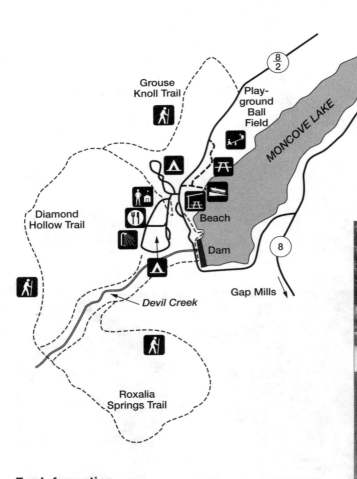

5 miles to Glace

Grouse Knoll Trail

Play-ground Ball Field

MONCOVE LAKE

8/2

8

N

Diamond Hollow Trail

Beach

Dam

8

Gap Mills

Devil Creek

Roxalia Springs Trail

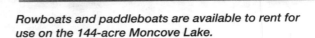

Rowboats and paddleboats are available to rent for use on the 144-acre Moncove Lake.

For Information

Moncove Lake State Park
P.O. Box 224
Gap Mills, WV 24941
(304) 772-3450

Location

   This state park was formerly a part of Moncove Lake Wildlife Management Area. The campground and recreational facilities were designated a state park in 1991. The 896-acre park is located east of Union; from US 219, follow WV 3 east for 9 miles toward Gap Mills, then 6 miles north on WV 8. Oak-hickory forest covers most of the area, which ranges from gently rolling hills to steep mountain sides with elevations from 2,503 to 3,100 feet. The 144-acre Moncove Lake provides swimming, warmwater fishing, and boating; boats are restricted to electric trolling motors or up to a 5-hp gasoline motor.

Facilities & Activities

50 tent/trailer sites
flush toilets/hot showers
dump station
2 group campsites
picnicking
playground/game courts
snack bar
lake swimming/beach
lake fishing
boating/boat launch/dock
paddleboat/rowboat rental
15 miles of hiking trails
seasonal nature/recreation program

Monongahela National Forest

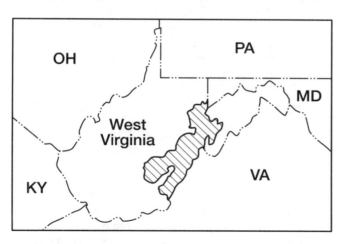

For Information

Forest Supervisor
Monongahela National Forest
200 Sycamore Street
Elkins, WV 26241
(304) 636-1800

Location

The Monongahela National Forest reclines against the eastern border of West Virginia. The Allegheny Front of the Appalachian Mountains forms the character of this 901,000-acre forest; the western side of the Front is moist while the eastern side is drier. The forest is administered by 6 ranger districts. US 33 and 250 traverse the forest east-west and US 219 runs north-south.

About the Forest

The Monongahela is the home to the headwaters of 5 major river streams and hundreds of miles of smaller streams. In the spring, during high water, some of the rivers may be run by whitewater enthusiasts. The lower summer flow is more suitable for lazy float trips or canoeing through scenic valleys. There are more than 700 miles of marked hiking trails, including 124 miles of the Allegheny Trail. Other recreational opportunities available to visitors include camping (primitive and developed), swimming, boating, fishing, rock climbing, and caving. In years of good snowfall, cross-country skiing is popular.

The highest point in West Virginia is located on the Monongahela National Forest in the Spruce Knob-Seneca Rocks National Recreation Area. Spruce Knob, the high point of Spruce Mountain,

rises to over 4,800 feet. The observation tower affords excellent views of the mountains to the east and west. The 100,000-acre National Recreation Area also includes Seneca Rocks, a 1,000-ft quartzite formation that rises above the North Fork Valley. Besides its interest to sightseers, Seneca Rocks is considered by many rock climbers to the best climb in the East.

Campsites are available at the following campgrounds through the National Recreation Reservation System (1-800-280-2267): Horseshoe and Stuart on the Cheat Ranger District; Big Bend and Seneca Shadows on the Potomac Ranger District; and Lake Sherwood on the White Sulphur Ranger District.

Information on **Spruce Knob-Senca Rocks National Recreation Area** appears on pages 174–176 rather than in this section. The Visitor Center, located near the intersection of US 33 and WV 28, provides information, exhibits on geology, history, rockclimbing, outdoor activities, and interpretive programs. It is open on weekends throughout the year and full-time during the summer season.

Wilderness Areas

The 35,864-acre **Cranberry Wilderness,** a part of the Allegheny Plateau, includes the entire drainage area of the Middle Fork of the Williams River and the North Fork of the Cranberry River. The mountains are broad, massive, and dissected by deep, narrow valleys. Elevation ranges from 2,400 feet to over 4,600 feet. Over 50 miles of maintained hiking trails are in or near the Wilderness.

Dolly Sods Wilderness is a 10,215-acre unroaded area high on the wind-swept plains on the Allegheny Plateau. At elevations of 2,600 to over 4,000 feet, the area has extensive flat rocky plains, upland bogs, and sweeping vistas. Red Creek and its tributaries have incised deep canyons into the plateau; several scenic waterfalls are along it course. There are over 25 miles of trails in the area.

The 12,200-acre **Laurel Fork Wilderness** combines the Laurel Fork North and South Wildernesses located along the headwaters of Laurel Fork. The Laurel Fork of the Cheat River is characterized

Monongahela National Forest (continued)

by its narrow valley floor with regularly dissected slopes and long narrow ridges. Numerous side streams occur along its length. Elevations vary from 2,900 feet to over 3,700 feet. The Laurel Fork campground is located between the Laurel Fork North Wilderness and the Laurel Fork South Wilderness, providing overnight camping opportunities as well as parking for day hikers.

The 20,000-acre **Otter Creek Wilderness,** a high, bowl-shaped basin, includes the entire drainage areas of Otter Creek and Shavers Lick Run. Nearly 50 miles of hiking trails are maintained; some lead along Otter Creek up to its origin, others along mountain ridges. The trails may be wet and muddy. Otter Creek usually is less than knee-deep where trails cross the streams, but it may be above the waist and fast-moving during high water following periods of prolonged rain. Extensive portions of the area are covered by nearly impenetrable strands of rhododendron, which make travel off the trails extremely difficult.

Special Notes

There are numerous points of interest on the Monongahela National Forest; the following are among them:

Highland Scenic Highway is a scenic drive featuring outstanding mountain and valley views in a remote area environment. The highway extends 44 miles from Richwood, follows WV 39/55 east to the Cranberry Mountain Visitor Center, then north on WV 150 to US 219 on Elk Mountain, 7 miles north of Marlinton. Azaleas, rhododendron, and abundant wild flowers are present along the roadside. Outstanding fall foliage displays are available in October. The 23 miles on WV 150 from the visitor center to US 219 is managed as a parkway; snow is not removed in the winter and this portion of the Scenic Highway is normally closed from mid-December to March.

Falls of Hills Creek Scenic Area, 16 miles east of Richwood on WV 39/55, is a 114-acre area that contains three waterfalls as Hills Creek drops over resistant sandstone ledges on its way to the Greenbrier River. A ¾-mile trail takes you 250 feet down a steep, narrow ravine to the three waterfalls. The lower waterfall is 63 feet high and is the second highest in West Virginia; the others are 25 feet and 45 feet high.

Cranberry Glades Botanical Area is about 20 miles east of Richwood on WV 39/55, then 2 miles north on a Forest Service Road. This 750-acre area

contains the largest area of bogs in West Virginia. Bogs are very wet, treeless areas whose plant and animal life is similar to that found in the Canadian bogs or "muskegs" of the North. The Glades consist of four bogs; a boardwalk has been constructed through two of the bogs so you can enjoy the area without disturbing this fragile community.

Cranberry Mountain Visitor Center, 21 miles east of Richwood on WV 39/55, provides exhibits and interpretive programs dealing with local ecology and history and is a source of information for the traveler. It is open daily during the summer and on weekends in May, September and part of October. A variety of movies and slide-tape programs are shown by request throughout the day.

Gaudineer Scenic Area is a remnant of a vast virgin spruce forest. The 140-acre primeval stand is about 300 years old. These spruce tower 100 feet and grow to 40 inches in diameter. To reach the area, travel west from Durbin on US 250 for 4 miles to FSR 27, then north on FSR 27 for 1½ miles to the Scenic Area.

Smoke Hole is a canyon through which the South Branch of the Potomac River flows for 20 miles; over half the distance is flanked by a quiet scenic road. The name refers to the caves along the mountainside where mist forms when cool air from the caves meets the moist warmer air in the gorge, giving the appearance of smoke. Smoke Hole is located on the Seneca Rocks Unit of the Spruce Knob-Seneca Rocks National Recreation Area. From US 220 travel west on WV 2.

The 140-acre Gaudineer Scenic Area is a remnant of a vast virgin spruce forest. A nature trail leads to this magnificent view.

Southern Ranger Districts
(Gauley, Marlinton, & White Sulphur)

For Information

Gauley Ranger District
Box 110
Richwood, WV 26261
(304) 846-2695

Marlinton Ranger District
P.O. Box 210
Marlinton, WV 24954-0210
(304) 799-4334

White Sulphur Ranger District
410 East Main Street
White Sulphur Springs, WV 24986
(304) 536-2144

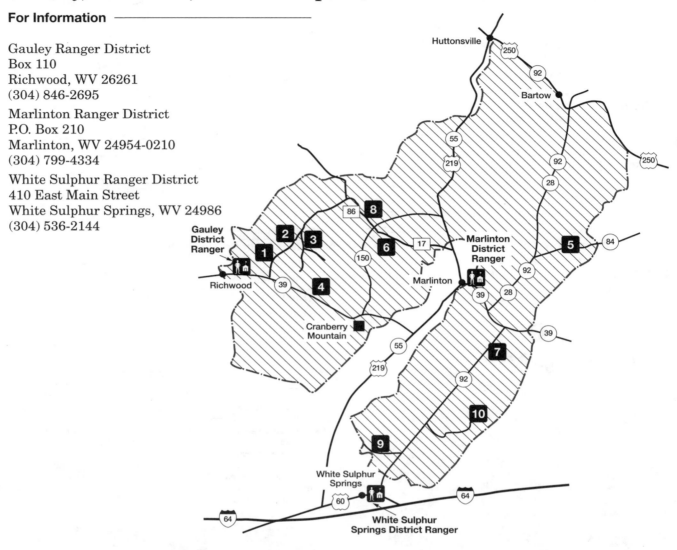

Location

The three ranger districts south of US 250 are Gauley, Marlinton, and White Sulphur. The Gauley Ranger District is situated in the southwestern portion of the national forest, mainly north of WV 39/55 and west of WV 150 (Highland Scenic Parkway). The ranger station is on WV 39/55 just north of Richwood. Campgrounds under the jurisdiction of the Marlinton Ranger District are located to the northwest, east, and southeast of the town of Marlinton. The ranger station is on WV 39 just east of Marlinton. The White Sulphur Ranger District is the southernmost district of the forest; the ranger station is located in White Sulphur Springs.

Directions to Recreation Areas with Campgrounds

Gauley Ranger District:

Big Rock Campground—On FR 76, about 5 miles north of Richwood.

Bishop Knob Campground—From Cowen, travel 1½ miles east on WV 20, turn right and go 4 miles east on WV 46, then 2½ miles on FR 101.

Cranberry Campground—Located northeast of Richwood; take FR 76 north and travel about 12 miles.

Summit Lake Campground—From Richwood, travel east on WV 39/55 for about 7 miles; turn left on a Forest Service Road at the North Bend Picnic Area and travel 2 miles.

Southern Ranger Districts *(continued)*

Marlinton Ranger District:

Bird Run Campground—From WV 42 at Frost, travel 1½ miles east on WV 84.

Day Run Campground—From Marlinton, go 4 miles north on US 219, turn left and go about 10 miles west on WV 17, then left on FR 216 for 1 mile.

Pocahontas Campground—About 14 miles from Marlinton on WV 92; travel southeast on WV 39/92, then south on WV 92.

Tea Creek Campground—From Marlinton, travel 6 miles north on US 219, 8 miles west on WV 150, and 2 miles west on FR 86.

White Sulphur Ranger District:

Blue Bend Campground—From White Sulphur Springs, travel north on WV 92 for 9 miles, 1 miles west on WV 16, and 2 miles west on WV 21.

Lake Sherwood Recreation Area—From WV 92 at Neola, turn east onto WV 14 and travel for 11 miles.

Lake Sherwood Recreation Area

Four of the campgrounds on the White Sulphur Ranger District provide camping facilities rated as "high level" development.

Map#/Recreation Areas	Development Level*	Camp Units	User Fee	Drinking Water	Picnicking	Fishing	Swimming	Boating
Gauley Ranger District								
1 Big Rock	3	5	•	•		•		
2 Bishop Knob	3	63	•	•				
3 Cranberry	3	30	•	•		•		
4 Summit Lake	3	33	•	•		•		•
Marlinton Ranger District								
5 Bird Run	2	12		•				
6 Day Run	2	12	•	•		•		
7 Pocahontas	2	10	•	•				
8 Tea Creek	2	29	•	•		•		
White Sulphur Ranger District								
9 Blue Bend				•	•	•	•	
Blue Bend	4	22	•	•				
Blue Meadow	3	18	•	•				
10 Lake Sherwood				•	•	•	•	•
West Shore	4	25	•	•				
Pine Run	4	35	•	•				
Meadow Creek	4	36	•	•				
Group	3	50	•	•				

***Development Level:**

2 = low level—usually accessible over primitive roads; spacing of camp units is irregular, pit toilets.

3 = moderate level—accessible by better unpaved or paved roads, camp units usually regularly spaced, paved and can accommodate RVs; toilets provided.

4 = high level—accessible by paved roads, paved roads and trails within area, camp units regularly spaced and can accommodate RVs; may have shower houses and playground equipment as well as some interpretive programs.

Northern Ranger Districts (Cheat, Greenbrier, & Potomac)

For Information

Cheat Ranger District
P.O. Box 368
Parsons, WV 26287
(304) 478-3251

Greenbrier Ranger District
Box 67
Bartow, WV 24920
(304) 456-3335

Potomac Ranger District
HC 59, Box 240
Petersburg, WV 26847
(304) 257-4488

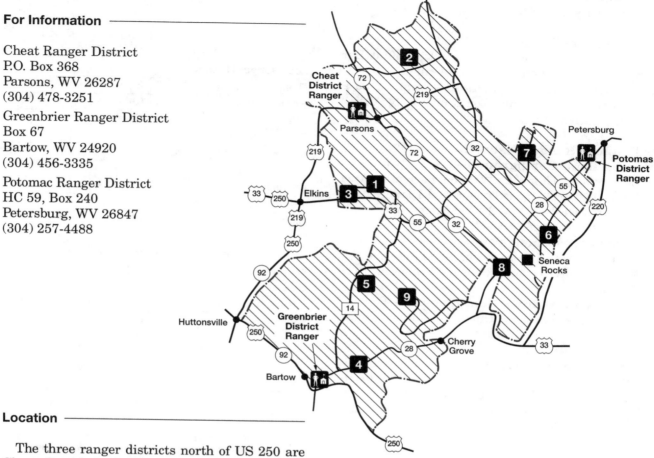

Location

The three ranger districts north of US 250 are Cheat, Greenbrier, and Potomac. The Cheat Ranger District is the northernmost district in the forest; the ranger station is located in Parsons. Greenbrier Ranger District is north of US 250; the ranger station is located on US 250 near Bartow. Potomac Ranger District is the easternmost district in the forest and encompasses the Spruce Knob-Seneca Rocks National Recreation Area. The ranger station is on WV 55 west of Petersburg.

Directions to Recreation Areas with Campgrounds

Cheat Ranger District:
Bear Heaven Recreation Area—From Elkins, travel 11 miles east on US 33, then 2 miles north on FR 91.
Horseshoe Recreation Area—From US 219 at Parsons, travel north on WV 72 to St. George; go 3 miles east on WV 1, then 4 miles northeast on WV 7.

Another example of a parent spending quality time with their child!

Stuart Recreation Area—From Elkins, travel 5 miles east on US 33, then ½-mile north on WV 6.

Greenbrier Ranger District:
Island Campground—From US 250 at Bartow, take WV 28 northeast for 5½ miles.

Laurel Fork Campground—From US 33 at Wymer, travel 10 miles south on FR 14, then 2 miles south on FR 423.

Potomac Ranger District:
Big Bend Campground—Located within the Seneca Rocks Unit of the National Recreation Area. From US 220 at Upper Tract, travel 1½ miles north and turn west on WV 2. The campground is 8½ miles at the end of the road.

Red Creek Campground—From WV 28/55 at Cabins, travel 4½ miles south, then 1 mile north on WV 4, 6 miles west on FR 19, and 5 miles north on FR 75.

Seneca Shadows Campground—Located within the Seneca Rocks Unit of the National Recreation Area. From US 33 at Seneca Rocks, go 1 mile south and turn right.

Spruce Knob Lake Campground—Located within the Spruce Knob Unit of the National Recreation Area. From WV 28 at Cherry Grove, travel 2½ miles southwest, then 9 miles north on CR 10, ⅔-mile northeast on FR 112, and ½-mile west on FR 1.

Map#/Recreation Areas	Development Level*	Camp Units	User Fee	Drinking Water	Picnicking	Fishing	Swimming	Boating
Cheat Ranger District								
1 Bear Heaven	2	8	•	•	•			
2 Horseshoe	3	13	•	•	•	•	•	
3 Stuart	5	27	•	•	•	•	•	
Group/Overflow	2	3		•				
Greenbrier Ranger District								
4 Island	2	6				•		
5 Laurel Fork	2	19	•					
Potomac Ranger District								
6 Big Bend	4	47	•	•		•		
7 Red Creek	4	12	•	•				
8 Seneca Shadows	5	38	•	•		•		
Walk-in	3	40	•	•				
Group	5	3	•	•				
9 Spruce Knob Lake	3	30	•	•		•		•
Walk-in	3	12	•	•				
Group	3	4	•	•				

*Development Levels:
2 = low level—usually accessible over primitive roads; spacing of camp units is irregular, pit toilets.
3 = moderate level—accessible by better unpaved or paved roads; camp units usually regularly spaced, paved and can accommodate RVs; toilets provided.
4 = high level—accessible by paved roads; paved roads and trails within area, camp units regularly spaced and can accommodate RVs; may have shower houses and playground equipment as well as some interpretive programs.
5 = very high level—beyond facilities in level 4; may offer electrical hookups, fish cleaning stations, flush toilets, hot showers, interpretive programs and other developed facilities.

Now this is a serious fisherman . . . he is dressed for the occasion and has the skills to go with it. Opportunities to fish on the Monongahela are abundant, whether it be stream, river, pond, or lake.

North Bend State Park

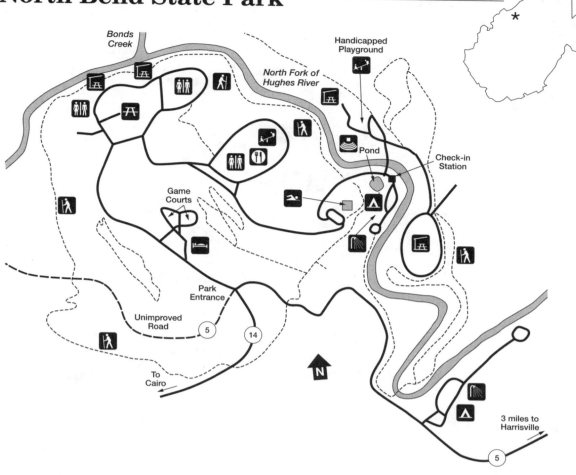

Bonds Creek

North Fork of Hughes River

Handicapped Playground

Pond

Check-in Station

Game Courts

Park Entrance

Unimproved Road

To Cairo

5

14

N

5

3 miles to Harrisville

For Information

North Bend State Park
P.O. Box 221
Cairo, WV 26337
(304) 643-2931

Location

This state park is south of US 50 that runs between Parkersburg and Clarksburg. Take either the Cairo exit or the Ellenboro exit off US 50 and travel south on WV 31; from Cairo, follow signs to the park. This 1,405-acre park, named for the horseshoe curve of the North Fork of the Hughes River, is West Virginia's major year-round park. Unique to North Bend is a playground and interpretive trail designed especially for the blind and physically challenged.

Facilities & Activities

80 tent/trailer sites
  26 sites with electric hookups
flush toilets/hot showers
dump station
8 modern cabins
29-room lodge
conference facilities
picnicking/shelters
playground
refreshments
swimming pool
tennis courts/miniature golf
game courts
stream fishing
hiking trails
interpretive trail
cross-country ski trails
restaurant
year-round nature/recreation program
amphitheater

Panther State Forest

For Information

Panther State Forest
Box 287
Panther, WV 24872
(304) 938-2252

Location

Panther State Forest is located southwest of Iaeger in the rugged hills near West Virginia's southern border with Virginia and Kentucky. From US 52 just north of Iaeger, head west and travel toward Panther; turn south on WV 3/2 before reaching Panther. This 7,180-acre state forest is extremely mountainous terrain with flat narrow ridgetops, almost completely forested. A modern group camp is available for retreats.

Facilities & Activities

6 campsites with electric hookups
pit toilets
group camp (capacity 60)
picnicking
playground
swimming pool
fishing
hiking trails

This state forest is located in extremely mountainous terrain; the campground has only 6 campsites, but, electric hookups are available.

Pipestem Resort State Park

River Trail

Bluestone River

Golf Course

River Trail

Tennis

Bluestone Canyon

Pipestem Lodge

Heritage Point (Overlook)

Golf Club House

Mountain Creek Lodge

Canyon Run Trail

Long Branch Creek

Mountain Creek

Canyon Tramway

LONG BRANCH LAKE

Park HDQ

River Trail

VC

Sled Run

Bluestone River

Recreation Center

Par 3 Golf Course

County Line Trail

Miniature Golf

Nature Trail Network

Nature Center

Indian Branch

Falls

Stables

12 miles to Hinton

N

20

Pipestem Knob Tower

14 miles to Princeton

For Information

Pipestem Resort State Park
Box 150
Pipestem, WV 25979
(304) 466-1800

Location

This park is located 20 miles north of Princeton and 12 miles south of Hinton on WV 20. From I-77 to the west, WV 20 is accessible via exit 14, and from I-64 to the north, WV 20 is accessible via exit 139. A windswept plateau provides the setting for this park's astonishing array of accommodations and recreational facilities. The unique name for this 4,023-acre resort is taken from the native pipestem bush whose hollow, woody stems were used by nine different Indian tribes in the making of pipes. The 16-acre Long Branch Lake, Bluestone River, and nearby Bluestone Lake afford a variety of fishing and boating opportunities. The park has two lodges: McKeever Lodge on the canyon rim, and Mountain Creek Lodge, located in the Bluestone Gorge and accessible only by tramway. Both lodges have complete conference facilities.

Facilities & Activities

82 tent/trailer sites
   31 sites with full hookups
   19 sites with electric hookups
flush toilets/hot showers
dump station
25 modern cabins
2 lodges (143 rooms)
conference facilities
picnicking
playground
snack bar
18-hole golf course/pro shop

Pipestem Resort State Park *(continued)*

9-hole (par-3) golf course/driving range
indoor & outdoor swimming pools
lighted tennis courts/miniature golf
game courts
fishing
boating
canoe/paddleboat rentals
16 hiking trails

cross-country ski trails/rentals
sled runs with rope tows
rental sleds/toboggans
horseback riding/bridle trails/overnight trail rides
rental horses/riding stables
restaurant
year-round nature/recreation program
arboretum
nature center
amphitheater
aerial tramway/observation tower

Pleasant Creek Wildlife Management Area

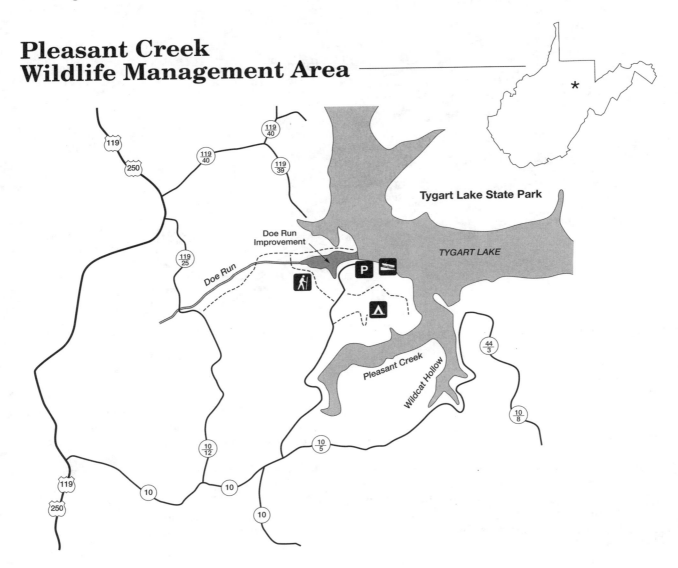

For Information

Pleasant Creek Wildlife Management Area
Route 3, Box 180
Philippi, WV 26416
(304) 457-4336

Location

Pleasant Creek Wildlife Management Area surrounds the southern tip of Tygart Lake and is adjacent to US 119/250; it is 6 miles north of Philippi and 9 miles south of Grafton. Entrance to this

Pleasant Creek WMA *(continued)*

1,623-acre WMA is recognized by a 120-foot high railroad trestle adjacent to US 119/250. The camping area is located 3 miles from the entrance. The slopes surrounding Pleasant Creek are steep and rise to 1,600 feet in elevation and include woodlands and brushy areas. Tygart Lake covers the land up to 1,094 feet in elevation during spring and summer, and may be drawn down to the 1,010-ft contour in late winter.

25 tent/trailer sites
pit toilets
fireplace or grill
group campsites
playground
lake swimming
fishing
boating/boat launch
hiking trails

Plum Orchard Lake Wildlife Management Area

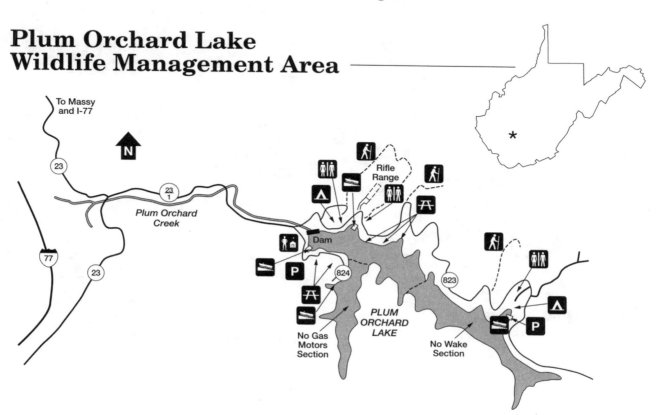

For Information

Plum Orchard Lake Wildlife Management Area
Route 1, Box 180
Scarbro, WV 25917
(304) 469-9905

Location

This wildlife management area is located near Scarbro; it can be reached by taking the Pax or Mossy exits off I-77 and following County Roads 23 and 23/1. Access from US 19 is via county road 15 from Oak Hall to Mossy, then 23 and 23/1. The 202-acre lake, which provides 6½ miles of shoreline, is nestled between Haystack and Packs mountains on Plum Orchard Creek. These mountains rise 700 to 900 feet above the lake to a maximum elevation of 2,665 feet on Packs Mountain. Camping facilities at this 2,953-acre WMA include 23 rustic sites at Beech Bottom and 29 at the dam.

Facilities & Activities

43 tent/trailer sites
pit toilets
fireplace or grill
picnic tables
trailer dump
fishing
boating/boat launch/rentals
rifle range
hiking trails

R.D. Bailey Lake

For Information

Resource Manager, Corps of Engineers
R.D. Bailey Lake
P.O. Drawer 70
Justice, WV 24851-0070
(304) 664-3220
(304) 664-9587 (lake information)

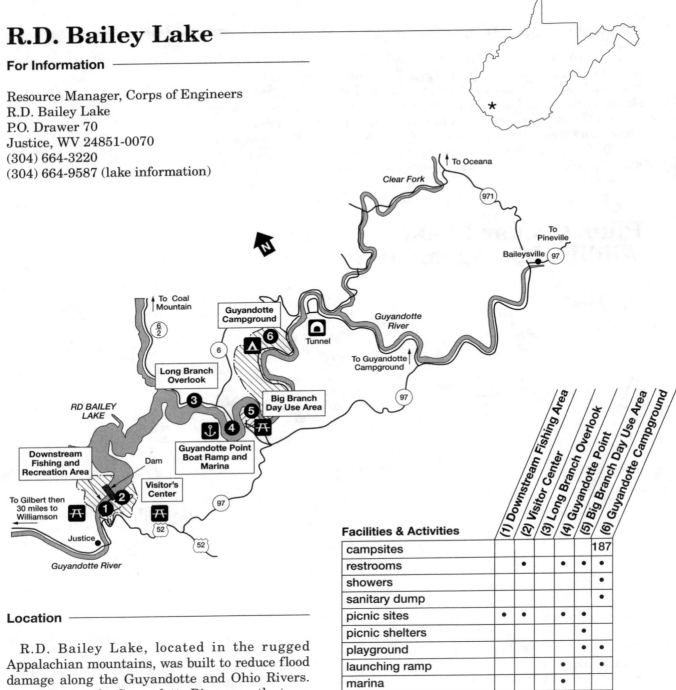

Facilities & Activities	(1) Downstream Fishing Area	(2) Visitor Center	(3) Long Branch Overlook	(4) Guyandotte Point	(5) Big Branch Day Use Area	(6) Guyandotte Campground
campsites						187
restrooms		•		•	•	•
showers						•
sanitary dump						•
picnic sites	•	•		•	•	
picnic shelters					•	
playground					•	•
launching ramp				•		•
marina				•		
fishing	•			•	•	
ranger station		•				
viewing area		•	•			

Location

R.D. Bailey Lake, located in the rugged Appalachian mountains, was built to reduce flood damage along the Guyandotte and Ohio Rivers. The dam is on the Guyandotte River near the town of Justice. The lake is open for boating year-round with a summer surface of 630 acres and 17 miles of shoreline. Under maximum storage conditions, the 7-mile lake would increase to 22 miles. Perched 365 feet above the lake, the visitor's center provides a breathtaking view of the dam, lake and surrounding forest. Tours of the dam and the 310-ft-high "control tower" can be arranged.

Spread along a scenic stretch of the Guyandotte River for 6 miles, the campground is divided into 4 segments, each with restrooms/showers, play-grounds and nearby trailer dump stations. Both tent and trailer sites have electric hookups. The campground is accessible from WV 97, about 3 miles southwest of Baileysville.

Seneca State Forest

For Information

Seneca State Forest
Route 1, Box 140
Dunmore, WV 24934
(304) 799-6213

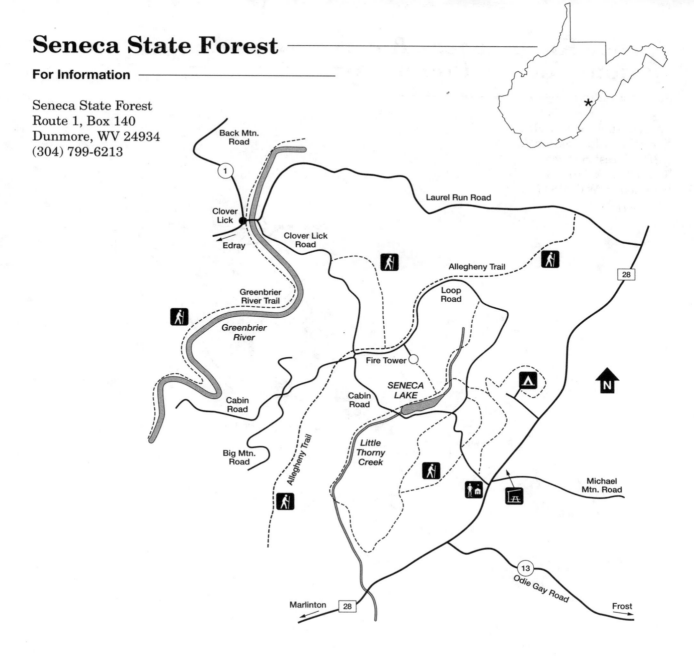

Location

Seneca State Forest is 4 miles southwest of Dunmore along WV 28. This 11,684-acre state forest borders the famed Greenbrier River. A pine-hardwood forest covers the gently sloping to hilly terrain ranging in elevation from 2,000 to 3,600 feet. The 4-acre Seneca Lake provides warmwater and trout fishing. Rustic guest cabins offer the grace and comfort of frontier living. The Allegheny Trail winds through the forest, and the nearby Greenbrier River Trail is easily accessible from Seneca.

Facilities & Activities

10 tent/trailer sites
drinking water
shower at forest headquarters
pit toilets
7 rustic cabins
picnicking/large picnic shelter
playground
fishing
boat rentals
23 miles of hiking trails

Spruce Knob-Seneca Rocks National Recreation Area

For Information

Spruce Knob-Seneca Rocks
   National Recreation Area
USDA Forest Service
Route 3, Box 240
Petersburg, WV 26847
(304) 257-4488

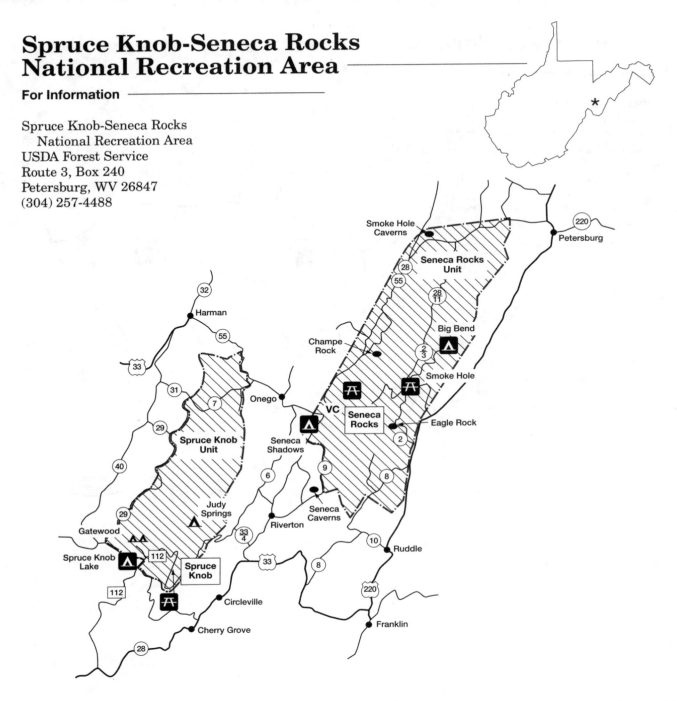

Location

The Spruce Knob-Seneca Rocks National Recreation Area on the Monogahela National Forest comprises 100,000 acres of lush backcountry. It includes the highest mountain in West Virginia, spectacular rock formations, fast-flowing streams, forested mountains, caves, and open meadows on the headwaters of the Potomac River. By its very nature, Spruce Knob-Seneca Rocks is suited to a wide range of outdoor recreation activities, and especially the more primitive types such as hiking, rock climbing,

caving, and whitewater canoeing. Major highways passing through the area include US 33 from Elkins, WV to Harrisburg, VA and Highway 28 from US 220 at Petersburg to US 250 at Thornwood.

Points of Interest

▲ Spruce Knob, the high point of Spruce Mountain, is the highest point in West Virginia, rising to over 4,800 feet. The observation tower affords excellent views of the mountains to the east and west. An interpretive trail is nearby.

- Seneca Rocks is a 1,000-ft quartzite formation that rises above the North Fork Valley. Besides its interest to sightseers, Seneca Rocks is considered by climbers to be the best rock climb in the East.
- The Smoke Hole is a canyon through which the South Branch of the Potomac flows for 20 miles; over half the distance is flanked by a quiet scenic road. The name refers to the caves along the mountainside where mist forms when cool air from the caves meets the moist warmer air in the gorge, giving the appearance of smoke.
- Eagle Rock, on the road to Smoke Hole, is a spectacular rock formation named for Colonel William Eagle, a Revolutionary War soldier who lived nearby and fought at Valley Forge; he is buried close to the base of the Rock.
- Seneca Creek originates on Spruce Mountain and courses northeast to empty into the North Fork at Seneca Rocks. It is a stream of scenic waterfalls and wild beauty, and has the reputation of being one of the best trout streams in West Virginia.

General Information

- An entry fee is not charged; camping fees are charged at all campgrounds except the Gatewood Group Camp and Judy Springs Walk-In on the Spruce Knob Unit.
- Seneca Rocks Visitor Center, located near the intersection of US 33 and Highway 28, provides information, exhibits on geology, history, rock-climbing, outdoor activities, and interpretive programs. It is open on weekends throughout the year and full-time during the summer season. Phone: (304) 567-2827.
- One developed campground is located on the Spruce Knob Unit, and 2 campgrounds are on the Seneca Rocks Unit. Campsites can be reserved at both campgrounds in the Seneca Rocks Unit (Seneca Shadows and Big Bend) through the National Recreation Reservation System. Phone 1-800-280-2267. Campsites not reserved in advance are available on a first-come, first-served basis.
- Developed campgrounds are equipped with tent pad, parking spur, toilet and water facilities, fireplace, and firewood. The parking spur is large enough to accommodate the average camp trailer.
- Some campgrounds open as early as mid-March; others in April and May. Seneca Shadows closes the end of October; others remain open through November or into December.
- Camping in the backcountry outside of developed sites is allowed; it has always been a popular activity in national forests. Campers are encouraged to practice no trace camping techniques. Permits are not required.
- Fishing in the North Fork near the visitor center is "fish for fun" only. All fish must be returned to the water and only artificial lures may be used. Before taking to the streams and lakes, check at the visitor center for state fishing regulations, licenses, seasons, and limits.
- Seneca Rocks provides some of the most challenging ascents on the east coast. Over 50 "routes" climb the many spires and crags of the Rocks. Only the well-equipped and skilled should attempt to climb.
- Hiking to the top of the Rocks can be a challenge. One route is to start at the Visitor Center and take the 1.3-mile trail that ascends the north edge of the Rocks to a viewing platform. This is a wide, easy-to-follow trail but it does climb about 900 feet and has many stairs. Other routes exist.

Seneca Shadows Campground has 40 walk-in campsites; each comes with a full view of Seneca Rocks.

Spruce Knob-Seneca Rocks NRA
(continued)

Facilities & Activities

Spruce Knob Unit
30 RV & tent campsites at Spruce Knob Lake
12 walk-in campsites
   vault toilets; drinking water
Gatewood Group Campground (40 max.)
   vault toilets; drinking water
Judy Springs Walk-in Camprgound
   no facilities; no drinking water
25-acre lake (trolling motors); boat launch
60 miles of trails
3-mile Gatewood Nature Trail
Spruce Knob Observation Tower
   ½-mile interpretive trail
   vault toilets; no water
11-unit picnic area at Spruce Knob
   vault toilets; water (hand-pump)
   picnic tables; grills

Seneca Unit
25 RV & tent campsites at Seneca Shadows
13 additional sites with electrical hook-ups
3 group camping areas (up to 40 each)
   flush toilets/showers
40 walk-in tent-only campsites
   vault toilets/water
50 RV & tent campsites at Big Bend Campground
   toilets/drinking water
17-unit picnic area at Smoke Hole
9-unit picnic area at Seneca Rocks
backcountry camping
whitewater canoeing/boating
fishing/icefishing/hunting
rock climbing/caving
hiking /backpacking
interpretive/nature trails
horseback riding
evening ranger programs/amphitheater
visitor center/exhibits/historical sites

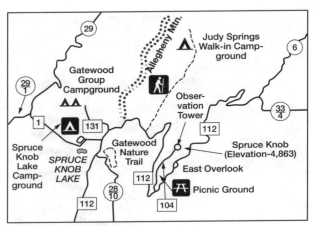

Detail of Spruce Knob Unit

Seneca Shadows Campground

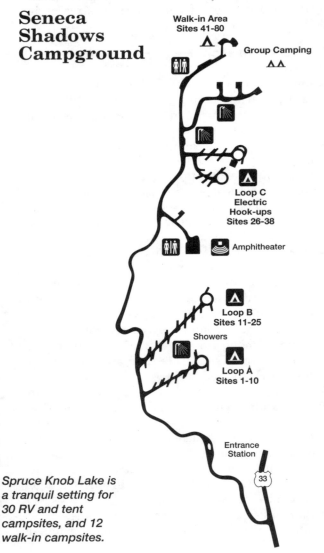

Spruce Knob Lake is a tranquil setting for 30 RV and tent campsites, and 12 walk-in campsites.

Stonewall Jackson Lake State Park

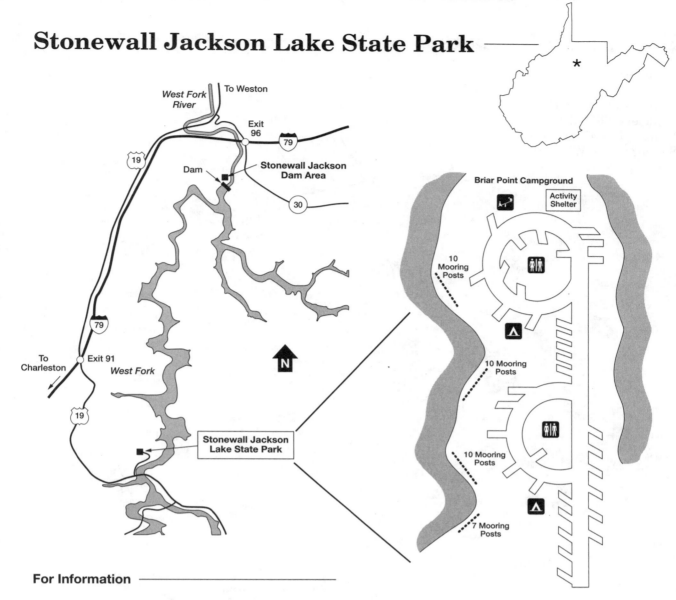

For Information

Stonewall Jackson Lake State Park
Route 1, Box 0
Roanoke, WV 26423
(304) 269-0523

Location

Stonewall Jackson Lake State Park is located about 13 miles south of Weston on US 19. From I-79, take exit 91 and follow US 19 south for 2½ miles to the park entrance. Stonewall Jackson Lake was formed by the damming of the West Fork River. This 2,650-acre lake is the main focus of Stonewall Jackson Lake State Park. The main room of the multi-purpose building is large enough to accommodate 400 people and the smaller conference room is suitable for a group of 50 to 75 people; a fully equipped kitchen is available.

Facilities & Activities

34 tent/trailer sites with full hookups
flush toilets/hot showers
picnicking
multi-purpose building
snack bar
lake fishing
fishing pier
boating/ramp/rentals
342-slip marina/bait shop
hiking /fitness trails

Summersville Lake

For Information

Resource Manager, Corps of Engineers
Summersville Lake
Route 2, Box 470
Summersville, WV 26651-9619
(304) 872-3412

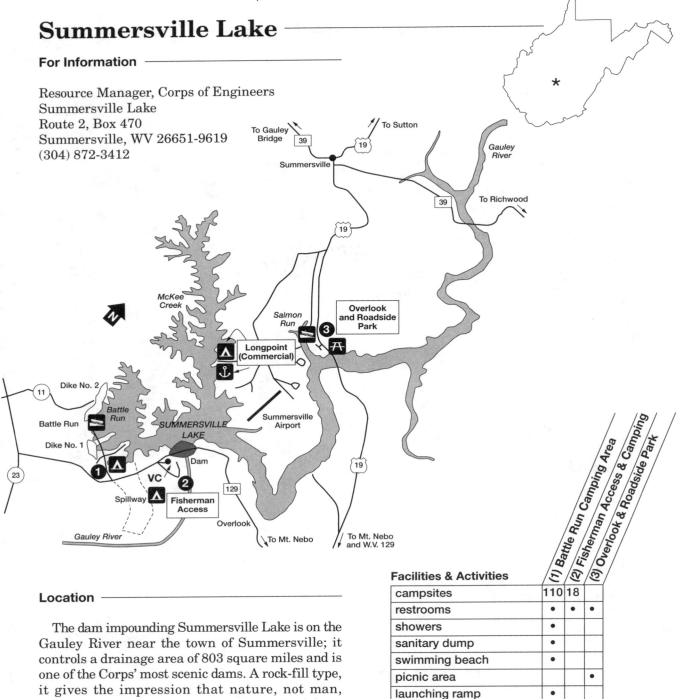

Facilities & Activities	(1) Battle Run Camping Area	(2) Fisherman Access & Camping	(3) Overlook & Roadside Park
campsites	110	18	
restrooms	•	•	•
showers	•		
sanitary dump	•		
swimming beach	•		
picnic area			•
launching ramp	•		
viewing area			•

Location

The dam impounding Summersville Lake is on the Gauley River near the town of Summersville; it controls a drainage area of 803 square miles and is one of the Corps' most scenic dams. A rock-fill type, it gives the impression that nature, not man, planned and placed it. During summer, the lake is raised to elevation 1,652 feet above sea level, which provides 2,790 surface acres of water for recreation. During late fall and winter, it is lowered to elevation 1,575 feet to provide maximum space for storage of floodwaters. The lake has 60 miles of shoreline; a scenic contrast of terrain ranging from rolling knolls to vertical rock cliffs can be viewed from various locations.

There are 2 camping areas at Summersville Lake: Battle Run and a primitive camping area below the dam. To reach the campgrounds, travel south from Summersville on US 19 for 7 miles, then northwest on WV 129 for 3 miles. The area near the dam site has a visitor's center, an observation area, a picnic area, and restrooms. A roadside park on US 19 provides another outstanding observation area; it is state maintained.

Sutton Lake

For Information

Resource Manager, Corps of Engineers
Sutton Lake
P.O. Box 426
Sutton, WV 26601
(304) 765-2816
(304) 765-2705 (lake information)

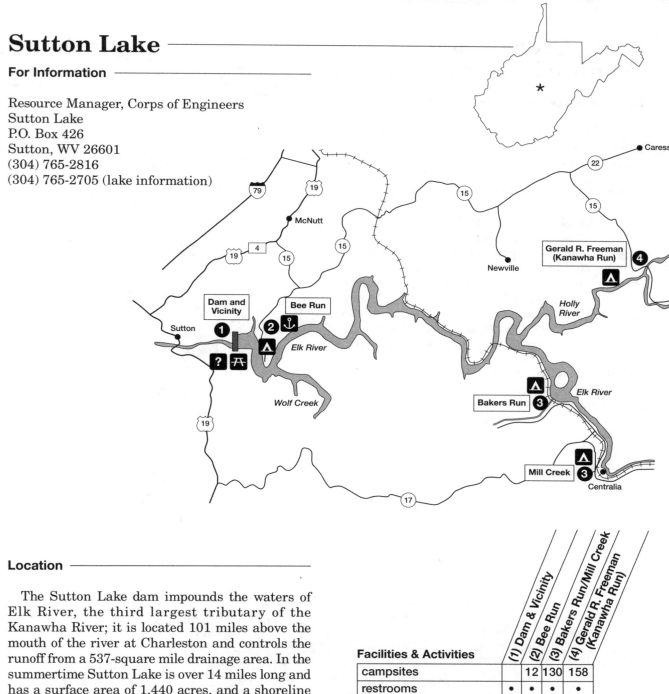

Location

The Sutton Lake dam impounds the waters of Elk River, the third largest tributary of the Kanawha River; it is located 101 miles above the mouth of the river at Charleston and controls the runoff from a 537-square mile drainage area. In the summertime Sutton Lake is over 14 miles long and has a surface area of 1,440 acres, and a shoreline of 40 miles—including several coves that make for good fishing. In the winter months the lake is lowered in excess of 27 feet to provide additional space for storage of potential floodwaters.

Sutton Lake has 4 camping areas: Bee Run, Bakers Run, Mill Creek, and Kanawha Run. The Bee Run camping area is on the north side of the lake near the dam; from US 19 between Sutton and McNutt, travel south on WV 15 for about a mile, then turn right and follow signs. Bakers Run and Mill Creek camping areas are located off WV 17; from US 19 south of Sutton, go east on WV 17 for

Facilities & Activities	(1) Dam & Vicinity	(2) Bee Run	(3) Bakers Run/Mill Creek	(4) Gerald R. Freeman (Kanawha Run)
campsites		12	130	158
restrooms	•	•	•	•
showers			•	•
sanitary dump			•	•
picnic area	•	•		
swimming	•			
launching ramp	•	•	•	•
marina		•		

about 10 miles. Kanawha Run (Gerald R. Freeman) camping area is on the north side of Holly River; from US 19 north of Sutton, take WV 15 east about 14 miles.

Teter Creek Lake
Wildlife Management Area

For Information

Teter Creek Lake Wildlife Management Area
Montrose, WV 26283
(304) 823-1043

Location

Teter Creek Lake Wildlife Managment Area is located 3 miles east of Meadowville, with access by a 3-mile-long blacktop road from WV 92 at Meadowville. This 137-acre WMA lies in the Allegheny Plateau and has an average elevation of about 1,800 feet. The hills around the lake have relatively gentle slopes and are wooded primarily with an oak-hickory type forest. The 35-acre Teter Creek Lake provides fishing for warmwater species and trout.

Facilities & Activities

26 tent/trailer sites
pit toilets
fireplace or grill
picnic tables
playground
fishing
boating/boat launch
hiking trails

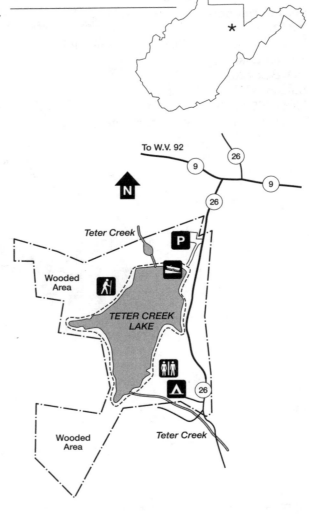

This fisherman is equipped for any lake that he may encounter in West Virginia, because some lakes allow only trolling motors, while others allow gasoline motors.

Tomlinson Run State Park

For Information

Tomlinson Run State Park
P.O. Box 97
New Manchester, WV 26056
(304) 564-3651

Location

This state park is located 7 miles north of Weirton on WV 2; take WV 8 north just past New Manchester where it intersects with WV 2, and follow signs to the park. The park's 1,398 acres extend along the stream from which the park gets its name, to within a mile of the stream's confluence with the Ohio River. Over 33 acres of water in the form of various ponds and lakes afford excellent fishing. The group camp features 10 cabins, which sleep 10 each, and counselor's quarters for 12. The camp also has a recreation building, a dining hall, and a fully-equipped kitchen; however, you do need to bring your own cooks. The rent-a-camp program provides the user with all the gear necessary for overnight tent camping in style: a 6-person lodge tent, 2 cots, a cooler, a propane stove and lantern, picnic table, and cookware.

Facilities & Activities

54 tent/trailer sites
    39 sites with electric hookups
flush toilets/hot showers
dump station
6 rent-a-camp sites
group camp (112 capacity)
    cabins/kitchen/dining hall/recreation building
picnicking/shelters
playground
snack bar
swimming pool/bathhouse
tennis courts/miniature golf
game courts
lake fishing
boating/boat docks
paddleboat/rowboat rentals
hiking trails
groceries
seasonal nature/recreation program

Twin Falls Resort State Park

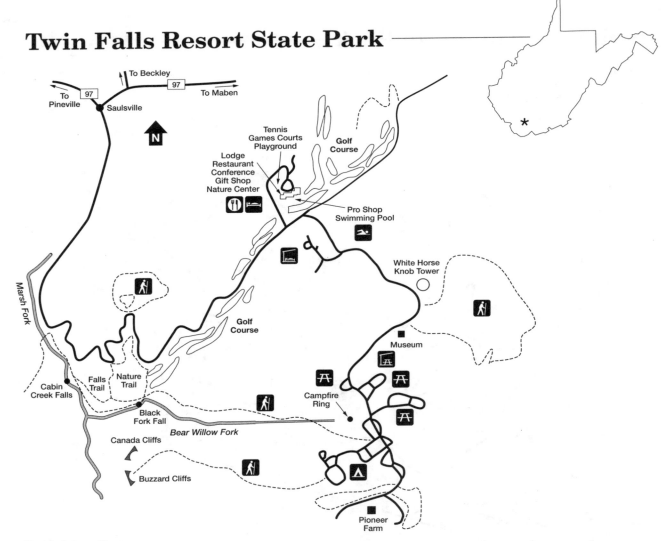

For Information

Twin Falls Resort State Park
P.O. Box 1023
Mullens, WV 25882
(304) 294-4000

Location

Twin Falls Resort State Park is located 27 miles southwest of Beckley. From I-77, take exit 42 and travel southwest on WV 16 for 4.2 miles to the junction of WV 54. Take WV 54 for 14 miles to Maben; turn right on WV 97 and drive 5.5 miles. At stop sign, turn left onto Bear Hole Road; the park entrance is less than a mile, and the lodge just over 4 miles. A sprawling 18-hole championship golf course and golf clubhouse/swimming pool complex provides a dominant centerpiece for the resort's recreational facilities. A restored, 19th-century pioneer farm creates a living museum; the park is open year-round.

Facilities & Activities

50 tent/trailer sites
  25 sites with electric hookups
flush toilets/hot showers
dump station
5 rent-a-camp sites
13 modern cabins
20-room lodge
conference facilities
picnicking/shelters
playground
refreshments
18-hole golf course/pro shop
swimming pool/golf clubhouse complex
tennis/game courts
9 hiking trails
camp store/restaurant
year-round nature/recreation program
living history farm

Tygart Lake State Park

For Information

Tygart Lake State Park
Route 1, Box 260
Grafton, WV 26354
(304) 265-3383
(304) 265-2320 (Lodge)

↑ To W.V. 9

Registration
Office

Boating
Area

Lodge

TYGART LAKE

To Dam Overlook
and U.S. 119 →

Location

This state park is located 5 miles south of Grafton off US 50. Take north/south US 119 or east/west US 50 to Grafton; from Grafton take US 50 to South Grafton and follow signs to the park. The outstanding feature of this 2,134-acre park is its 13-mile lake, winding through wooded valleys. The Tygart Lake Lodge sets on a promontory overlooking the lake; it is ideal for small group meetings and conventions. The spacious restaurant provides a panorama of the lake and seats up to 100 for meals. The Tygart Lake Marina offers complete boat servicing and launching facilities.

Facilities & Activities

40 tent/trailer sites
    14 sites with electric hookups
flush toilets/hot showers
dump station
10 modern cabins
20-room lodge
conference facilities
picnicking
playground
game courts
refreshments
lake swimming
lake fishing
waterskiing/scuba diving
boating/launch ramp
ski and fishing boat rentals
full service marina
hiking trails
restaurant
seasonal nature/recreation program

The size of the marina at Tygart Lake reveals the popularity of this state park. Ski boats and fishing boats can be rented.

Watoga State Park

For Information

Watoga State Park
H.C. 82, Box 252
Marlinton, WV 24954-9550
(304) 799-4087

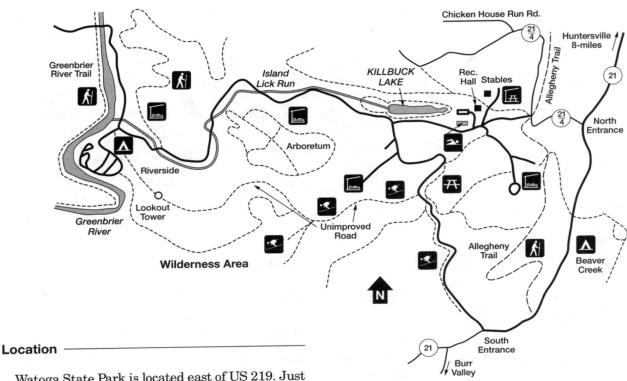

Location

Watoga State Park is located east of US 219. Just north of Hillsboro and south of Mill Point on US 219, a sign directs you to the park's western entrance via a 2-mile paved secondary road. An alternative route is to turn south from WV 39 at Huntersville and travel 9 miles to the park's north entrance. First and largest of West Virginia state parks, Watoga encompasses 10,100 acres; it is a sprawling, verdant woodland located in the Appalachian highlands. The park's unusual name is a derivative of the Cherokee word, *watauga,* which means "the river of islands." Indians gave this name to the Greenbrier River area, which forms several miles of the park's boundary, due to the river's wide, shallow nature, which causes many sandbars and islands to be formed.

Facilities & Activities

50 tent/trailer sites at Riverside Campground
    19 sites with electric hookups
38 tent/trailer sites at Beaver Creek
    12 sites with electric hookups

flush toilets/hot showers
dump station
8 modern cabins/25 standard cabins
picnicking/shelter
playground
refreshments
swimming pool
tennis/game courts
stream/lake fishing
boating
paddleboat/rowboat rentals
hiking trails
cross-country ski trails
horseback riding/bridle trails
rental horses/riding stables
groceries
restaurant
seasonal nature/recreation program
arboretum

Resources for Further Information

Delaware

Delaware Division of
Parks & Recreation
89 Kings Highway
P.O. Box 1401
Dover, DE 19903
(302) 739-4702

Delaware Department
of Agriculture
Forestry Section
2320 South Dupont
Highway
Dover, DE 19901
(302) 739-4811

Delaware Tourism
Office
99 Kings Highway
P.O. Box 1401
Dover, DE 19903
(302) 739-4271
1-800-282-8667
(in-state)
1-800-441-8846
(out-of-state)

Virginia

Virginia Department
of Conservation and
Recreation
Division of State Parks
203 Governor Street,
Suite 306
Richmond, VA 23219
(804) 786-1712
1-800-866-9222
(in-state, not in
Richmond)

Virginia Division of
Tourism
1021 East Cary Street
P.O. Box 798
Richmond, VA 23219
(804) 786-4484
1-800-VISIT VA

State Forest
Superintendent
Route 1, Box 250
Cumberland, VA
23040-9515
(804) 492-4121

State Bicycle
Coordinator
Virginia Department
of Transportation
1401 East Broad
Street
Richmond, VA 23219
(804) 786-2983

US Army Corps of
Engineers
Norfolk District
803 Front Street
Norfolk, VA
23510-1096

**State Park Camping
& Cabin
Reservations:**
Virginia State Parks
Reservation Center
P.O. Box 1895
Richmond, VA
23215-1895
(804) 225-3867
Richmond Area
1-800-933-PARK
(7275)

Maryland

Maryland State Forest
& Park Service
Department of Natural
Resources
Tawes State Office
Building
580 Taylor Avenue, E-3
Annapolis, MD 21401
(410) 974-3771

Maryland Office of
Tourism Development
Redwood Tower, 9th
Floor
217 East Redwood
Street
Baltimore, MD 21202
1-800-543-1036

**Official Highway
Map, and the
Scenic Highway
Map (free):**
Maryland Highway
Administration
Map Distribution
Section
2323 West Joppa Road
Brooklandville, MD
21022

US Army Corps of
Engineers
Baltimore District
P.O. Box 1715
Baltimore, MD
21203-1715

West Virginia

West Virginia Division
of Tourism and Parks
Parks and Recreation
State Capitol Complex
Building 6, Room 451
1900 Kanawha Blvd.,
East
Charleston, WV
25305-0314
1-800 CALL WVA

**State Park Camping/
Cabin/Lodge
Reservations:**
(same as above or
phone park directly)

**For Wildlife
Management
Areas**
West Virginia Division
of Natural Resources
Wildlife Resources
Section
State Capitol Complex
Building 3, Room 814
1900 Kanawha Blvd.,
East
Charleston, WV
25305-0664
(304) 558-2771

US Army Corps of
Engineers
Huntington District
502 8th Street
Huntington, WV
25701-2070
(304) 529-5258

Other

**Reservation System for National Park
Service:**
MISTIX
P.O. Box 85705
San Diego, CA 92138-5704
1-800-365-CAMP (2267)

Reservation System for US Forest Service:
National Recreation Reservation System
P.O. Box 900
Cumberland, MD 21502
1-800-CAMP (2267)
FAX: 301-722-9802

INDEX

A

Appalachian National Scenic
    Trail, 14–15, 63–64
Appomattox, VA, 106
Asheville, NC, 74
ASSATEAGUE ISLAND
    NATIONAL SEASHORE,
    36–37
ASSATEAGUE STATE
    PARK, 38
AUDRA STATE PARK, 139

B

BABCOCK STATE PARK,
    140–141
Backcountry ethics, 19–20
Barboursville, WV, 142
Bartow, WV, 165–166
Bassett, VA, 123
Bear, DE, 31
BEAR CREEK LAKE STATE
    PARK, 73
BEECH FORK STATE
    PARK, 142
Berlin, MD, 36, 38
Big Pool, MD, 49
BIG RUN STATE PARK, 39
BLACKBIRD STATE
    FOREST, 25
Blacksburg, VA, 109–110
BLACKWATER FALLS STATE
    PARK, 143
BLUE RIDGE PARKWAY,
    74–76
BLUESTONE LAKE WILDLIFE
    MANAGEMENT AREA, 145
BLUESTONE STATE PARK, 144
Boonsboro, MD, 50, 52, 63
Boydton, VA, 114
BRANDYWINE CREEK STATE
    PARK, 26
Breaks, VA, 77
BREAKS INTERSTATE PARK,
    77–78
Bridgewater, VA, 102–103
Bruceton Mills, WV, 152

Buckhannon, WV, 139
Buena Vista, VA, 92, 101
BULL RUN REGIONAL
    PARK, 79
Burnsville, WV, 146
BURNSVILLE LAKE, 146

C

CABWAYLINGO STATE
    FOREST, 147
Cairo, WV, 167
Caldwell, WV, 154
Camp Creek, WV, 148
CAMP CREEK STATE
    PARK, 148
Camping equipment supplies
    checklist, 20–21
CANAAN VALLEY RESORT
    STATE PARK, 149
Cape Charles, VA, 115
CAPE HENLOPEN STATE
    PARK, 27
CARPENTER STATE PARK, 28
CATOCTIN MOUNTAIN
    PARK, 40–41
CEDAR CREEK STATE
    PARK, 150
Centreville, VA, 79
Charleston, WV, 157
CHESAPEAKE AND OHIO
    CANAL NATIONAL
    HISTORICAL
    PARK, 42–44
Chesterfield, VA, 124
CHIEF LOGAN STATE PARK,
    151
Clarksburg, MD, 55
Clarksville, VA, 122
CLAYTOR LAKE STATE
    PARK, 80
Clifftop, WV, 140
Clifton, MD, 45
CLINCH MOUNTAIN
    WILDLIFE
    MANAGEMENT AREA, 81
Confluence, PA, 71
Cooking equipment checklist, 22

COOPERS ROCK STATE
    FOREST, 152
COSCA REGIONAL PARK, 45
Covington, VA, 88, 92, 101
Crisfield, MD, 54
Cumberland, VA, 73
CUMBERLAND GAP
    NATIONAL HISTORICAL
    PARK, 82–83
CUNNINGHAM FALLS STATE
    PARK, 46

D

Davis, WV, 143, 149
DEEP CREEK LAKE STATE
    PARK, 47
Delaplane, VA, 133
Delaware information, 3–4
DELAWARE SEASHORE
    STATE PARK, 29
Denton, MD, 56
DOUTHAT STATE PARK, 84
Dublin, VA, 80
Duffield, VA, 120
Dunlow, WV, 147
Dunmore, WV, 173

E

East Lynn, WV, 153
EAST LYNN LAKE, 153
Edinburg, VA, 102–104
Elk Garden, WV, 156
Elkins, WV, 161
ELK NECK STATE PARK, 48
Ellicott City, MD, 58

F

FAIRY STONE STATE PARK,
    85
FALSE CAPE STATE PARK, 86
Federal Duck Stamp, 12
Federal Recreation Passport
    Program, 12
Felton, DE, 30

FLANNAGAN (JOHN W.) DAM & RESERVOIR, 87
Flintstone, MD, 61, 65
FORT FREDERICK STATE PARK, 49

G

GAMBRILL STATE PARK, 50
Gap Mills, WV, 160
GARRETT STATE FOREST, 65–66
GATHRIGHT DAM & LAKE MOOMAW, 88–89
GEORGE WASHINGTON NATIONAL FOREST, 90–92, 101–104
Glen Arm, MD, 53
Glenville, WV, 150
Golden Access Passport, 12
Golden Age Passport, 12
Golden Eagle Passport, 12
Grafton, WV, 183
Grantsville, MD, 39, 57, 65
GRAYSON HIGHLANDS STATE PARK, 105
Green Bay, VA, 136
Greenbelt, MD, 51
GREENBELT PARK, 51–52
GREENBRIER STATE FOREST, 154
GREENBRIER STATE PARK, 52–53
GREEN RIDGE STATE FOREST, 65–66

H

Hacker Valley, WV, 155
Harrisonburg, VA, 90
HART-MILLER ISLAND STATE PARK, 53
Haysi, VA, 87
Hiking/backpacking checklist, 22–23
Hinton, WV, 144
HOLLIDAY LAKE STATE PARK, 106
HOLLY RIVER STATE PARK, 155
Hot Springs, VA, 88, 92, 101
Huddleston, VA, 134

HUNGRY MOTHER STATE PARK, 107
Huttonsville, WV, 158

I

Indian Mills, WV, 145

J

JANES ISLAND STATE PARK, 54
Jarrettsville, MD, 67
JEFFERSON NATIONAL FOREST, 108–113
JENNINGS RANDOLPH LAKE, 156
Justice, WV, 172

K

KANAWHA STATE FOREST, 157
KERR (JOHN H.) DAM & RESERVOIR, 114
KILLENS POND STATE PARK, 30
KIPTOPEKE STATE PARK, 115
KUMBRABOW STATE FOREST, 158

L

Laurel, DE, 32
LAUREL LAKE WILDLIFE MANAGEMENT AREA, 159
Lenore, WV, 159
Lewes, DE, 27
LITTLE BENNETT REGIONAL PARK, 55
Logan, WV, 151
Lorton, VA, 125
LUMS POND STATE PARK, 31
Luray, VA, 130

M

Map symbols, 23
Marbury, MD, 62

Marion, VA, 107, 116
Marlinton, WV, 163–164, 184
MARTINAK STATE PARK, 56
Maryland information, 4–6
Middlesboro, KY, 82
Millboro, VA, 84
MONCOVE LAKE STATE PARK, 160
MONONGAHELA NATIONAL FOREST, 161–166
Montrose, WV, 180
Montross, VA, 137
MOUNT ROGERS NATIONAL RECREATION AREA, 108, 116–118
Mt. Solon, VA, 119
Mouth of Wilson, VA, 105
Mullens, WV, 182

N

Natural Bridge Station, VA, 112–113
NATURAL CHIMNEYS REGIONAL PARK, 119
NATURAL TUNNEL STATE PARK, 120
Newark, DE, 28
New Castle, VA, 112–113
NEW GERMANY STATE PARK, 57
New Manchester, WV, 181
New River Gorge, 16–18
NORTH BEND STATE PARK, 167
NORTH FORK OF POUND LAKE, 121
North East, MD, 48

O

Oakland, MD, 65, 68
OCCONEECHEE STATE PARK, 122

P

Panther, WV, 168
PANTHER STATE FOREST, 168
Park Pass, 12
Parsons, WV, 165–166
PATAPSCO VALLEY STATE PARK, 58–59

Petersburg, WV, 165–166, 174
Philippi, WV, 170
PHILPOTT LAKE, 123
Pipestem, WV, 169
PIPESTEM RESORT STATE
    PARK, 169–170
PLEASANT CREEK
    WILDLIFE
    MANAGEMENT AREA,
    170–171
PLUM ORCHARD LAKE
    WILDLIFE
    MANAGEMENT AREA, 171
POCAHONTAS STATE
    PARK, 124
POCOMOKE RIVER STATE
    PARK, 59
POHICK BAY REGIONAL
    PARK, 125
POINT LOOKOUT STATE
    PARK, 60
POTOMAC STATE FOREST,
    65–66
Pound, VA, 121
PRINCE WILLIAM FOREST
    PARK, 126–128

R

R. D. BAILEY LAKE, 172
Rehoboth Beach, DE, 29
Reservation system, 13
Resources for further
    information, 185
Richwood, WV, 163–164
Roanoke, VA, 108
Roanoke, WV, 177
ROCKY GAP STATE PARK, 61

S

Saltville, VA, 81
SAVAGE RIVER STATE
    FOREST, 65–66

Scarbro, WV, 171
Scotland, MD, 60
Scottsburg, VA, 135
SEASHORE STATE PARK AND
    NATURAL AREA, 129
SENECA STATE FOREST, 173
Sharpsburg, MD, 42
SHENANDOAH NATIONAL
    PARK, 130–132
SKY MEADOWS STATE
    PARK, 133
SMALLWOOD STATE
    PARK, 62
SMITH MOUNTAIN LAKE
    STATE PARK, 134
Smyrna, DE, 25
Snow Hill, MD, 59
SOUTH MOUNTAIN STATE
    PARK, 63–64
SPRUCE KNOB-SENECA
    ROCKS NATIONAL
    RECREATION
    AREA, 174–176
Staunton, VA, 92,101
STAUNTON RIVER STATE
    PARK, 135
STONEWALL JACKSON LAKE
    STATE PARK, 177
Stuart, VA, 85
Summersville, WV, 178
SUMMERSVILLE LAKE, 178
SUSQUEHANNA STATE
    PARK, 67
Sutton, WV, 179
SUTTON LAKE, 179
SWALLOW FALLS STATE
    PARK, 68
Swanton, MD, 47

T

TETER CREEK LAKE
    WILDLIFE
    MANAGEMENT AREA, 180

Thurmont, MD, 40, 46
TOMLINSON RUN STATE
    PARK, 181
TRAP POND STATE PARK,
    32–33
Triangle, VA, 126
TWIN FALLS RESORT STATE
    PARK, 182
TWIN LAKES STATE PARK, 136
TYGART LAKE STATE
    PARK, 183

U

Upper Marlboro, MD, 69

V

Virginia Beach, VA, 86, 129
Virginia information, 7–9

W

WATKINS REGIONAL PARK,
    69–70
WATOGA STATE PARK, 184
WESTMORELAND STATE
    PARK, 137
West Virginia information, 8–11
White Sulphur Springs, WV,
    163–164
Wilderness areas, 90, 109,
    161–162
Wilmington, DE, 26
Wise, VA, 111–112
Wytheville, VA, 109–110

Y

YOUGHIOGHENY RIVER
    LAKE, 71